Sharing

To Hilda Valerie (Val) David
1939–2016

Sharing
Crime against Capitalism

Matthew David

polity

First published in 2017 by Polity Press

Polity Press
65 Bridge Street
Cambridge CB2 1UR, UK

Polity Press
350 Main Street
Malden, MA 02148, USA

ISBN-13: 978-1-5095-1322-2
ISBN-13: 978-1-5095-1323-9 (pb)

A catalogue record for this book is available from the British Library.

Typeset in 10.5 on 12 pt Plantin by Servis Filmsetting Ltd, Stockport, Cheshire
Printed and bound in the UK by CPI Group (UK) Ltd, Croydon

The publisher has used its best endeavours to ensure that the URLs for external websites referred to in this book are correct and active at the time of going to press. However, the publisher has no responsibility for the websites and can make no guarantee that a site will remain live or that the content is or will remain appropriate.

Every effort has been made to trace all copyright holders, but if any have been inadvertently overlooked the publisher will be pleased to include any necessary credits in any subsequent reprint or edition.

For further information on Polity, visit our website: www.politybooks.com

Contents

Acknowledgements

Thanks are due to the various coauthors whose thinking on sharing I have shared (Jack Birmingham, Debbie Halbert, Jamie Kirkhope, Andrew Kirton, Peter Millward and Natasha Whiteman); to those authors whose work I coedited (and thereby internalized) for the *Sage Handbook of Intellectual Property* (all fifty of you); to those who shared their wisdom in editing this and earlier works of mine on post-scarcity sharing (in particular Anna Davies, Bill Dutton, Richard Giulianotti, David Held, Julia Knight, James Milton, Eva-Maria Nag, Raphaël Nowak, Chris Rojek and Andrew Whelan); to the many nameless but invaluable peer reviewers down the years; to Durham University's Institute of Advanced Study for hosting discussions that facilitated this work; and to those participants in discussions at Cardiff University, CUNY, SUNY, London's City University and Queen Mary College, Oxford's Internet Institute and Department of Music, the University of Utrecht's Workshop on the Sharing Economy, and Durham University's Café Politique, where the ideas presented in this book were presented and critiqued. Particular thanks to Sarah Dancy, Rachel Moore, Jonathan Skerrett and Amy Williams at Polity Press for getting things into shape. Finally, I would especially like to thank all the students over the years who have taken my various cybercrime and cyberculture modules. They taught me a lot and I hope they learned something from all the free downloaded versions of my work they seemed always able to find.

1

Introduction

Sharing: Crime against Capitalism sets out to examine the pros and cons of property, market and sharing-based economies in terms of innovation, production and distribution of informational goods. The book will address this comparison in terms of efficiency, efficacy and incentive. By informational goods is meant books, music, computer software, visual media, journalism, academic journal articles and scientific research (including pharmaceutical research and development). In contrast to the over- and misused notion of 'the tragedy of the commons' (Hardin 1968), which outlines how goods held in common can be overexploited and undermaintained in the absence of counterbalancing forces, but which then (erroneously) asserts that the only viable counterbalance is private property rights, my book (in line with the work of Heller 1998 and 2008) illustrates 'the tragedy of the anti-commons', wherein private ownership and competition inhibit the maintenance of public goods and reduce overall efficiency, efficacy and incentive. *Sharing: Crime against Capitalism* also highlights the superiority of a sharing-based economy in maximizing the public good and overall utility.

Free music online reduces opportunity costs (e.g., the inability to purchase one thing – such as a concert ticket – if one has just spent one's money on something else – such as a recording), increasing spending on live performance; and when freely shared recordings boost live concert ticket sales, and, consequently, ticket prices, musicians get better paid. The Internet and World Wide Web illustrate the primacy of collaborative programming over commercial coding, and open-source networks of hackers have broken all silo-made corporate encryption. Newspapers and broadcasters draw upon freely shared content provided by digital 'citizen witnesses', and this has allowed them to cut costs and sack staff. Yet, such organizations are challenged by the Internet when freely shared content surpasses traditional media claims to be the ones who bring the news and, in particular, who are the first to bring it to audiences (uncensored). Academic journals are increasingly owned by commercial publishers, which profit from content produced by public science, science which is made available without charge by researchers but which is then sold back to the research community in terms of rapidly escalating journal prices. Non-commercial funding (whether in the domain of pure science or of applied science such as in pharmaceuticals) underpins the research that creates most of the value in what may later be fenced off through patent.

While only too willing to cut costs to some degree by means of using freely shared content online (or from other non-property/non-market-based networks such as academic science), commercial intermediaries are threatened by free distribution of content if it is *too* effective in reducing cost. Success in reducing cost can also reduce scarcity and, if that cannot be controlled, may then lead to a radical reduction in price (potentially to nothing). This 'threat' (or promise – depending upon how you see things) underpins the pressure for legislation to further criminalize sharing. In conditions of global network capitalism, sharing information is a 'crime against capitalism'. Nonetheless, despite stringent efforts, such legislative strategies have been radically unsuccessful in actually containing the level and significance of sharing.

In this context, where criminalization has largely failed to prevent sharing, alternative business models have emerged. These new business strategies have attempted to 'compete' in the spaces created by sharing as an alternative to capitalist business-as-usual. What has emerged, as this book will document, is a form of post-scarcity 'sharing economy'. This is, at least, at the level of informational goods. In suspending intellectual property rights in practical terms (the law still formally protects IP), and in bypassing the need for markets (free-sharing is not the same as direct reciprocation in the form of exchange by barter), what emerges is something not fully capitalist. However, there still remains the potential for people to get paid and even for some people to make a 'profit'. Yet, this is in conditions where content is open and accessible to ever greater numbers; and in many cases for nothing.

Sharing: Crime Against Capitalism?

The significance of free-sharing across global digital networks needs to be seen in the light of the emergence of global network capitalism (Castells 1996, 2009). The contradictions within global network capitalism are both the spaces in which free-sharing arose, and those that are intensified by free-sharing. The first contradiction lies in globalization itself. On the one hand, globalization extends market and property relations. Globalization has meant expanding markets by means of a deregulation of trade barriers and the integration of distribution chains within global distribution networks. Globalization has also extended property rights protection beyond national jurisdictions. This is particularly true for IP, where the harmonizing of national laws has been achieved in recent years through a combination of multi- and bilateral treaties (Yu 2015). Globalization also reduces costs through global outsourcing of production to cheaper labour markets (Chon 2015). On the other hand, globalization affords an exponential expansion in pirate, counterfeit and generic 'outsourcing' in production and distribution (Rojek 2015).

In similar fashion, digital networks expand markets and reduce costs for copyright holders and counterfeiters alike – this is the second contradiction of global *network* capitalism. This is true in music, film, publishing, software and computer games, as well as in television (Kirton and David 2013). Digital compression, distribution and processing have afforded the expansion of legal markets and have also allowed widespread bypassing of the legal channels for gaining access, as well as the bypassing of the technical means of preventing access to those who do not pay – i.e., encryption (David and Kirkhope 2004).

Third, the 'capitalism' within global network capitalism shows an intensification of the tension between markets and property rights, which is a generic contradiction – but one that global digital networks take to new levels. Intellectual property protection is designed to limit market entry and so to suspend competition. However, pirate capitalists operate illicit markets at the expense of IP-based monopoly profits. In so doing, they reduce prices. Whether 'capitalism' is primarily defined by 'markets', as Weber (1930) argued, or whether 'capitalism' is primarily defined by 'private property', as Marx (1995/1867) held, remains disputed. This is not just a dispute between theories. It is a dispute enacted in the conduct of IP defenders, pirates and sharers across global digital networks.

The free circulation of information challenges IP-based business models, because in such models it is information that is the commodity being sold, or at least it makes up the greater part of the value being sold relative to the physical packaging in which the informational content is delivered. This is true in relation to copyrighted software, music, published works and live sports broadcasts, as well as in patent-protected scientific research. If the price being charged is largely determined by the market value of the informational content and not by its packaging, then when that informational content is freely available elsewhere, the price collapses.

Knowledge has always been valuable and, in part at least, defines human social and economic activity in distinction from animal behaviour (Gouldner 1976). What is understood today as intellectual property law emerged alongside capitalism and the industrial revolution (May and Sell 2005). The significance of innovative technologies and novel creative expressions, in giving economic advantage, is not new. Nor is the drive to protect such innovation/novelty as something akin to 'property'. The emergence of what Castells calls a network society (1996, 2009) does give greater significance (as a cost of production) to information over physical raw materials, physical labour power and/or energy inputs. However, it is an error to simply assume that an 'information society' is one where informational content inevitably becomes more valuable than physical objects, effort and energy. Where once information-rich commodities (such as novels, films, musical recordings and so on) required physical carriers to be manufactured and distributed, networked computers allow such content to be circulated without the need for traditional modes of packaging and distribution. In the past, someone seeking to sell books or records would look to protect themselves from commercial rivals by means of copyright. Now it is possible for every networked computer user to copy and share content that would have once required expensive printing or record presses.

Because the challenge to IP control has shifted from commercial to non-commercial copying, it is sharing that has been criminalized all the more forcefully in recent years. The rise of the tape-cassette first saw a shift in attention from commercial piracy to personal infringement (Marshall 2004), but digital network sharing has taken this challenge to far greater levels (David 2010). However, while efforts have been made to prohibit sharing as a threat to network capitalism, there is also evidence of a more fluid relationship between sharing and business, which this book will highlight. Legally speaking, sharing, in the sense of making free copies of IP-protected content without permission, is an 'alternative to business'. Yet it can also be the basis for 'alternative business models'. Freely distributed content is being profited from by some, even as freely shared content is undermining profit from the sale of such content by those who retain the traditional IP-protected business model. Sharing (in the sense of lending) an individual's physical goods and/or giving up their time may lead to an extension of market relations (if that lending is done in the form of paid 'renting'). However, IP infringement, in the form of free-sharing (making copies) of formally IP-protected content, challenges capitalism as a system of property rights. In this way, free-sharing of digital content challenges us to rethink our theoretical accounts of property, exchange relations, production, distribution and incentive.

Since the end of the Cold War, a 'global network capitalism' has been constructed. At the heart of this new 'regime' has been the deregulation of labour combined with an intensified regulation of property protection, particularly intellectual property protection. In 'global network capitalism', monopoly rights over informational content have been extended in time, space, scope and depth (David and Halbert 2015). This is true at least at the level of formal law, even if enforcement of such a regulative framework has not been fully achieved. The World Trade Organisation (WTO) was created in the years just after the collapse of the Soviet Union. The WTO's first act was the 1994/95 Agreement on Trade-Related Aspects of Intellectual Property Rights (TRIPS). TRIPS required all signatories to the WTO to pass into domestic legislation the treaty's harmonization of global IP protection. At that point in time, the perceived threat to intellectual property was still commercial infringement. Only one year later, the World Intellectual Property Organization (WIPO) produced a revised Copyright Treaty (1996). This treaty first addressed the perceived global threat of free digital sharing. In 1996, it was the increased availability of cheap CD copiers to the general consumer that was considered the primary emerging challenge (Krueger 2004). Simply having two CD players built into one stereo system, and the fact that one of these had a record function, meant the 'digital revolution' that had been such a benefit to the music industry since the advent of the CD in 1982 (Sandall 2007) suddenly started to look like a threat. Yet the 'threat' from CD burners was as nothing when compared to what came next: online file-sharing.

Free digital sharing arose in the copyright domain. Its development from music (discussed in Chapter 3) to film and onto live visual content (see Chapter 4) in part followed, but also drove, technical developments. The same is also true of computer software (see

Chapter 5). In a further development of technical capacity, the 3D printer revolution (Rifkin 2014) will make IP-rich physical goods available to 'download'. Where film and television followed music, downloading objects will follow the downloading of purely informational content. However, for the moment, 'free' sharing of (patent-protected) information (such as is contained in generic medicines and 'fake' designer handbags) does not 'give' you the pill or the bag. For this, for now, the end-user still requires what IP holders call 'pirate capitalist' intermediaries (Rojek 2015).

While the copyright industries' war on downloading has commanded the headlines regarding the potential challenge of sharing, significant issues also exist around sharing in the domains of IP covered by patent and trademark. Two-thirds of pharmaceutical science is funded by non-commercial actors (Boldrin and Levine 2008). Scientific innovation is built upon the principle of free-sharing of knowledge (Merton 1972/1942). Sharing-based knowledge production makes large private profits only if pharmaceutical companies can place end-products under patent controls, or if counterfeiters can sell unlicensed copies at inflated prices – something itself only possible because the monopolies they infringe keep prices higher than would be the case if competition were legal. In both cases, shared knowledge production fuels private profits only if its shared origins can be controlled.

On the other hand, trademark holders, when seeking to reduce costs by outsourcing production, also make life easier for counterfeiters. Counterfeiters can use the same cut-price outsourced manufacturers used by lawful rights holders to make identical, but IP-infringing, 'fakes' (Chon 2015). However, at the level of selling these pills and bags and so forth, the struggle is between legal and pirate capitalists.

Manufacturing generic drugs in developing countries is another example of the relationship between IP control and infringement. Unlike counterfeit drugs, generic drugs replicate the chemistry of the patented product but not the trademarked packaging of its owner's brand. Generics undercut patent monopoly prices, just as they also undermine the market for counterfeits. This enables safe and affordable access to medicine in the global South (Darch 2015; Millaleo and Cadenas 2015; Thomas 2015). Again, we see that what was produced in conditions of freely shared knowledge can become private property; and what was private property can be appropriated and sold by others. Medical research produced by publicly funded science may be patented, and this may then be infringed by generic drug-makers. (Of course, such things as medicines and designer goods cannot be simply shared freely at the current time, but free access to the information required to make them does enable radically more affordable generic products.)

This book is for the most part concerned with the free-sharing of informational content. It is not, therefore, primarily concerned with commercial generics, counterfeiting and piracy. The 3D printer revolution is increasing the scope for the free downloading of information-based physical goods. However, at the present time, for all but the simplest of objects (and only for the very small minority of people with access to a 3D printer), information-rich things still require manufacturers and distributors (lawful or otherwise), and these are for the most part commercial – not sharing-based. As such, a large part of this book focuses upon the free-sharing of content protected under copyright. This includes music, visual media, software and publishing, including scientific publishing. However, to the extent that sharing is central to scientific knowledge production, this book does address genetics research and pharmaceuticals.

Alternative Business Models or Alternatives to Business?

The collaborative production and free distribution of code (protocols) enabled the production of the Internet (Abbate 1999), as well as of the World Wide Web (Berners-Lee 2000). Nevertheless, such foundations do not mean that the Internet and the Web cannot be used to make money.

Facebook streams advertising to its users when they freely share their lives on its platform, and this business model is hugely profitable. Similarly, selling eyeballs to advertisers is the basis for Google's business. This is despite the fact that most of the information being sought via Google's search engine is not for sale as such (Vaidhyanathan 2012). Services like YouTube (itself owned by Google) also make their money from advertising linked to the freely shared content that users upload, or look for and then look at, via these search services. A range of very lucrative alternative business models work on the basis of linking end-users to freely shared content, but then also linking both to advertising content.

Traditional business models, such as those of record companies, film studios, publishers and broadcasters, have suffered as a result of the rise of free-sharing. Nevertheless, during the first wave of the digital revolution, these businesses benefited greatly from reduced costs and wider distribution networks, fuelling a wave of global cross-media integration. The largest recording, filmmaking, publishing and broadcasting businesses are today owned by global cross-media corporations (Castells 2009). More often than not, one arm of the same corporation will be selling the Internet access that enables the infringement of content produced and/or distributed by other arms of that same corporation (David et al. 2015).

This book documents how sharing-based production and distribution underpin the greater part of informational content in today's network society. This ranges from science to publishing and the arts. Collaborative production is the wellspring of profit in pharmaceuticals, biotechnology, print and television. It also underpins the wider 'creative industries', although this is in large part due to the non- and underpaid nature of much creative work, under conditions of copyright control and royalties rather than real wages and secure employment (O'Brien 2015).

Free-sharing is good for business if content is free to *business* while remaining scarce to customers. However, this condition cannot be easily maintained in a network society. Free-sharing cannot be kept scarce when it can be freely copied and distributed online. This potential for post-scarcity threatens, or promises (depending on your point of view), to turn a reduced cost of production into a radical driver of price reduction. Such price reduction is potentially to zero if the cost of making each new copy by any given computer user is too small even to be measurable (Rifkin 2014; Mason 2015).

Where marginal cost, the cost of making the next copy, approaches zero, there can no longer be said to be any scarcity in such a good. In these conditions, the need for allocation mechanisms such as markets and property rights is brought into question. In relation to informational goods, that 'zero marginal cost' situation has become a reality. Nonetheless, even if the marginal cost of informational goods falls away in a network society, the prior development costs remain. Those who defend IP argue that it is in the need to recover these fixed and upfront costs that a justification for property rights and markets remain.

Markets and property rights may be warranted after all if free-sharing of outcomes does not incentivize individuals and organizations to produce efficient and effective products and distribution mechanisms for them. The three related issues of efficiency, effectiveness and incentive are therefore recurrent ones in this book. At least in relation to informational goods, *Sharing: Crime against Capitalism* will show that free-sharing outperforms markets and property rights on all three fronts.

The Economics of Sharing and of Capitalism

'Economics is the science which studies human behaviour as a relationship between ends and scarce means which have alternative
uses' (Robbins 1935: 15). As this quotation suggests, economics
primarily concerns itself with producing and distributing rivalrous
goods. Rivalrous goods are things where 'use' by one person limits
or even exhausts use by one or more others (Phythian-Adams 2015).
Institutions designed to deal with the rivalrous quality of time and
things include property rights (which may or may not be 'private'
property) and markets. Other institutions include state planning,
communal regulation and familial obligation. All such arrangements
for dealing with the rivalrous quality of time and things are 'social
institutions', including markets and property rights. Goods where
one user's use does not limit further use are, in contrast, referred to
as non-rivalrous goods (Phythian-Adams 2015: 33). Non-rivalrous
goods are, for the most part, non-physical 'creations' of human activity, such as technical knowledge and artistic expressions. Depending
upon a good's rivalrous or non-rivalrous quality, 'sharing' it relates
in different ways to markets and property rights. The 'sharing' of
rivalrous goods may be enacted through renting, free-lending, disin-
termediated exchange and/or barter. Nevertheless, referring to such
direct and instrumentally calculated exchanges as 'sharing' has been
brought into question by some writers (Hern 2015). New forms
of rental, lending, direct exchange and barter may extend market
relations through digital network services. In some such situations,
property rights are upheld in the manner of someone offering to
rent out a physical object that they own. However, markets may be
extended even while undoing property rights. This might occur when
the distribution of generic medicines and counterfeit designer goods
are extended by means of online marketing. Market expansion at the
expense of property rights also occurs in the production and distribution of 'pirate capitalist' CDs and DVDs (Rojek 2015).

Moreover, free-sharing, when limited to the private family and
friendship sphere, represents no challenge to markets and property rights. In fact, unpaid domestic labour provides an essential
foundation to markets and property-based allocation mechanisms
(Crompton 1997: 83–98). It is the 'private' character of such actions
that reproduce the undervaluation of such provision of resources.
Digital networks, on the other hand, create scope for high levels
of free-sharing within a global 'public' domain, a domain in large

part created by such sharing. As Habermas argues (1992/1962), free speech was central to the emergence of a public sphere in the long eighteenth century. Today, in similar fashion, it is free-sharing that is pivotal to the creation and defence of a global public sphere. This public domain stands in opposition to ongoing attempts at a proprietary enclosure of all domains of human interaction today (Dutton 2009). Free-sharing of time and things within specified (high-trust) communities can be enabled by digital networks. Where there is no physical limit to multiple and simultaneous use, such as in relation to fully non-rivalrous informational goods, digital networks enable forms and levels of free-sharing that challenge both markets and property rights.

Whether free-sharing of informational content represents an existential threat to market- and property-based arrangements depends rather upon the capacity of sharing, not just to undermine conventional economic arrangements, but to *provide alternatives*. This question of alternatives can be broken down into three elements: *efficiency*, *efficacy* and *incentive*.

Efficiency concerns the *cost* of producing a good. Efficiency can itself be divided into five dimensions (Heyne 2008): production and allocation efficiency, informational and transactional efficiency, and 'Pareto optimization'. Production efficiency, as its name suggests, relates to the cost of making particular goods. Allocational efficiency connects to production efficiency, but is specifically about *optimizing investment of resources*. Production and allocational efficiency together provide a narrow conception of efficiency within the immediate process of production. Informational efficiency, meanwhile, describes the level of resource expenditure required to *make an optimal rational decision* about which available option best meets one's needs. Transactional efficiency relates to the expense involved in *actually fulfilling a preference* once it has been selected (there may be various expenses involved in actually taking hold of and/or using an item).

Efficacy is closely connected to efficiency. However, efficacy refers to the *utility* of goods, not the cost of producing them. It is concerned with the 'quality' of particular outcomes and the overall quality of all the outcomes achieved (the overall quantity of such quality achieved). In this connection, production and allocational efficiency are linked within a narrow definition of efficiency in terms of costs of production, while informational and transactional efficiency extend the concept of efficiency to the domains of circulation (i.e., distribution). Informational and transaction costs have a significant impact on the *efficacy* of decisions made, in terms of their quality and access (i.e., their overall utility).

'Pareto optimization' is a term used to refer to a condition of overall efficiency where no more utility can be achieved through relocating resources without then creating a more significant loss of utility by making that alteration. In relation to non-rivalrous goods, this zero-sum calculation is irrelevant. However, time remains limited even where digital plenitude makes a near infinite amount of informational content available for nothing. Indeed, in such conditions the scarcity of time becomes ever more apparent. This continued scarcity of time in conditions of informational non-scarcity is highly significant in the economics of free-sharing.

Whether in relation to techno-scientific innovation or artistic creativity, incentive, meanwhile, refers to levels of *motivation*. Free-sharing, or so the argument commonly goes, may diminish incentive/motivation if creators/inventors thereby receive no reward for their efforts. However, free distribution also offers scope for promoting paid performance, peer recognition and the display of abilities that are better rewarded than direct creators and innovators actually receive from copyright and patent. Indeed, *Sharing: Crime against Capitalism* demonstrates how free-sharing of non-rivalrous informational goods outperforms market- and property-based systems on all counts: efficiency, efficacy and incentive.

The Structure of the Book

This book sets out the case for sharing as an alternative to markets and property-based forms of allocating informational goods across seven domains: libraries, music, visual media, computer software, publishing, genetic science and pharmaceuticals. These seven themes are addressed one by one, in Chapters 2–8.

Chapter 2 addresses libraries and the digital world, the idea of a library as a repository of free (at the point of use) access to information, and its migration from walled spaces to networked infrastructures. Where once the best libraries were free to access only to the most privileged groups in society, today's digital repository of knowledge extends access to unprecedented numbers, even while digital divides (around access to the Internet and quality of access to/skill in use of the Internet – see David and Millward 2014) continue to limit this availability. Information is either capital or culture, private asset or public good, depending upon its level of accessibility. The struggle between the principles of 'the bookshop' and those of 'the library' become the defining conflict of the network society. The struggle for literacy, education and for public libraries is a long one. Today's struggle for a free culture online is only the latest manifestation. Two digital revolutions do in fact coexist, one enabling the technical locking down of access to and distribution of content, the other allowing the breakdown of these barriers. This double digital revolution can be seen in the recent history of libraries, as well as in the wider domain of online information selling and sharing.

Chapter 3 addresses peer-to-peer music-sharing online. The recording industry business model in the second half of the twentieth century became centred on the idea of the 'recording artist'. The advent of file-sharing has seen this (largely illusory) common sense fall apart. The first digital revolution in music was the CD, creating a commercial profit storm. That the affordances of digital storage, distribution and processing should have so radically turned the recording industry upside down was not predicted by those who laid its foundations. The history of file-sharing has been a legal and technical, cat-and-mouse struggle, not the unfolding of any linear logic of technology. The case of recorded music most clearly illustrates the mythic nature of the claim that rendering information as property (rather than as freely shared culture) benefits creators or that it is the key to stimulating creativity. The copyright-based record contract leaves almost all artists in a condition of debt bondage to their record company in return for recordings that *may* get them noticed, and hence gain them a live audience whose ticket purchases *do* offer the artist a better reward for their time. That such an audience can more efficiently and effectively be gained for nothing online, and when free access to material eliminates the opportunity costs between record sales and ticket sales/prices, artists are better off when their music circulates with no price tag attached.

Chapter 4 engages with live-streaming of television content. Where the CD replaced an earlier commodity (the vinyl disc), the first digital revolution in television was the replacement for free-to-access (state- or advertiser-funded) 'terrestrial' broadcasting with subscription-based cable and satellite television. The scope to erect technical monopoly controls over access and to increase audience size by global digital distribution technologies allowed the first digital revolution to outbid terrestrial rivals for legal monopoly rights, especially over live sports events. Technical monopoly control was assured early on by the fact that the domestic Internet bandwidth was insufficient to stream live events with any clarity. Rupert Murdoch's UK Sky and

US Fox networks were built up on the basis of this set of monopoly conditions. Only with the development of a faster domestic Internet bandwidth was it possible to bypass such monopoly control. Live-streaming now offers a second digital revolution that is beginning to challenge the first.

Chapter 5 looks at open-source software and proprietary software, and argues that it is wrong to assume that copyright is the best way to incentivize the production of such software. Those producing code in corporate research and development departments have never successfully produced encryption code that open-source-based and free-sharing-based communities of hackers have not been able to break – almost as soon as it has been released. What Himanen calls 'the hacker ethic', and what Söderberg calls 'play struggle', represent forms of incentive and creative space that allow for far more innovation than takes place in corporate silos. Even within the silos of corporate coding, such as those making commercial computer games, the claim that the prevention of free-sharing by means of copyright is either necessary or significant is questionable. These industries stay alive by bringing out new products rather than protecting old ones with legal monopolies. At the cutting edge of gaming, the scope for free-sharing increases as the scope for proprietary control falls away. The history of the Internet, the World Wide Web, Wikipedia, Facebook, Google, Apple and Microsoft all illustrate the primacy of free-sharing over the capacity to lock down ideas. The creation of non-profit organizations in the digital commons has been essential not just for the creation of the standards and protocols on which the network society operates, but also for maintaining scope for future development, as well as for meaningful and informed choice for end-users.

Chapter 6 unpacks the complex and diverse world of publishing: academic, journalistic and trade. Academic publishing is the most extreme case, with no payment to authors for journal articles, even while commercial purchase of academic journals in recent decades has seen exponential increases in journal prices. Authoring, editing and reviewing are all done for little or no payment as part of a sharing-based academic economy structured around peer recognition. Journalism (print and broadcast), meanwhile, has been radically challenged by digital media networks, although the Internet is only a secondary part of a longer-running digital revolution in print and broadcasting. Digital proliferation of media channels has seen advertising revenues spread thinner, while the rise of citizen journalism online offers cheap copy and yet also a threat to the value of traditional journalistic authority. Horizontal integration in publishing houses and vertical integration of these within larger media companies in general has been combined with an increased outsourcing of the agent function, creating increased pressure to deliver 'big books'. An ever-shrinking number of big players produce a similarly shrinking pool of such repeaters ('franchises'), pot-boilers, cookbooks and tie-ins. Free-sharing remains the wellspring for new writers. Beyond the tiny layer of big book celebrity authors, most writers make money from types of activity that free circulation of their work actually encourages.

Chapter 7 offers an account of free-sharing in science, with a particular focus upon contemporary genetics. At one level, genes are fundamentally 'free', in the sense of being a common heritage of all humanity, both those of our own bodies and those of the non-human 'nature' around us. At another level, genetics (as scientific knowledge of genes) is best furthered through the free-sharing of research, rather than through commercial patenting. Genetic diversity, in non-human nature and within human bodies, pre-existed scientific 'discovery', even as traditional knowledge of certain properties and conditions also preceded today's scientific accounts. Whether by means of patent or by new forms of rights over traditional knowledge, attempts to regulate access to such content, and knowledge of it, have proven highly problematic. The defence of genes as a common or shared heritage of humanity continues not only in relation to human genetics, but also in the defence of farmers over claims made, and practices undertaken, by agribusiness in relation to genetically modified crops. It is argued that not only is free-sharing an ethical imperative; it is also essential in the production of scientific knowledge in the first place. The Human Genome Project and related public and private gene mapping and patenting strategies highlight both the superiority of publicly funded and freely shared scientific research, and the dangers of private patent thickets in closing down knowledge production.

Chapter 8 looks at the case of pharmaceuticals. Medical research requires large scale, upfront investment. Patents are said to incentivize such investment, so free-sharing of pharmaceutical research findings reduces the willingness to invest. As Chapter 8 will show, this argument is doubly misleading. First, the greater part of innovative pharmaceutical research is funded directly, or indirectly (via tax breaks and other mechanisms), by non-commercial sources; meanwhile, the greater part of what commercial actors do spend is done so on 'down the line' development (i.e., reverse engineered, 'me too', patent-evading emulation), as well as on clinical and post-clinical trials, all of which turn out to be far more expensive when conducted commercially than is the case when they are undertaken by publicly funded agencies. Privately funded research is also far more prone to corruption, price inflation and even medically harmful conflicts of interest. Second, private patents limit research development and collaboration, where the foundation for innovation is shared access to past and cutting-edge findings. Beyond the question of scientific production of new drugs, which is best served by free-sharing of knowledge via public science, generic drugs (drugs made by freely appropriating patented or formerly patented formulas) are actually the best way to maximize distribution, undercut monopoly prices and limit the market for dangerous counterfeit medicines that seek to profit from deceit in relation to existing patent and trademark monopolies. The cases of HIV/AIDS and Ebola illustrate the primacy of publicly funded medicine in both initial drug development and in delivering results to those most in need.

Chapter 9 will draw together the evidence presented in the preceding chapters to answer the question: is sharing a crime against capitalism, or is capitalism capable of absorbing and adapting to the challenge of sharing? This final chapter highlights the failure to contain sharing within the bounds of a property-based profit system. As such, sharing represents an existential challenge to capitalism today, even as the pre-figurative spaces of such a new mode of production have not yet abolished the fetters of the old.

What Sharing? And (more to the point) What is Sharing?

Two questions are important to address at this point. First, why have the seven domains that make up the substantive content of this book (libraries, music, visual media, computer software, publishing, genetic science and pharmaceuticals) been chosen. Second, how does this book seek to apply the category 'sharing' when it is a term that means so many different things to different people (and sometimes even to the same people)? The answers to both questions relate to one another. This book focuses upon the sharing of informational goods first of all because these goods are central to today's informational or network society, and, second, because the non-rivalrous nature of such goods renders them so much easier to share and, in so doing, challenges traditional conceptions of value, scarcity and price. Attention to libraries arises as a pre-digital form of informational sharing that prefigures contemporary struggles, while attention to music, visual media, software and publishing in the digital age addresses the most powerful fault lines in the conflict between free-sharing and a market based on property rights and prices. Discussion of scientific and medical research highlights how this struggle is growing even in those domains where non-rivalrous informational content still requires physical carries and procedures (pills, seeds, etc.), as was once the case – but increasingly is not – in the domains of books, records, films, newspapers and the like. My choice to address genetics and pharmaceuticals, but not designer goods and patented jet engine components, etc., is deliberate. Pills, tests, procedures and seeds still require physical interventions or making, and cannot simply be 'downloaded' by the average Internet user. This makes them more similar to designer clothing and engine parts than to the digital download of a film, game or book, etc. However, the science behind genetic and pharmaceutical inventions are predominantly created by scientists working within a culture of shared knowledge production, not the commercial domains that often claim credit for their creations, nor to the commercially driven fields of designer goods and of commercial manufacturing. This is not to say that the study of design, fashion and engineering would not also highlight significant foundations for creativity coming from shared cultures, and to that extent further study of these fields certainly warrants attention.

The second question, of what is being meant here by sharing, has already been answered in part. This book addresses the sharing of non-rivalrous informational goods, and to that extent what is being talked about here is the making of free copies, not the dividing up or lending out of physical objects. The notion of giving and taking that apply to singular objects – such that taking removes the thing from the person giving it – does not apply when making copies of infinitely reproducible code. In place of giving and taking, what exist in relation to informational goods are domains of production and reception, enabled by systems of transmission in between them. Sharing may occur at the level of coproduction, free circulation of copies or in the free reproduction of such copies by end-users. The distinction between sharing as peer coproduction and sharing as free copying is significant, but porous. These dimensions may complement or contradict, diverge or mesh. Some informational content is produced through peer-to-peer coproduction (as in hacker software, Wikipedia, the Web and Internet platforms, scientific research, citizen journalism and fan fiction), and circulated freely beyond its producer community. Other content is produced by commercial actors (such as film, television and music companies and commercial publishers and drugs companies), but is then circulated freely by sharers against the wishes of IP holders. Sometimes, content produced by scientists, academics, authors and others (such as citizen journalists, Facebook and Google users, etc.) may be created and given away for nothing, only for it to be sold or profited from by third parties. While IP holders present sharing primarily as being 'theft' by non-producers, circulating and copying content produced for commercial use and so 'harming' such producers, this book presents a very different story. Free-sharing, even in relation only to non-rivalrous informational goods, represents at least three different things (coproduction, circulation and making copies). However, even when not everything being freely circulated and copied was produced with the intention of its being freely shared, or was made by means of peer-to-peer sharing communities, a sharing economy is neither contradictory nor merely a parasite. At one level, this book both highlights the power of sharing-based coproduction in software, publishing and fundamental science, and also shows the power of sharing-based transmission and copying in the domains of music, visual media and pharmaceuticals. Incentives to create may not always appear to coincide with efficiencies and overall efficacy at the level of distribution and use. At a deeper level, it must be noted that this is a false divide. Fans downloading music freely spend more on concerts and so help coproduce the live musical experience. Fan fiction invigorates creation, and creates opportunities for authors to get better paid than most do through royalties on their work. Distinct forms of sharing can operate in parallel – such as when public science leads to knowledge that is then released from IP control by those manufacturing generic medicines.

As such, this book seeks to focus upon the sharing of non-rivalrous informational goods, and to examine at least three dimensions of such sharing, in production, circulation and copying. Production, circulation and copying map onto the questions of incentive, efficiency and efficacy that will also shape the evaluative framing by which it is asked whether free-sharing represents a viable economic alternative to property rights and markets – which this book shows it does. This multi-field and multi-levelled approach creates a diverse array of interactions, affordances and outcomes. This diversity ranges from reinforcing commercial monopolies, creating space for new and highly profitable companies, to radically challenging the possibility to own property or to maintain scarcity (and hence prices) in the digital age. While this book does conclude that sharing is a significant threat to a system (capitalism) that is based on property, scarcity and prices, this is by no means a simple, linear and singular fact. The threat is sufficient to mean that although those who seek to govern and maintain global network capitalism increasingly seek to criminal-ize sharing, such efforts have largely failed. Whether a post-scarcity network society will become a post-capitalist one is a possibility, not an inevitability.

2

Libraries and the Digital World

Introduction

This chapter addresses the parallel between the library as store of knowledge and today's Internet-connected network of shared resources. While the library, in its physical manifestation, was and is limited both in its content and in who is able to access that content, today's digital networks offer greater content and greater access. Even while Internet access is not universal or equitable, it is more so than any previous cultural repository. The principle of free access at the point of use – what makes a library different from, for instance, a bookshop – stands in stark opposition to a pay-per-use model of culture. While the 'best' libraries have often been closed to those who were not already privileged (free to those who can afford it, very expensive to those who cannot), today's network library promises or threatens to extend the principle of free access to all cultures, to anyone who can log onto a computer. Given that this demographic maps directly onto that part of the human population that might otherwise have been able and willing to pay for access to cultural goods, the digital network library (the World Wide Web of shared human culture) poses a serious threat to 'business as usual' – or at least the possibility of extending a capitalist business model based on private ownership, scarcity and the price mechanism, from the realm of physical goods, to informational goods. However, if the digital library represents the possibility of an information society, it also disrupts the possibility of an information economy, at least in the way economics is currently understood.

This chapter begins by drawing out Alvin Gouldner's (1976)

distinction between information as either *culture or capital*, and the significance of this distinction in contemporary disputes over power and freedom. The history of literacy, education and libraries is then touched upon in connection to what can be called the dual and contradictory revolutions associated with information in the digital age: one revolution in the direction of increased commodification of formerly free-to-access culture, and the second revolution freeing access. The works of Siva Vaidhyanathan and Claudy Op den Kamp are then used to highlight both the potential for, and the attempts to limit, free access to culture in the digital age. Vaidhyanathan explores the 'anarchic' potential for a free culture that arises in an age where the principle of libraries as a free resource expands radically. Contrariwise, Op den Kamp highlights the chilling impact of copyright extension in expanding the domain of 'orphan works', works that are not being made formally available by archives for fear of prosecution by unknown claimants upholding rights initially held by the long since dead. Of course, archives and libraries did and do play a role in maintaining private ownership, such as in the case of libraries of record and of patent libraries. However, the former are now largely redundant, and new archives are emerging to preserve and assert the common culture against patent appropriation. It is true too that patent libraries, while designed to protect private rights claims, are also the repository of the common culture once each particular patent claim expires. Furthermore, it is essential to note that libraries operate according to academic principles linked to the assertion of an author's moral rights, not simply their copyrights. While copyright law does apply to copying whole works, the content of libraries is there to be used freely, in exchange for appropriate referencing of the author's name (if that work is 'used' by its reader), not payment to the work's publisher. As such, attempts by copyright holders and IP protection lobbyists to equate copyright infringement with plagiarism should be resisted.

In conclusion, this chapter suggests that the global network society has witnessed the rise of a new form of digital archive of the world's culture, and that this should be celebrated and protected from those who would close down free-sharing to preserve scarcity and, hence, maintain the scope to profit from selling information. The question that arises, in a post-scarcity free culture of sharing, is not how to allocate scarce resources. It is, rather, *how to locate and choose information in conditions of plenty*. Scope exists in such conditions for manipulation and even exploitation; the struggle between a free culture and a fee culture is not simply abolished by the Internet. Nonetheless, the radical potential of sharing does here expand.

Information: Culture or Capital

For Alvin Gouldner (1976), knowledge and information are the foundations for practical action in the world and can be applied in various different ways. On the one hand, knowledge privatized – where information is packaged within the parameters of intellectual property rights – becomes a form of capital, an asset whose application can demand some form of rent, profit or private return. On the other hand, information and knowledge shared become the common culture, from which all can benefit and which all can use to whatever advantage they wish without the need to pay to access or use it. This distinction between private capital and shared culture, both drawing upon and disputing access to knowledge and information, is a thread running through this book. It is the same distinction – drawn initially by Castells but developed in this work – between today's dominant networks of power built upon and defending private property and new forms of counterpower based upon sharing.

This tension between culture and capital goes to the heart of today's global network society. For Gouldner, the axiom that all human economic and social activity has its roots in 'knowledge' (in as far as human 'action' can be distinguished from animal behaviour) goes back much further than simply the rise of today's knowledge economy, information society or so-called post-industrial society. The conflict between culture and capital recurs across all human history. Nonetheless, this dispute becomes particularly acute in today's global network society, as the distinction between physical capital and informational content (i.e., in terms of the kinds of products that are being produced) becomes less significant, as does the distinction between physical labour and informational content (i.e., in terms of the kinds of work that is being done). Nonetheless, orchards and tools needed tending, and even the most brute features of the industrial revolution never fully removed the need for brains beneath the workers' caps (Braverman 1974). The very notion that we have undergone a simple transition from agricultural to industrial, and then another from industrial to post-industrial societies (Bell 1976), is misleading. The most advanced science and technology are applied to farming, and it is the service sector that retains most of the old principles of craft and personal 'service' (Castells 1996). The abstracted knowledge, in the form of formal information/content, that governs farming, manufacture and service work is now largely stored and distributed digitally. What is interesting is not the distinction between agriculture, manufacturing and service work, but rather the globally distributed nature of such knowledge/information deployed in all these sectors, and the disputes over access to and application of such knowledge and information within a global network society.

In this regard, an interesting example of the disputed nature of knowledge and information in the global network society comes in the form of libraries. In recent years, digitization has allowed publishers to create academic journal articles first and foremost in a digital format. The creation of paper (physical) copies comes later (if at all). This has radically reduced costs of both production and, even more so, distribution. It is now common practice for academic libraries, at least in relatively affluent societies, to buy their journal subscriptions from publishers in 'electronic bundles'. Rather than subscribing to individual paper titles, a library or a consortium of libraries negotiates to receive a set of titles from a particular publisher. This may involve a base set of paper copies (for a limited number of titles) as well as a larger set of electronic titles made available 'on top'. Not only does such electronic access increase the number of titles that a particular library can make available to its readers, it also (most often) means that the particular library gains access to the (digitized) back catalogue of that journal, even if it had not previously subscribed to that title. This allows a significant 'catch up' for relatively new or relatively under-resourced libraries (David 1996, 1998), as they are now able to offer their users as great a back catalogue of content as older and better-resourced libraries (at least to the extent that older content has been digitized). This offers up an immense democratic potential, not only within developed countries, but also for less developed countries, especially where digital access means a far more fundamental 'catching up'. However, there is a (significant) catch. For those titles that are only accessed electronically, such access may be removed, unlike when a physical copy has been acquired. Having fewer, if any, hard copies distributed increases control, even as it also increases the risk of loss/corruption of the original work. To the extent that publishers sell libraries access to digital content, including back catalogues of past content, the danger arises that if a library ceases to pay its subscription, it will lose not only its future issues of a particular title, but also access to current and past content. This double-edged sword, between digital distribution and centralized control, neatly captures the tension between information as culture and as capital in today's global network society. The potential exists for a radical democratizing of access to information. However, at the same time, the potential for privatization of information also grows.

Literacy, Education and Libraries

The contradiction between access and exclusion that can be seen played out in the example of journal subscriptions above cuts across the wider fields of literacy, education and libraries more generally. The history of all these forms of accessing, processing and storing of abstracted forms of knowledge witnessed a struggle between attempts to use knowledge to further the interests of dominant groups in maintaining the exclusion of the majority, and attempts to use knowledge as a vehicle for promoting a more democratic society.

The rise of literacy rates in the nineteenth and twentieth centuries is, in part, associated with increased democratic participation, although this is a rather ambiguous relationship. Worker self-education was part of the trade union and labour movement's struggle to democratize newly emergent capitalist societies, and nation states' responses to these attempts. The creation of free (and compulsory) education for all was, at a certain level, an attempt to indoctrinate citizens into acceptance of an unequal social order (Anderson 1983; Rose 1985). Authoritarian regimes in the twentieth century took such measures to control through literacy and education to even further extremes. Such examples show how literacy and education can be used to promote inequality, just as much as they can be used to reduce it. The sociology of education more generally indicates how 'education cannot compensate for society' (Bernstein 1970: 344). Education reinforces just as much as it removes disadvantage. The rise of a more educated society has not created a fairer one (Boliver 2010, 2013). 'The rise of the meritocracy' (Young 1958), a society that warrants its self-assured and self-justifying extension of inequality on the basis of uneven levels of educational outcome (even while claiming – mainly erroneously – some level of equality of educational opportunity), sees universal education and literacy being presented as simply the level playing field upon which unequal talents find their just desserts. (For detailed critiques of the illusions of meritocracy, see Brown 2000, as well as Halsey et al. 1980.)

Libraries too have a history that has as much inhibited as it has advanced equality. The movement to create public libraries from the nineteenth century onwards was part of a democratizing process (UNESCO 1949), but for all such efforts, from antiquity to the present day, the world's most prestigious libraries have closed their doors to all but the very elite of society; and such access as was afforded to elites was then used to perpetuate their advantage. In having access to knowledge that was denied to others, elites could then use such knowledge as cultural capital to warrant unequal rewards (Bourdieu 1992). How far then does the metaphor of the library, and the actuality of its principles of free – yet often also exclusive – access to, and use of, knowledge extend into today's global network society? Will a digital network society extend free access to all, such that all knowledge becomes the common culture? Or will the principles of closure and distinction prevail, leading to further privatization of knowledge into capital?

Digital Revolutions One and Two

The digital revolution involves 'code', a term that is associated with recording and transmitting information in a form that keeps content secret in some fashion or another. Initial use of radio transmission by the British military in the 1920s was abandoned because the messages being sent were 'broadcast' and hence open to the enemy to listen in to (Kittler 1997). This broadcast capability was taken up by commercial and state radio shortly afterwards. German military planners later figured out that radio broadcasting could be militarily useful as long as messages sent were encoded. Digital communications are always already encoded, although not in a sense that automatically affords secrecy, and the 'coding' used to send messages on the Internet in fact undermine attempts to keep secrets.

Today's digital revolution, in storage, processing and communication, is largely based on shared code. (For further discussion of storage and processing code and its origins in shared code writing, see Chapter 5.) In relation to digital communications, and in particular the Internet, the capacity for a network of networks to function depends upon a non-proprietary system of shared codes called protocols; these protocols do create the potential for control in distributed systems (Galloway 2004), but, importantly, such control is limited (David 2010: 24–25). The network of networks that is the Internet, built upon a set of shared protocols that allow a network to function around and beyond any particular blockage along any particular pathway, makes earlier forms of hierarchical and parochial control very nearly impossible.

Digital code creates divergent affordances within the global network society, and these differences have coalesced around what can be called two digital revolutions, each standing in stark contrast to the other. The first digital revolution draws upon the capacity of digital codes to facilitate both encryption and surveillance, the two combined making up what is referred to as *digital rights management* (DRM) (May 2007). Encoding markers within digital content can allow encryption to prevent access to those without authorization, while other encoded markers may be used to locate or follow particular content and particular users. DRM – such as the encrypting of music files, or in requiring access codes to watch digital television coverage, or when usernames and passwords regulate a person's access to email accounts and Internet usage – transform access to content and communication; relative, that is, to older forms of analogue television and radio, records, and video cassettes, as well as to using telephones or posting letters. In the past, no password was required to listen to the news, visit the cinema, watch television, read a newspaper, make a telephone call or post a letter. As will be documented throughout this work, the rise of the first digital revolution has seen new forms of control and monitoring over culture. This is what Lawrence Lessig (2002) refers to as 'code as law', a situation where technical barriers and eyes replace legal process in deciding what can be seen and who has the right to see what (and whom).

Set against this first digital revolution, a second digital revolution moves in quite the opposite direction, exploiting and developing other affordances within digital code, most particularly the shared and sharing-enabling foundations of new digital media, that is, the shared protocols that enable every networked computer to communicate with every other networked machine. The nature of such shared code is that it is designed to enable all machines to interact and, as such, any blockage between any two machines can be bypassed as messages can be broken down, rerouted and reassembled at their destination. The second digital revolution is manifested in music and film file-sharing, live content streaming, the sharing of games software, hacking collectives, and in the citizen journalism that has bypassed state censors and commercial editorial controls, and has, in a way, created a global digital library beyond all the walls and limits of former libraries, containing the sum of all previous repositories.

Internet and Access

Where the first and second digital revolutions fight it out online over the closing down or the opening up of information as either capital to be exploited or as culture to be shared, a primary question that precedes all such action is that of access to the Internet in the first place. It is one thing to say that the Internet creates a digital library for a global age, a free repository of knowledge for a free society, even despite attempts to keep digital channels proprietary; it is another, and a quite incorrect, thing to say that everyone has access to the Internet. There are a number of digital divides (David and Millward 2014: section 2). What was first called the digital divide referred simply to the overall numbers of people who had no access to the Internet as distinct from those that did. This divide could and can be mapped within countries, and between developed and less developed societies. Even beyond this division, and once basic access in at least the most advanced societies reached very high levels, what was referred to as the second digital divide remains – that of quality of access and competence to use simple access to maximum benefit (see David 2001). Access to the Internet is not universal, nor is the quality of such access equal, or the ability of all users to maximize the benefits of their use. Nonetheless, access to the Internet has expanded to far greater numbers within all societies relative to the numbers able to afford pay-to-view television, or to attend university and hence have access to their libraries/archives (Dutton et al. 2013). While far from universal, the Internet today does make available more information to more people than any other medium or institution in the history of human civilization. This is not to say that the Internet can or should replace other institutions, not least schools. It is, rather, a supplement to more elementary or established forms of learning – one that creates the greatest ever expansion of shared human knowing since the invention of writing and the rise of general literacy.

A large part of the physical infrastructure of the Internet is in private hands, and, for those outside education, most access to the Internet is through private payment. Yet, at the same time, once online, the Internet affords access to the greatest repository of freely shared content ever to have existed. This is the tension at the heart of the global network society, that between a free culture and a fee culture. The question of content and access is neatly captured in another parallel with the world of contemporary libraries. The advent of the Internet and digital archives has seen most of the world's university libraries digitize their catalogues. These catalogues have also been put online. In research on libraries in London early in the development of such processes (Zeitlyn et al. 1999), one consequence of online public access catalogues (OPACs) was found to be an increase in requests to view works in prestigious and well-resourced university libraries – in particular, to view rare, old and expensive content (both books and journals). With more than 100 institutions of higher education within the greater London area, the creation of a consortium to share information about resources led to disquiet among the more affluent institutions, which believed that their resources were being used by staff and students of other institutions with no reciprocal benefit to the staff and students of elite institutions. As a result, many of the more prestigious libraries introduced electronic swipe-card entry systems in the early to mid-1990s to prevent 'members of the public' from taking advantage of the knowledge of contents now available online by actually coming along and wandering in. Primitive as this example of OPACs and swipe-cards is, it neatly captures the tension between the two digital revolutions, both using digital affordances, but each using them in divergent ways – to open/close access to the library of human knowledge. Today, if a creative, scientific or academic work is available in a commercial form somewhere in the world, it is likely also to be available electronically everywhere by various non-commercial means. This virtual and global library combines lawful postings and copyright-infringing versions. This digital commons exists despite various attempts to close it down. It is a shared repository of human knowledge, a library of humanity for a global world.

Digital Commons: The Anarchist in the Library

The possibility of a friction-free global library of all human culture is a promise to some, but is certainly a threat to those for whom scarcity is the basic starting point for charging prices. Siva Vaidhyanathan (2004) suggests attempts to build friction into the Internet have been driven by the desire to clamp down on the potential for anarchy in the library and to prevent an anarchic library from spilling out into the rest of social life. For Vaidhyanathan, anarchy has always stood as the opposite of oligarchy in the organization of social and political life. The Internet simply creates new potential for realizing the anarchist dream of a horizontal and self-organized society. The claim that society needs order and that order can only come from 'above' has always been used to warrant hierarchy (Hobbes 1991), usually by those higher up in any such arrangement.

In the nineteenth century, moral panics about 'anarchists' presented any threat to dominant interests as, at root, the work of 'mindless' anarchists, and the stereotype of anarchists as bomb- or rock-wielding 'angry young man', bent on pointless destruction, has come down to us today. For Vaidhyanathan, anarchy should be understood rather as an invitation to create a self-organizing and flat social system. The digital commons and the possibility of a free-sharing of the world's cultural resources makes just such a society seem far more achievable than in past times. That is why moral panics about anarchy on the Internet encourage an impression that unregulated 'access' would simply descend into a flood of pornography, hate-speech, cyberterrorism and paedophilia. The population is to be protected on the assumption that to be exposed to a cultural free-for-all would corrupt them. Yet, those who claim the right to decide what is acceptable and what is not are not neutral in their choices.

Vaidhyanathan documents how attempts to introduce 'friction' (censorship is another name for it) into the global commons, the worldwide digital library, have been done through a combination of national security and property-based regulative frames that does little to protect citizens. Rather, such regulation protects an oligarchic state as well as corporate actors who equate their protection with that of everyone else. In the name of protecting children, citizens are denied rights to choose and are, rather, infantilized themselves (with authorities in loco parentis). To protect freedom, new controls are introduced. To preserve security, 'citizenship' – something requiring informed, free choice – is put at risk.

Orphan Works: The Capitalist in the Archive

The radical extension of the problem of orphan works in recent years powerfully illustrates the tension between a free culture and a fee culture. Since the formation of the World Trade Organisation in 1994/95, and its first act, the creation of the Agreement on Trade Related-Aspects of Intellectual Property Rights (TRIPS), copyright extensions to between fifty and seventy years after the death of the author have been rolled out across almost the entire world. This treaty requires all signatories to follow the United States' lead – which was, with the Sonny Bono Copyright Extension Act, otherwise known as the Mickey Mouse Protection Act (Vaidhyanathan 2003) – to extend copyright to maintain ownership over creative works that date back to the very earliest years of the twentieth century. This has huge implications for libraries and archives of creative works.

An orphan work is a creative work where a legal rights holder may exist but has not been identified. Copyright extending up to seventy years beyond the death of the author means a long chain of potential claimants is able to come forward to demand damages in the event of any work, perhaps long out of print, being made available without their prior permission. This problem is particularly acute in the case of film archives, but the same problem exists for all creative works. Film archives hold vast stores of old films, both fictional and documentary-based, often on nitrate film that is prone to deterioration and is even dangerous (being highly inflammable). Claudy Op den Kamp (2015: 407) notes estimates of the scale of the orphan works problem have ranged from 40 per cent of British Library holdings, and as much as 58 per cent of Cornell University's library, with various European audio-visual archives estimating that between 5 and 21 per cent of their stock is orphaned. In the domain of older works, the problem is most acute, of course. It has been estimated (Hediger 2005) that 75 per cent of films made in the silent era are now no longer in existence. Of what remains, a similar proportion is estimated to comprise orphan works.

As long as a work is believed to be orphaned (i.e., to remain potentially under copyright, but where the potential rights holder remains unidentified), it is unlikely to be copied by an official archive, whether for storage or release purposes. This is because the issue of uncertain legal ownership raises very serious financial risks. For the oldest film materials, where 100-year-old film companies may have long ceased trading, and where the director and producer are also long dead, the question of whether the work still remains in copyright – and, if so, who would own it – becomes deeply opaque. Any descendant of a director, screenwriter, producer or company owner can make the case for ownership up to seventy years after the death of their relative. Currently, copying a work that, subsequently, sees a copyright claimant come forward and successfully challenge the copying as an infringement of their rights, would be subject to punitive damages that are both extremely high and unpredictable (see Phythian-Adams 2015). Across the world, the sum of all the archival material that remains unavailable for reproduction and circulation is vast. Op den Kamp documents attempts to create protocols for archives that would fix in advance the price of a copyright claim if one were to arise. Such prices would be set at a realistic proportion of any revenues that might arise from reproducing a work otherwise out of circulation. This form of licensing arrangement would end the current orphan works problem, which combines uncertainty over whether copyright still stands with uncertainly over what such copyright would cost if it were infringed simply because no rights holder could be identified prior to the infringement. Sadly, the existing film and wider copyright industries, those that have pressed hardest for worldwide and ever-longer temporal extension to copyright, have also been successful in resisting such licensing arrangements.

Efforts towards the digitization of all film archives have been restricted by the orphan works problem, which has itself been exacerbated by copyright extension. The problem of orphan works is also made worse by the fact that copyright requires no registration. It was once the case, in many countries at least, that copyright required the publisher to 'lodge' copies of the work with a library of record in order to assert its rights (Johns 2009). This is something that has been done away with in the rush towards global copyright harmonization and extension (in depth, duration and geographical reach). As such, another positive function of libraries (the recording of when copyright started so at least to be able to know exactly when it would end) was lost. Copyright-infringing, free circulation online (beyond the legal and physical constraints of established archives) is one solution; but the need to digitize the content in the first place does mean that physical archives need to revise existing laws to allow them to make this common heritage of humanity accessible to such digital distribution.

Libraries as Records of Ownership and/or the Common Heritage of Humanity

As was suggested above, libraries occupy a contradictory position in relation to intellectual property. On the one hand, libraries make the ideas expressed in copyrighted (and patented) works freely available to see. However, on the other hand, libraries have functioned (in relation to copyright), and continue to function (in the case of patent), in 'publicly' asserting rights holders' claims over ideas as 'private' property.

Pradip Thomas (2015) describes the creation of an archive of Indian traditional knowledge (TK) – the Traditional Knowledge Digital Library (TKDL). This project documents an array of existing knowledge, covering food, health and traditional medicine – relating, in particular, to yoga. Thomas notes (2015: 363–364) that, in the United States, more than 130 patents and 1,000 trademarks were given to yoga postures and products in 2007 alone. The Indian government has fought many legal battles with US and EU corporations regarding attempted patent claims over such things as the basic genetic qualities that distinguish basmati rice, neem and turmeric. The TKDL has begun to limit the scope for bioprospecting/biopiracy

(Shiva 1997; Mooney 2000). Such limitation is achieved insofar as this new archive documents 'prior art' – which basically means what is already known. In this way, the library functions to protect the common culture from private ownership claims, by documenting the fact that it was already common knowledge. Chidi Oguamanam (2015) has similarly outlined attempts by farmers in the global South to protect – through archiving and documenting – local, indigenous and traditional forms of knowledge, alongside information about seeds and farming practices (see also Chapter 7 below).

Asserting that knowledge was already common knowledge some-where does not, however, ensure that such knowledge will remain free to share everywhere. Despite pressing for global extension of IP rights, the United States does not recognize demonstrations of 'prior art' made in other countries (Halbert 2014). Also, while patent librar-ies make individual claims to innovation into 'public' knowledge, in the sense that all can know what has been invented, this public knowledge does not mean the knowledge made known belongs to the public. In fact, patent library registration is a condition for making such new knowledge private property, at least for a limited duration (around 20 years). Nonetheless, public registration in return for a limited private monopoly is exactly that: limited. After the expiry of the patent's duration, the knowledge, held in public (in the patent library), does become public knowledge, part of the common culture. Graham Dutfield and Uma Suthersanan (2005) note that technol-ogy, computing, medical and agribusiness companies have sought, where possible, to register innovations under copyright rules rather than under patents, precisely to avoid the need to disclose their inno-vations and because copyright gives far, far longer terms of private control.

Plagiarism vs. Piracy

Using a library to access content for free stands in stark contrast to attempts to sell access to content on a pay-to-view basis. The rise of peer-to-peer file-sharing in the 2000s saw record and film companies target schools, universities and colleges that gave stu-dents access to the Internet, which those students then used to share content online with one another. Record and film companies sought to equate such copyright-infringing file-sharing with plagiarism in an attempt to suggest that these companies and educational institutions had a common purpose in preventing such supposedly equivalent

'cheating' (David 2010: 104–106). These claims are highly spe-
cious, and serve here to highlight the very difference such campaigns
sought to obscure: that between a free culture, based on recognition of authors, and a fee culture, based on payments made to their
publishers.

Students, when writing an essay, are encouraged and required to
access content using libraries. They are not required to pay to use
library materials. Rather, they are taught to reference the author when
they use the author's work. Not to reference correctly constitutes
plagiarism, where one person's work contains the words of another
but where the impression is created that this second author's work is
that of the first. More particularly, plagiarism is the failure to clearly
demonstrate when content derives from another source. Plagiarism
is not the same as copyright infringement. Correct referencing of
an original author eliminates plagiarism. Copying a sentence or a
short paragraph from a work would not constitute copyright infringement, but in an essay it would be plagiarism if it were unreferenced.
Similarly, copying with attribution would not be plagiarism, while,
even with an acknowledgement of authorship, copying a whole song
or large segment of a book would breach copyright. In this connection, downloading and meticulously documenting a music archive
from sharing sites would not be plagiarism; as such, a music collection would be fully referenced. (If students were as meticulous in
their essay referencing as they are in their music archiving, that would
be a good thing, from an educational point of view at least.)

Plagiarism is rooted in theological principles regarding attributing
authorship (initially in the word of god), not in commercial consid-
erations of payment. Libraries, in this regard, follow the Hegelian
principle of an author's moral rights, rather than a Lockean conception of copyright as a property right. Moral rights (something more
fully articulated in statute law systems) and copyright (something
more developed in common law – Anglo-Saxon – legal systems) are
distinct; in post-WTO/TRIPS treaties and agreements, it is the latter
that has come to dominate worldwide (Ghosh 2015). An author's
moral rights – based on the romantic principle of the embodiment of
an author's personality in their work – assert that the author's name
should always be associated with the work and that their dignity
requires this as it does a defence of the integrity of the work itself.
Referencing correctly, and hence avoiding plagiarism, stands in line
with this framework. In contrast, copyright, in the Lockean tradition, derives from a supposed natural right to ownership based on
the labour undertaken in creating the work. This model assumes that

control over use and payment for use – rather than author recognition – is paramount. Students who learn to share the common culture in exchange for a referencing of (showing respect for) authors follow the moral rights tradition, even while the following of very similar practices in the context of file-sharing (such as in the aforementioned music archiving example) constitutes copyright violation.

Libraries are required to abide by copyright. Read the copyright licence agreement above the photocopier next time you are infringing copyright yourself. By informing you of what you should *not* do, the library is itself avoiding liability for what you *are* doing on 'their' photocopier; yet, in putting a copying machine right next to a huge room full of books, what did they think you were going to do? Of course, as long as a poster telling you not to infringe copyright is placed above the photocopier, regardless of whether or not you ever read, never mind heed it, at least *the library* is not breaking the law. (Just copying this page will not constitute copyright infringement, so please send me a picture of yourself next to the photocopier and under the licensing agreement.) This legal principle has significant consequences for online sharing service providers, as this book will go on to highlight.

From Scarcity to Authority

The digital affordances of today's global network society extend the principle of the library to the whole world of human culture. We are, for the first time in history, creating the possibility of an end to scarcity, at least in relation to informational content; and, with the development of 3D printers, the same logic is pressing ahead in the domain of physical objects that embody abstract knowledge in their composition. An end to scarcity, a library of all human culture, freely available to all who can access a computer (a limit that must be addressed) everywhere, always and forever, would fundamentally challenge a social order based on the principle of scarcity and the price mechanism that currently regulates access to scarce goods.

While the price mechanism and the idea of private property are justified on the grounds that they enable the allocation of scarce and rivalrous things, their maintenance acts to perpetuate the very scarcity used to justify their existence. Beyond scarcity, the question arises not as to how to allocate, but rather as how to choose between the near infinite array of possible options available to choose between. This has been a longstanding question for library users: not how to afford a book, but how to find the one you need when confronted by plenitude (Zeitlyn et al. 1998, 1999).

The question that then arises is whether an age of free access will see the rise of new forms of control, controls that may replicate the rise of the editorial nexus within state and commercial media in the nineteenth and twentieth centuries. What had initially been the radical political organs of a challenger class, the newspapers of the emerging urban bourgeoisie soon became dominated by commercial interests – in particular, the interests of advertisers and proprietors. This shift from political radicalism to economic dominance, effected through the controlling power of editors in binding content with the needs of these vested interests, turned the public sphere into an increasingly commercial one (Habermas 1992/1962). Might the same enthusiasm for a new freedom through a new media today not find itself similarly constrained by commercial and/or political forms of power?

This is not a foregone conclusion and so requires analysis, not presumption. On the one hand, the kind of editorial nexus that Jürgen Habermas describes when documenting how newspapers (and, by extension, radio and television later) moved from 'alternative voice' towards 'commercial management' does not exist online. While advertisers abound on the Web, content is not limited to that which editors believe will best complement the needs of their advertisers' profits. Content is not regulated by an editorial nexus. To this extent at least, the future will not simply mirror the past.

On the other hand, in an age of digital plenty, the possibility exists for manipulation in the way that users search for content. Whereas, in principle, a librarian is not working on commission, commercial search engines stand accused of programming their search algorithms in such a fashion as to either prioritize some sites over others, or, at best, to make it very easy for powerful players to design their websites to come higher up any particular search than less well-resourced sites. Graeme Kirkpatrick (2008) usefully highlights the hidden scope for such manipulation, while Siva Vaidhaynathan (2012) details why Google, in particular, poses a significant threat to an open and equal digital culture (see Chapter 5 for further discussion).

Conclusions: Free Culture or Fee Culture

The Internet as a library for a global network society manifests the tension between two digital revolutions: one towards increased enclosure by encryption code, in the creation of a global fee culture; and the second towards increased access by shared code, in the creation of a global free culture. This tension between fee and free culture, between enclosure and sharing, between information as capital and information as culture, is part of a longstanding struggle: for universal versus elite education, between general literacy and class distinction, and between closure of and access to culture – such as was embodied in the distinction between private and public libraries.

On the one hand, the global network society has seen the rise of swipe cards, pin codes and centraliszed control, as well as of surveillance over ever-greater swathes of everyday life (Lyon 2001). On the other hand, this same global network society affords free access, greater autonomy and even anonymity. The rise of a digital commons represents a threat to the business of selling access to scarce goods as it renders scarcity itself something rare. Yet, the rise of increased intellectual property duration, extension and depth, as illustrated in the case of orphan works, makes the possibility of archives, and of the Internet as a universal archive of human culture, harder, if all the more essential. The need to document the common culture becomes increasingly important in an age of aggressive prospecting and rights assertion.

The idea of the library, and the ways in which students are encouraged to use it, to reference rather than to pay for use, upholds the principle of authors' moral rights to receive recognition for their work, rather than direct payment – and, as such, supports a Hegelian rather than a Lockean conception of possession. In this regard, it is important to reject erroneous equations between plagiarism and intellectual property infringement. Plagiarism, as a form of intellectual *identity* 'theft', is not the same thing as intellectual *property* 'theft'; and even the conception of IP infringement as 'theft' is a metaphorical stretching of the truth.

The struggle for a free culture does not simply stop when access is made possible. In an age of plenitude, questions still arise as to how to find things, and whom to believe when searching for content. As such, the model of an impartial librarian should be upheld when sizing up the (im)partiality of search engines and websites.

3

Peer-to-Peer Music-Sharing Online

Introduction

The history of peer-to-peer music-sharing and its impact on the music industry, from the birth of the first file-sharing service in 1999, through a series of peer-to-peer and peers-to-peer services until the present, is relatively short. However, it has been perhaps the most visible manifestation of the challenge posed by sharing to an economic system based upon monopoly control of copyright and the consequent possibility of selling informational goods as commodities. The idea of the recording as the meal, rather than simply being the menu, however, has itself only had a relatively brief history; and what came to be the standard business model in the later decades of the twentieth century is no more natural or necessary than what has come to challenge it. The myth of the recording artist, relative to the performing artist, is explored in this chapter. The notion that musicians are the beneficiaries of the system of copyright that protected, and thereby enabled, the recording industry to develop is debunked. Most recording artists end up owing their record labels money, as the bulk of recording costs are offset against a royalty payment that is only ever a tiny fraction of the actual net income from sales of their recorded works. Of the tiny number who break even, most make less than a living wage from such recordings, and the number making more from recording than they do from live performance dwindles to single figures. As musicians take a better share of live performance revenues than they do revenue from recording sales, and as declining record sales have gone hand-in-hand with increased attendance at and ticket prices for live concerts, it is in fact in artists' interests that recordings circulate freely rather than for a price. Recording-as-information becomes the menu, and the live event as performance becomes the meal. Not only is sharing the best way for artists to get paid; its proliferation also demonstrates the failure of technical, legal and cultural attempts to stop it – something that highlights not just the efficiency and efficacy of sharing, but also the relative creativity of sharers compared to the non-innovativeness of corporate research and development teams seeking to stop sharing. This software development theme is the focus of Chapter 5. The current chapter will, rather, suggest that the shift to live music as revenue stream offers alternative business models based on a revaluation of place and performance/labour relative to abstracted information/capital within global networks (a shift that is further evidenced in Chapter 4's discussion of live-streaming and digital television).

From CDs to Napster: The Rise of Peer-to-Peer

The rise of peer-to-peer music-sharing combines many elements, primarily those of *digital storage* (including compression), *digital distribution* and *digital searching*. The first part – digital storage – starts with the development and adoption of the compact disc (CD). This development was both profound and deeply contradictory. The CD revolutionized the established recording industry, but also led to its profound crisis. The CD was developed through collaboration between commercial actors (Phillips and Sony, amongst others) and was introduced as a commercial format for selling recorded music in 1982. It was cheaper to manufacture than vinyl, could be sold at a higher price, was less prone to breakages in transit, was more durable in use and – once popular – had the profoundly beneficial effect for record companies that consumers not only bought new music on CD but also needed to 'reformat' their existing record collections – i.e., buying digital copies of what they already owned in older formats. Reduced costs, higher prices and increased sales (due to reformatting) resulted in a perfect profit storm for the recording industry between 1982 and 1999 (Sandall 2007), when file-sharing services first arose and took the efficiencies of digital storage in a fundamentally different direction.

Digital storage was supplemented by digital compression and distribution mechanisms – also initially within the recording industry (and film/television sectors). Compression formats (MP1 and 2) had been developed to aid in the transmission of television images via digital satellite and cable services, where large amounts of data needed to be transmitted over what were, by today's standards, relatively narrow bandwidths. MP3 compression is something of a fiction, as a work in progress between MP2 and MP4 (developed for combining music and video transmission); but it was MP3 that became the standard format for compressing music files for relatively efficient digital transmission. Initially, compression was developed to aid in the production, mastering and manufacturing processes, whereby record companies could distribute content around the world for various technical and financial reasons. Again, while this aided in the profit storm of the 1982–99 era, the MP3 format would become the base element in free-sharing after 1999.

The Internet and World Wide Web are also significant elements in the configuration of affordances that allowed for the rise of peer-to-peer music-sharing, and their history is addressed in more detail in Chapter 5. In essence, from 1982 to 1999, the commercial recording industry revelled in the efficiency of digital storage and distribution. This period saw the rise of new multimedia conglomerates, with record companies being highly prized arms and/or foundations of bigger empires of global, vertically and horizontally integrated businesses (Castells 2009). Suddenly, it became normal for the same company that produced a record to also own the company holding an artist's publishing rights (Hull 2004), the music video channel, and the factory making both the CD and the machine to play it on. In the 1980s and 1990s, such companies were too busy counting their profits (and using them to buy out their competition) to notice that, in distributing digital copies of musical content, they were in effect giving away the master copies of their own intellectual property (Sandall 2007: 30).

From Napster to Now

Shaun Fanning's Napster combined the efficiency of the MP3 compression format with the Internet's ability to distribute content – and the simple addition of a relatively easy-to-use Web-based search engine site that allowed users to make their personal music collections accessible to others such that downloaders could make copies of content made available by uploaders. The seventeen years of profit growth that had followed the introduction of the CD suddenly went into reverse in 1999. It is possible to dispute the 'causal' relationship between increased sharing and falling sales of recorded music at the individual level (David and Kirkhope 2006); those who share music are more likely to buy music than those who do not share music. However, it is the case that such music fans started buying less recorded music from 1999 onwards than they had done before (and at a lower price) (Krueger 2004).

Napster's central server model was an easy target for legal action, as copyright-infringing files were exchanged directly through the software provider's computers. (In this way, Napster was not a fully peer-to-peer service.) For this reason, it was successfully prosecuted and closed down. However, Napster was immediately replaced by a new generation of more fully peer-to-peer services that evaded the legal liability for which Napster had been successfully prosecuted. This began a legal cat-and-mouse struggle between sharers and those seeking to defend copyright. Peer-to-peer, then peers-to-peer (torrents) and then streaming services meant each attempt to target a legal bottleneck in the latest sharing network simply saw that bottleneck removed, allowing for continued sharing. In this cat-and-mouse struggle, the mouse kept on winning.

While Chapter 5 suggests that this cat-and-mouse battle evidences the superior creativity of sharing-based hacker programmers relative to commercial actors when it comes to developing software, this chapter seeks to address a different question. If the cat never manages to catch the mice, surely the cat will starve. The recording industry seeks to present itself as defending the 'cool cats' (the romantic artists) against the thieving mice who, record companies claim, will leave artists broke. In truth, the profound slimming down of the recording industry's 'fat cats' has not harmed artists, who were themselves the losers in the established business model where 'romantic' artists were 'paid' (if that is the right word when debt is far more often the actual outcome) royalties based on a copyright, rather than wages based on performance.

The Myth of The Recording Artist (Then and Now)

The decision by The Beatles in 1966 to stop performing live – a decision arrived at through a particular configuration of personal and technical reasons – led to the production a year later of the 'studio album' *Sgt. Pepper's Lonely Hearts Club Band*. The Beach Boys' album *Pet Sounds*, released in 1966, was also a 'studio album'; and the two can be seen as the first 'concept albums'. This shift from a series of songs to an integrated concept album was also a shift in ideology from the pop artist as performing artist to becoming primarily a recording artist. The idea of the recording artist, reclusive and detached from their audience, making a living from the sale of recordings, is not the reality for the vast majority of musical artists, even those who are 'rich and famous' – which very few are. The very great majority of musicians who make a living in the music business do so from live performance, not from recording revenues. In this regard, though hardly typical themselves in other respects, it is The Rolling Stones who exemplify the life of a musical artist. Despite making money from recordings (which few artists do), The Rolling Stones still tour and still make more money from touring than they do from record sales.

While the performing artist gets paid to perform, the recording artist records works, copies of which are then sold by a record company. The record company then returns a royalty to the artists for each copy of the work sold. In order to have the right to sell copies of the artist's work, the record company has signed a contract with the artist. The artist signs over copyrights in their intellectual property to the record company, which, in exchange, pay the artist a royalty based on the number of copies sold. Rather than getting paid for their time, such as might be expected for a session musician or for a performing artist whom audiences pay to see perform, the recording artist lives on royalties. An artist may receive an advance on future royalties, and may use some part of this to live on, but, for the greater number, money advanced is not paid to the artist at all. Rather, for most artists, the whole advance (and, for the rest, most of any advance) is offset against the costs that labels themselves run up in producing, promoting and managing the artists' work. These artists are not, then, paid for their work, but receive a royalty on sales. However, this royalty will be used to repay the advance. As such, even when 'earning' royalties, artists rarely actually 'receive' them. Rather than being a creative worker or performer, the recording artist has been framed within a 'romantic' conception of creative work (Marshall 2004). The record company deals with the commercial side of things, thereby claiming to 'protect' the artist from the instrumental and uncreative side of 'the business'. Much has been written criticizing the mythology of the 'romantic' genius in music and elsewhere (Marshall 2004). It is also true that the particular myth of the detached romantic genius popularized in the music industry underplays the extent to which early romantic poets and artists sought to express community, nature and collective 'creativity', not just the brilliance of the unique individual (David 2006). Wordsworth did not wander lonely as a cloud in spring, but rather read about the experience in his sister's diary

(Byatt 1997). Early in his life, Wordsworth wrote against individual claims to authorship as individual possession. Yet, when older, he set about campaigning for stronger and longer copyright terms to protect his inheritance in cash terms (May and Sell 2005) on the premise of the idea of individual genius. It is that later conception of the identifiable (and hence lawfully exclusive) author that copyright industries (such as the recording industry) have become attached to. Yet, the romantic artist is mythical in numerous ways, in terms of both the origins of creativity itself and in how best to protect the creative artist. Creativity comes from multiple sources: community, individual introspection, performance with other artists, engagement with an audience and/or technical production (such as can be added in a recording studio). The myth of the recording artist fuses the individualized version of romantic genius with the technical production process in a studio, while community, live performance and audience interaction contributions are marginalized. This is one very particular construction of 'creativity'. As this chapter will suggest, this construction does not perform well in rewarding artists, nor therefore in 'incentivizing' creativity; neither is it the only possible foundation for creative works. A sharing-based model of distributing recordings that promotes live performance also values community, artist interaction and audience engagement, in both the commercial and the cultural sense of value. Such an alternative model of valuing and fostering creativity would not produce another *Sgt. Pepper* or *Pet Sounds*, but then these works have already been created, so to repeat them would hardly be 'creative'.

The 'Romantic' Myth of the Recording Artist

The 'romantic' business model of artists insulated from the business of selling themselves directly for money through the 'protection' afforded by the sale of their copyright (to record companies in exchange for royalties, and even an advance on those royalties) is deeply exploitative, and misleading if it fosters a view of the artist benefiting from such 'protection'. In almost all cases (Holmes 2003), this model does not benefit the artist; and, even where artists make money in this business model, they make more from live performance (Krueger 2004) – and such earnings are further advanced by free circulation of their work, as this chapter will outline.

The case against the 'romantic' advance/royalties model has been detailed well enough elsewhere (Albini 1994; Love 2000), but the evidence debunking the model is easily summarized. A contract with a record company will involve a commitment to invest in the artist in exchange for copyright on their work. The investment will be called 'an advance', and out of this advance will be taken almost all the costs required to produce, promote and manage the artist. The advance may or may not include an income for the artist to live on. Note that almost all the costs record companies sink into the artist's work is in this 'advance', and the advance needs to be 'repaid' from later sales. This might seem fair enough, but there is a catch. The advance is not simply repaid from future net sales income. Future net sales income returns to the record company, which now owns the copyright. The 'investment' must, for the most part, be repaid not from the sum of net sales, but rather from the sum of the artist's royalties, which will themselves be only a very small percentage of the net sales – 5–15 per cent, depending on their negotiating position when they signed. Repayment of the advance/investment out of the tiny fraction of sales income that the artist is actually assigned in royalties is called 'recouping', not 'repayment'. But 90 per cent of records never 'recoup' (Kirton 2015) – that is to say, the advance/investment exceeds the 5–15 per cent of net sales paid in royalties, and so the artist remains indebted to the record company. This is not to say the record did not repay the investment made in the artist, only that the royalties earned failed to 'recoup'. This may be because the royalty rates were so small, not because the record 'failed' to sell. The popular example is the one-million-dollar record deal (Albini 1994; and Love 2000). This million is spent on production, promotion and management (with an allowance for the artist to live on). If the work then sold a million copies, it would still 'fail to recoup' even when net sales were many millions of dollars. This is because the one-million-dollar advance is still more than the 5, 10 or even 15 per cent of net sales (itself only about 60 per cent of retail) assigned as royalties. One million sales at $US10 per sale (meaning $6 to the record company) would generate six million dollars for the label. Even if artists were to be getting the maximum royalty rate (15 per cent), they would only then receive $900,000 in royalties. As such, they failed to recoup. The record company takes the 85–95 per cent of net sales, and so still profits – even from works that do not recoup. All the royalties earned are paid back to the label because these earnings are set against the money advanced to invest in the work. A million-selling album then leaves the artist, who has 'enjoyed' an allowance (akin to minimum wage levels – Albini 1994) while making the work, in debt. Most records do not sell anything like that number of copies and most contracts do not offer any living allowance. Most musicians do not have record contracts; most of those who do have contracts do not have advances that extend to a living wage. Most artists with a contract fail to recoup; failure to recoup leaves the artist powerless to negotiate the terms of any subsequent contract. The first thing to be cut with such future contracts is the artist's living allowance, if one were ever offered in the first place. The point remains the same. Because artists have to repay almost the full cost of the investment made in them by record companies from the very small fraction of net sales they 'receive' in royalties, they are in almost all cases left owing money to their record companies. The record company can claim that the artist has failed to recoup even when overall net sales generated significant profits for record companies. Those who fail to recoup but who still remain under contract will be compelled to accept worse contractual conditions for subsequent works.

The standard argument in favour of this dispensation is that investing in records is a gamble, with most records failing to cover their costs from total sales, let alone recouping, and hence record companies claim they need to take the lion's share of net sales to cover themselves against such losses (Rossman 2010). Many records do lose money for all concerned. However, sleight of hand between 'recouping' and 'repaying' allows this argument to be grossly exaggerated. (See Light and Warburton 2005 for a parallel example of exaggeration in the claims made by pharmaceutical companies.)

Once signed to a record company, and once in a position where royalties fail to recoup advances, artists find themselves in a position of debt bondage to their record companies. Such debt bondage leaves them unable to renegotiate the terms of further investment in subsequent recordings, leading to lower advances and lower royalty rates, which then deepen the conditions of debt bondage going forward. Artists are effectively trapped in debt. Note that, as advances are mostly paid by the record company for their own expenses (investments) – and when these are very often for the use of their own studios, staff and services – the costs, profits and debts can again be further exaggerated and stacked against artists in the interests of record companies.

This model fails artists at every level. New artists are told that the model is designed to reward success and so not to expect to get paid if they are not already a star. Stars are told that 85–95 per cent of net sales income is retained by the record company to support the struggling younger artist, whose work has a greater risk of not selling. When, as is even the case for most 'stars', their royalties 'fail' to recoup investment (for the above reason – despite high sales), stars are told that at least their records generate the publicity necessary to make them a living from live performance (Dredge 2013). As will be suggested below, if all record contracts are good for is generating publicity, this is a long since redundant and highly inefficient mechanism that all artists would benefit from seeing the end of. Just as the failure of record sales to pay artists any reasonable earnings even at the height of their careers, so any suggestion that artists benefit from royalties on record sales when they are old is again largely false. Artists do receive some income from performance rights (such as when songs are played on the radio) and from author rights (when works are covered), but these are not the copyright that is connected to the sale of copies and around which the record industry centres. While artists have experienced a long history of exploitation and downright theft in relation to publishing rights (Heylin 2015), it was only the profit frenzy of the 1980s and 1990s that saw record companies buying up all the large publishing houses, with the result that publishing rights fell into their hands. This was a situation that would harm artists, as it meant failure to recoup in record sales would see record companies able to take income from publishing rights in lieu of insufficient record-sales-based royalties to repay the debts that were owed to them. Previously, publishing rights had been a separate and insulated source of earnings when such rights were managed and collected by a different company from that of the artist's record label (Hull 2004). That record companies can now take earnings from airplay and covers, in lieu of insufficient sales income, is also of no benefit to artists (Rojek 2011). The so-called '360-degree contract' enables record labels to recover their costs from all the artist's sources of earnings, even while retaining the greater part of record sales revenues. That standard record contracts create such a vicious circle of debt bondage is used to justify claims by record companies over all alternative income streams (airplay, live performance, covers, merchandising, tie-ins and so on).

In one study, only 2.5 per cent of those artists with copyright-based royalty claims – i.e., those who had been successful enough to have a record deal – earned the equivalent of the minimum state benefit level (exclusive of housing cost) (Holmes 2003). Of such artists, Albini (1994) notes that only a handful earn more from record sales than they would be able to earn working for the minimum wage in a convenience store. Alan Krueger (2004; Krueger and Connolly 2006) calculates that, of those who did earn reasonable earnings from record sales, only two or three a year earn more from this than they did from live performance. As a business model, the claim that the romantic advance/royalty model rewards artists and hence incentivizes creativity is simply not credible.

Why Sign?

The rather obvious question then arises. If royalty-based record deals are so onerous and exploitative, why on earth would anyone sign one? The record company defence of their standard business model is simple enough. They claim the right to take the lion's share of all net sales, and more if they own the publishing company as well, which most now do (Hull 2004), because they claim they do the lion's share of the work. There are millions of songs, singers and musicians in the world. Only some make money, and to make money out of music takes more than just 'raw' talent. Record companies identify five core functions they perform in the transformation of a prospective artist into a commercial success (David 2010: 130–141). It is perhaps an extension of the very 'romantic' conception of the artist, which has been critiqued here and elsewhere (Marshall 2004), that the artist might consider themselves the sole source of value, when so much else besides goes into their development, at least as a commercially viable artist.

For artists to be saleable, and hence to have any economic value to which they then may feel entitled, the record company can claim to have contributed a good number of things. First, the saleable work must be produced; second, the work needs to be manufactured; third, it needs to be distributed (a two-way street, if manufactured product is to be sent out and payment for it is to come back in); fourth, the work needs to be promoted; and finally, the artists' rights need managing to ensure that earnings can be secured on all possible intellectual property rights (in terms of performance, publishing, recording, appearance and merchandising). If artists add just themselves to the equation, while the record company adds all these five dimensions, perhaps, then, it is only fair that the record label receives at least five-sixths of net sales (in fact, it always takes even more than this). However, this calculus is seriously flawed. First and foremost, artists do not 'receive' this one-sixth (or less) anyway, as these earnings are set against the very costs of production, management and promotion that labels claim constitute three of their five contributions. Second, in a digital age, production, manufacture, distribution and promotion do not require the kinds of fixed capital that might once have made such a distribution of earnings seem fair or at the very least unavoidable. Regarding rights management, it is only recently that many of these rights have fallen to record companies to manage (see above) and this has certainly not been to the advantage of artists. Record companies simply became horizontally and vertically integrated to remove this layer of autonomy that artists previously had. In the past, it was next to impossible to gain any radio airplay if your work was not signed to a major label, as it was to get any bookings with large and/or prestigious performance venues. That a record deal afforded you publicity was as much testament to the negative power of record companies to exclude anyone without their backing as it was evidence of their beneficial value. Given that most artists never saw earnings from the sale of their work anyway, the capacity of record companies to get record shops to actually pay for stock sold (no mean feat, it is true) was of little comfort. Thus, now, in an age of digital production, manufacture, distribution and promotion, and where record companies' management of the wider field of an artist's rights is of no particular benefit to artists, as well as where the traditional business model saw so little return to the artist, the case for signing a record deal seems pretty much dead and buried. Yet, a record deal is still valued: why?

Why Not Sign?

If a record deal tends to leave the artist not getting paid, at least in terms of royalties on record sales (royalties being swallowed up by the unbalanced relationship between the costs to be set against them and the percentage of net sales they are set at), a record deal was – at least, until now – the only way to gain the exposure and popularity needed to secure an audience to come to live events from which the artist could at least hope to earn a living. Some additional earnings could be made from publishing rights, sales of merchandise and performance rights, if the record company did not tie those up as well within a 360-degree contract. In the end, recording, which could be regarded as unpaid work, could be seen instead as free advertising. While record companies like to claim that the record is the 'thing', the finished product, it primarily remains just a menu, at least from the artist's point of view, with the live event being the meal. If having a record deal was this mythical sign that got you noticed (got your work reviewed in the music press, got your music played on the radio, and secured you live bookings), while it may feel galling not to receive payment for it, in the absence of an alternative, why not sign? As Courtney Love (2000) puts it, if the tips are big enough, it can pay to go to work for nothing. Yet, Love is here talking about peer-to-peer file-sharing. She notes that as record deals are, for the most part, no more advantageous to artists than having their work circulated freely, and if publicity is really all that is being gained from them, such deals are no better than free-sharing. Given the choice, she would rather her fans got her recorded music for nothing. At least their ticket purchases do pay her bills. Her record company uses her record sales to pay their own bills, not hers, so if someone is going to have her music for nothing, she is pretty clear who she thinks it should be. As will be outlined in the next section, if fans do not buy records and therefore have more money in their pockets to go see artists live, this is all the better for artists.

The Rise of Live

Objection to being exploited by one's own record company – such that the greater part of a company's investment in an artist is to be repaid by that artist from their royalties, but where such royalties are only a tiny percentage of net sales, so leaving the artist in debt even when the remaining net sales pass to the company and leave it in profit – is understandable. Hence, if most artists do, in effect, end up working for nothing, at least when it comes to recording, then having this work taken and shared for free by fans may be seen as no better or no worse a situation with which to contend.

However, it is in fact *better*, in many respects, for artists to experience the situation of not having their recordings bought by their fans (because of free-sharing), than it is for them to experience the situation of not getting paid by their record companies. This is because record companies do charge fans for access to recorded music, and if that money does not find its way back to artists, it still means fans have less money to spend than they otherwise would. This creates opportunity costs, the inability to purchase one good if you have just paid your money out for another. Fans who have paid money for recorded music have less disposable income left to go to see artists performing live, and so the demand for concert tickets will be less and the price elasticity of tickets will increase (meaning fans will be more likely to withdraw demand at higher prices). At least, this is what classical micro-economic theory of demand would predict.

In reality, such a pattern is indeed borne out in the loss of competition between live and recorded music purchases that can be identified when recorded music is available to freely share – i.e., in the form of subsequent increases in concert ticket sales. Krueger (2004; Krueger and Connolly 2006) used long-term survey data on concert ticket prices and volumes of sales in the United States to track the causal effect of free music-sharing on the price fans were willing to pay for tickets and the volume of tickets being sold. Using regression models, Krueger goes beyond simply mapping the correlation over time between live performance revenues and the advance of free digital copying – first of all, via cheap CD copiers for the domestic market (from the mid-1990s), and then with the development of file-sharing services from 1999. The minor shift caused by domestic CD copiers and the far greater shift brought about by the rise of online file-sharing saw, then, the sale of recorded music fall. Importantly, this fall led to diminished opportunity costs and hence to increased ticket sales and prices.

Not all the money saved by not buying records is spent on concert tickets. Today, people spend a lot more money accessing digital networks than they did a generation ago. While record sales reduced, overall spending on music (live and recorded) has not declined (Krueger 2004), so spending of network access is not simply consuming what was previously spent on physical recordings. Similarly, the rapid rise in spending on computer games, which has overtaken spending on musical recordings and film in recent years (Lastowka 2015), does represent 'competition' for spending on recordings (audio and visual), but again the increased spend on live performance shows that spending on games has not simply eaten up what was previously spent on music (or film).

Similarly, the claim that 'the rise of live' is overly romanticized – while containing some truth – should not itself be overstated. Existing inequalities have not disappeared in terms of who gets paid. Mega-stars who sell millions of records are also more likely to sell the most concert tickets and at the highest prices. However, the growth in the live musical economy since 1999 does mean that more performers are getting paid more money, even if it is certainly not being paid out equally. Digital networks make it easier for less well-known artists to find an audience willing to pay for live performances, but it has not created a totally level playing field. It is just more level than before.

Given that recording artists so rarely actually receive a payment from the sale of their records, and if a decline in record sales produces an increase in ticket sales and prices, as long as artists get paid to perform (which they are more likely to do even if this is not always true), musicians do, in fact, benefit from free-sharing.

Record companies might respond by saying that money lost by them from reduced sales, even if it were unlikely to have ended up directly in the pockets of artists, would have been the money used to pay the royalties that would themselves have paid for production, management and promotion (as discussed earlier in this chapter). It would also have paid to top up those royalties, as this small percentage of net sales value rarely covers all these costs to be set against royalties. Nevertheless, even if all the 85–95 per cent of net sales retained by the record company was spent on production, management and promotional work (which is nothing like the truth – although I do not say all this money goes up managers' noses in the executive toilets of record companies, as it has been suggested I argue; see Rossman 2010: 692), there is no reason to believe that this benefits artists. The rise of live performance has reduced the value of hyper-controlled studio production even as digital technology makes studio production and mastering less and less the preserve of commercial 'studios' and exclusive producers. Digital distribution and promotion also undermine the need for record companies and, in fact, break the monopoly control such players had over artists in the past – so making it easier to get noticed. If free distribution is more effective in generating a paying audience, the ability of record companies to extract revenue from retail outlets remains only as important as it is harmful to artists in creating counterproductive opportunity costs.

Adaptive (iTunes and Spotify) vs. Alternative (Sharing- and Selling-Based) Business Models

As has been observed above, sharing music online is the best way for artists to get paid, even if it is not good news for record companies. Sharing recordings bypasses the need for old media distribution models like record companies. To the extent that record companies were highly exploitative of artists, their bypassing is no loss to musicians. Sharing copies does not preclude the possibility of payment. The rise of file-sharing has seen a range of adaptive and alternative business models. Adaptive business models are those premised upon selling access to recorded music through media that still uphold intellectual property rights. Alternative business models, in contrast, are those that seek to come to terms with the logic of sharing, while still looking to make a living in such conditions.

Perhaps the most obvious example of an adaptive business model is iTunes. Record companies had been deeply resistant to licensing the distribution of their catalogues of recorded works, and were very keen instead to retain control. However, the failure to prevent the spread of file-sharing, and with attempts to prevent file-sharing simply encouraging new forms of distribution that were even harder to target, meant the option of making digital distribution go away was simply not available. Attempts to operate record-company-specific download services failed. Because free file-sharing services used a single unencrypted MP3 format, multiple and divergent corporate platforms were doubly unattractive – users having both to pay and in return getting only partial selections and products incompatible with other interfaces. For record companies, iTunes required a release of control, but, as control had already been lost, it was the lesser of two evils. iTunes is a commercial, non-sharing-based, platform, but it only exists (or at least only contains the spectrum of content that it does) because free file-sharing forced the hand of record labels. iTunes is commercially successful, generating significant profits for Apple and record companies – although the payments to artists are as bad as those made from physical sales (England 2015). For all its commercial success, sales on iTunes are dwarfed by the scale of free distribution on file-sharing sites (David 2010: 90). While iTunes is good news for the beleaguered recording industry, it is not any kind of return to past times, and is, at best, a limited adaptation and acceptance of the dominance of free-sharing in relation to recorded music consumption today.

A further extension of this fact is exemplified in Spotify. While iTunes arose when record companies realized they could not stop file-sharing and thus sought a commercial imitation of it, so record companies were persuaded to license their music to a free-to-access streaming service – Spotify – when confronted by the failure to stem the tide of (post-peer-to-peer) torrent and streaming services. Spotify offers users free access to music in exchange for being fed streamed advertising (although around a quarter of subscribers choose to pay a monthly subscription to avoid the need to be fed these adverts). Advertising revenue is used to pay rights holders, which does mean income for record companies – if not artists. Spotify claims to be taming the free access culture, making it possible to do business in an environment where users expect content without having to pay for it. In Norway, it is claimed that the introduction of Spotify coincided with a decline in the use of copyright-infringing services, while, in other locations, research suggests that Spotify simply eats into CD sales and iTunes downloads (David 2016). The recent purchase by iTunes of Beats (a US-based equivalent of Spotify) may be explained by iTunes's fear that Beats's streaming service will mainly be fishing in iTunes's pond, as users of such newly legal free-streaming services are often those that had previously used legal pay for downloading services. As such, Spotify and Beats may be simply extending the logic of free access that was made possible by free-sharing services. To say that this is taming the digital frontier is a nice way of saying that the logic of free-sharing has actually colonized the mainstream.

Spotify would like to move all its users towards paying a subscription to use its service. However, although overall numbers using the service have risen, only a quarter pay such fees. The company has found it impossible to force users to pay, as they can easily migrate back to free (copyright infringing) services if so pressed. The limits on what services like Spotify offer (streaming, not downloading for free; and advertiser interruptions on free-to-use versions) also mean they cannot fully replace alternative (infringing) services that give users more control.

Radiohead's 'honesty box' approach, of abandoning their record label and releasing their album *In Rainbows* via their publishing company in exchange for whatever fans are willing to pay, netted them higher earnings than had their previous work's royalties. Radiohead showed it was possible to manage recording, publicity and distribution in the digital age in a fashion far more advantageous to artists than was the case using traditional record companies. However, once freed from record company control, the band have gone on to release work 'themselves' at a fixed price. If Radiohead can fill stadiums without fear that record sales will diminish concert revenues, other less high-profile artists, like the Charlatans (see David 2010: 150–151), continue to give their recorded music away to boost live audience attendance and spending. The music industry is at least less of a winner-takes-all sector than it once was. A range of other successful alternative business models have emerged (see David 2010: 147–154). However, what may be more interesting is the general acceptance today of free access. Free-sharing is now dominant. Artists benefit from this situation whether they are signed to record companies or not. While free digital distribution means record companies have less income and hence less control over the market, this is not to the disadvantage of artists, and creates a more open field than would have otherwise existed. Back catalogues and older consumers keep the existing business models afloat even as the power and significance of these businesses decline gradually after each round of crashes, bankruptcies and take-overs. A shift to tie-ins of music within computer games, films, television and adverts, over selling copies of content directly to customers, alongside advertisement-funded free-streaming services, does mean the traditional record industry model is fading away, even while this extension of the logic of free access, heralded by file-sharing, is a gradual process. No total and instantaneous collapse of the old order has occurred. Just as those who introduced the CD in 1982 were too busy counting their profits to realize they were laying the foundations for a fundamental transformation of the recorded music industry, so it is that those who have promoted sharing would not have been aware of the new business opportunities that a culture of free-sharing would open up.

Radiohead's last royalties-based (record company-owned) album *Hail to the Thief* (2003) contained the track *We Suck Young Blood*, which equated record labels with parasitic vampires exploiting creative artists. Releasing their next album *In Rainbows* 'themselves', via their publishers, meant Radiohead received the greater part of the sales income, not just a small percentage in royalties. Fans could buy the album online for whatever price they chose: 38 per cent only paid the processing fee of 45 pence (Buskirk 2007). This led critics of the 'honesty box' approach to suggest that such fans were themselves parasitic leeches who, in effect, were giving nothing to the band. However, Buskirk cites Comscore data, which suggests that, of those who did pay more than the processing fee, the average amount paid was six dollars, earning the band more than two and a half million dollars in the first three weeks after release, with millions more earned subsequently through downloads and physical sales of the album. With freely available versions of subsequent albums being available online in any case, Radiohead have, since 2007, reverted to setting a fixed price for their subsequent albums, which they still control and release through their publishers, and not via a royalties-based contract with a record company. As such, fans still choose whether or not to pay. The idea that the weight of non-contributing 'free-riders' (Olson 1965) within 'sharing' networks, those who take but do not co-create or offer anything themselves, will undermine the incentive for artists to create new work, is simply false. 'The tragedy of the commons' (Hardin 1968), so often presumed by those that would prohibit sharing to secure capitalism, scarcity and profit, is proven false in relation to music here, as it is throughout this work.

Conclusions: Reversing the Menu and the Meal

The boundary between adaptive and alternative business models is not clear, nor absolute. While iTunes was an adaptive strategy retaining the model of selling copies of IP-protected content to customers, sharing-based services, and streaming services (legal and otherwise), no longer charge for IP access, but rather sell advertising space to support free-access distribution platforms. Artists who give away content to increase live audiences represent another alternative business strategy. The mix of approaches that make up the everyday choices of music fans blends all these things. However, what is most significant is the overall environment that now exists. This is one where free access is accepted, artists are better paid for live performance and access to audiences is less controlled by the monopoly power of a small set of record companies than was once the case.

The relative balance between capital and labour has shifted, with greater reward now being given to live performance, and less reward being given to the owner of fixed capital, i.e., property – in this case, intellectual property in the form of the copyright over recorded works. This is not to say that capital has ceased to exist – in live venues, for example, and through the whole spectrum of the music business, from record companies, radio stations, the music press and TV: in essence, the whole cross-media global entertainment industry. It is not as though 'capitalism' has ended yet. Nonetheless, the rise of free-sharing and the greater valuation of live performance over recorded capital does mean that both audiences and artists have a greater capacity to limit the power over them exercised by capital.

4

Live-streaming and Television Rights Management

Introduction

Live-streaming combines compression formats developed for the transmission of live television over dedicated digital cable and satellite channels with the faster broadband speeds of today's Internet. Initially, livestreams were used by Internet users to broadcast their own lives 'live' in the form of 'lifecasts'. However, with the development of global digital media broadcasting empires built on 'pay-to-view' access to live sporting events, rerouted free-to-view livestreams of such broadcasts became popular. The rise of commercial pay-to-view digital television represents the first digital revolution in sports media coverage. The subsequent development of free live-streaming channels represents its opposite, a second digital revolution in sports media coverage based on sharing. These divergent affordances of similar technical assemblages highlight interesting tensions within what Manuel Castells calls the global network society (1996, 2009). In turn, this allows for an exploration of the strengths and limits of Castells's work, particularly the extent to which his account has highlighted the rise of a new set of core players, but has neglected the very real potential for 'support labour' (marginalized and exploited by the first digital revolution) to exercise new forms of economic counterpower – an economic counterpower based on sharing. Central to Castells's account of communication power within the network society is what he calls 'Murdochization', the emergence of a new breed of corporate 'networks of networks' that bind together economic, political and cultural networks in their digital empire building. As pay-to-view live sports broadcasting is central to the Murdoch model of power, so sharing live sports broadcasts becomes significant as a mode of economic counterpower. Attempts to prohibit such sharing networks have been numerous. However, they have all failed. New network enterprises and their users evade legal, technical and cultural (editorial) control.

The success of the Murdoch model must be set against the failure of all attempts by others to emulate it. To assert the paradigmatic nature of News Corp is problematic if it is in fact unique. The established position of News Corp's subsidiaries, Sky and Fox, in major markets, combined with the availability of free-sharing alternatives, has meant it has not been possible for others to generate the kinds of profits gained by Murdoch, and, as such, his networks are not so much paradigmatic as they are unique. Even within his network of networks, the success of the first digital revolution is uncertain. In the case of the English Premier League (EPL), the most extreme example of Murdochized 'success', increased revenues have alienated many fans and still left half its clubs technically insolvent. Sharing puts power back into the hands of fans who were excluded by the first digital revolution, but this second digital revolution has not replaced the first, at least not yet.

The First Digital Revolution in Television: Pay-to-View Enclosure

As was noted in Chapter 3, the music industry has experienced two digital revolutions. A very similar set of processes took place in television. In the case of Time Warner, these two were one and the same. However, the first digital revolution in television came a decade after that in music. The dating being suggested here is from the launch of major digital satellite channels – such as Sky – in the early 1990s. The launch of satellite television was a major transformation.

Castells (2009) suggests that the rise of a new form of power in the network society is exemplified by the new breed of global digital network businesses. These business empires bind together networks of cultural, economic and political nodes across the globe. Their power, what Castells calls 'communication power', lies in the ability to generate income from the sale of digital content, but at the same time to shape wider political and cultural processes through binding politicians and consumers within their business models. In essence, Castells suggests that the whole of society is thereby 'reprogrammed' by the rise of this new set of digital channels.

Underpinning the success of Rupert Murdoch's transformation, from newspaper magnate to global digital media entrepreneur, has been his ability to build audiences for his new channels with a range of new programming. The core of this new programming has been live sport. Essentially, what Murdoch began, and what others have tried to follow, is to buy up the rights to popular national (and, increasingly, international) sporting tournaments. Prior to the rise of global digital broadcasting technology, in the form of satellites, live sports events were mainly broadcast to national audiences (with international linkage between national broadcasters for worldwide events such as the Olympics and the football World Cup). Satellites meant that a bigger audience could be reached, and this increased the potential economic return on broadcasting such events. What companies like Sky and Fox did was to buy up exclusive broadcast rights for tournaments at rates in excess of what nationally based terrestrial channels were previously paying. These events were then made available by subscription to those who paid for new digital services, where previously matches had been broadcast free-to-air on analogue channels. This led to a form of digital enclosure, whereby digital media became the means by which formerly free access became increasingly expensive and accessible only to those who could afford to pay.

The phenomenon was not just confined to Rupert Murdoch's Sky and Fox in the United States and United Kingdom respectively. Across the world, subsidiaries of the Murdoch empire, and others, have followed the example set, and today, sports as diverse as Indian Cricket, Australian Rules Football, various divisions of motor sport, various versions of rugby, sailing, golf and many others besides have migrated from free-to-air towards digital pay-to-view (Kirton and David 2013). The most extreme manifestation of this has been in Association Football, where exclusive rights deals with digital service providers have seen a price and income spiral across the globe. In many respects, this parallels the 'profit storm' in the record industry that lasted from 1982 to 1999.

With their parallel launches in 1992, the EPL (a reconfiguration that included the top twenty clubs in the English Football League) and Rupert Murdoch's BSkyB (Sky) service are the most developed case in point here. Since migrating away from terrestrial and national television rights sales to exclusive digital rights to live match broadcasting, initially exclusive to Sky, the EPL now sells digital broadcast rights to 211 territories around the world (Millward 2011). Rights revenues have moved from approximately one hundred million pounds per year in 1992, to two billion a year today (David et al. 2015).

The Second Digital Revolution: Free-Sharing Livestreams

Just as the first digital revolution in live television broadcasting was ten years after the equivalent in music, so the second digital revolution came a decade after Napster's 1999 launch. The reason for this time lag is fairly straightforward. Although the CD was launched in 1982, it took another decade to launch large-scale live satellite broadcasting. The bandwidth had to be sufficient to carry the live feed at a level of resolution that customers were willing to pay for. The development of the first and second generations of data-compression (MP1 and MP2) made this possible in the late 1980s, and then the satellite and receivers had to be made ready. The MP3 compression format was key to enabling music downloads over the Internet; time permitting (given modest broadband speeds at the time), it was possible to do this in 1999 (as Napster showed). However, it was not for another ten years that domestic Internet broadband speeds would allow for live visual content to be streamed over the Internet with any degree of clarity. When tennis was first broadcast on the BBC in 1936, very limited audiences were only able to see the players darting about in white flannels against a dark background. They were entirely unable to see the ball, but simply followed the movement of the players to estimate where it must have been (Barnett 1990). This was almost always the experience of anyone seeking to view a live sporting match via the Internet prior to the late 2000s.

Live-streaming over the Internet originated as 'life' streaming. Users simply broadcast their lives and thoughts to the world. It was only in the very late 2000s that users of such services began using channels to reroute and stream live, digital, television broadcasts of sporting fixtures. These live broadcasts were very often initially sourced from pay-to-view service providers, and, as such, rerouting them to be distributed freely online was an infringement of the copyright monopoly in which the commercial broadcaster had invested with the hope of profiting from their exclusivity. Streaming channels that had originally been used to broadcast live feeds of personal content were increasingly used to share copyrighted content, both recorded content and live events. This second digital revolution was therefore in direct contravention of the basic premise of the first. Digital broadcasting had been a means of securing monopoly control over what had previously been free-to-air content. Now, new digital affordances were placing content back into the domain of free access.

The extent of live-streaming is hard to gauge, precisely because it is often deemed a breach of the law and so people who use this technology may not seek to publicize the fact. However, estimates by various sources suggest that the numbers accessing such services to watch EPL matches had reached into the millions by 2008 (Birmingham and David 2011: 73), and some individual matches were being streamed by more than a million viewers by the following year (Smith 2009). Individual fixtures may have upwards of thousands of streams being transmitted while the event is ongoing, with every stream being watched by potentially limitless numbers of viewers. Every live sporting fixture that is being broadcast digitally somewhere in the world today is likely to be being restreamed everywhere. In essence, streaming is now endemic.

Just as the years of digitally inflated profit between 1982 and 1999 stored up the seeds of subsequent crisis for the music industry, so the years from 1992 to 2009 saw companies like Sky and Fox build up ever-larger markets for their exclusive access to key sporting leagues and fixtures. However, that very success, plus the exponential increase in prices that this success was built upon and the global reach of the digital services that arose, was what fed both the demand for, and the ability to supply, free-streams once broadband speeds rose sufficiently. While Sky and Fox remain profitable, others that have sought to emulate their success have failed – trapped as they are now between established monopolies and the free-streaming that limits the scope for expanding the customer bases of new commercial players. In 2009, the bankruptcy of Setanta – the first player to successfully bid for EPL rights after the UK government decided Sky's total control over all EPL matches was unduly restrictive of competition – indicated that, while Murdoch's model worked for him, it could not be emulated in new conditions. To date, all subsequent attempts to enter the field have ended in failure. Sky remains in business, but the first and second digital revolutions have created a standoff between an established monopoly and new and unlawful sharers. Given the centrality of Murdoch's Sky and Fox digital sports broadcasting channels to Castells's account of network power, it is worthwhile to examine the extent to which free-streaming does represent a form of economic counterpower.

Justin.TV, First Row Sports and Wiziwig:
Network Enterprises and their Users

As has been noted above, the first digital revolution in sports broadcasting combined legal monopoly control over rights with technical monopoly control over means of distribution. With Internet broadband speeds being unable to support live broadcasts of any visual quality, commercial 'pay-to-view' service providers had control over programming (i.e., content) and over switching (the ability to link content), and hence the ability to choose and exclude who they liked in terms of access. This did not last. By the late 2000s (as documented above), the Internet was able to support live-streaming. EPL's head Richard Scudamore (2009) branded the rise of free-streaming of EPL matches as nothing short of 'theft', and, in his estimation, 'theft' on a grand scale.

A range of legal challenges have been undertaken by digital broadcasters with monopoly rights to broadcast matches against streaming channel service providers. The case of Justin.TV usefully illustrates the failure of early actions, while an examination of the later cases against First Row Sports and Wiziwig illustrates the failure of later legal strategies. Justin.TV is a streaming channel service provider that offers its users channels through which they, the users, stream content of their choosing. This content is very often rerouted from commercial broadcasters. At any one time, Justin.TV will be supporting many thousands of such channels. Every live broadcast of sporting content anywhere in the world (content that is more often than not being broadcast in a pay-to-view form in the first instance) is likely to be so rerouted by someone using a Justin.TV channel, and a very wide range of alternative service providers as well. Even matches that are not being broadcast live domestically, for fear that this might weaken gate receipts, will often be broadcast live commercially elsewhere in the world, and can then be rerouted via a streaming channel to users everywhere – including in the home territory where the match is being played (but not always shown). As such, streaming services are more comprehensive than any particular commercial provider, and, indeed, more comprehensive than all commercial providers combined – at least in terms of the domestic content available to any given user (due to domestic restrictions on broadcasting some matches live). Sky and the EPL were, and remain, very keen to shut down such infringing channels. Justin.TV does not actively promote copyright infringement, and seeks to comply with copyright holders' wishes when an infringing channel is brought to its attention. Unfortunately, at least from the point of view of rights holders, for a channel to be shut down it must first be checked to confirm that it is infringing copyright. This process means that many streams run for the duration of the event being broadcast before they are closed, and, even when closed down mid-stream, viewers can switch to thousands of other channels streaming the same content. Because Justin.TV seeks to comply with the law, and does not advocate infringement as such, it has 'safe haven' legal protection, and cannot be held liable for what users choose to use its services for.

The viability of services like Justin.TV show the viability of such free-sharing channels as a mode of economic counterpower. Moreover, the rise in use of live-streaming services encouraged the development of *dedicated* sports streaming services. The case of First Row Sports illustrates this, as it became the largest of such services and so became a subsequent target for legal attack after the failure to prevent Justin.TV. The difference between Justin.TV and First Row Sports is that the latter does actively promote the use of its service as a means of accessing live sports broadcasts for free. Content is still streamed by users of its service, and not the service provider itself, but the active promotion of accessing 'infringing' content as a means to draw an audience to its services (and hence to generate a mul-timillion pound annual advertising income) did make a difference in the reaction of the courts. In 2013, the High Court in London agreed to the request of the EPL and Sky that all UK Internet service providers (ISPs) be required to block access to First Row Sports's website. Moving beyond the closing down of individual channels when they are shown to be infringing IP, this court decision has acted to pre-emptively block the streaming channel service provider itself, seeking thereby to drive the cork back into the bottle at the narrowest point. (This move went further than previous actions by US courts, which had ordered the 'seizing' of particular web addresses used by the service in that country.) The Spanish courts took similar action against another service provider (Wiziwig), and for similar reasons, at the start of 2015.

While Internet service providers in both the UK and Spain complied with the above demands, the blockages were immediately evaded. First Row Sport users simply logged onto alternative versions of the same services 'located' in other countries. Sometimes this requires the use of virtual proxy networks (VPNs). VPNs allow a user in one jurisdiction to log onto a server in another country so as to then be able to log on from within that second jurisdiction to sites that would be blocked in the first. Ian Brown (2015) notes that the use of VPNs has risen most rapidly in countries where such site-blocking actions as occurred in the case of First Row Sports have been undertaken. VPNs were designed in part to enable business users to evade national restrictions when working outside their home country, and for political protesters in repressive regimes; however, they can just as well be used to facilitate economic counterpower relative to attempts to maintain dominant monopoly controls over IP. Even without using VPNs, those looking to stream content can simply find an array of alternative websites operated by the same service providers. Being the emblematic 'network enterprises' that they are, streaming channel services hop, skip and jump to new addresses – much as content does between channels within any such service when sharers seek to evade regulation. Even beyond the scope of particular services to swap web addresses, users can simply look for alternative sharing service providers, of which there is a great, and ever-growing, number.

Live-streaming channel service providers are 'network enterprises'. Live-streaming channel service providers exploit the affordances of global digital media networks in a fashion very distinct from what Castells identifies as the paradigmatic network of networks – News Corporation – with its pay-to-view model of IP-rich programming and switching. Such alternative 'network enterprises' directly challenge the pay-to-view model. Nonetheless, streaming-channel-service-providing network enterprises are businesses, only ones based on advertising revenue generation, not on the control of intellectual property. Free-sharing directly challenges a business model based on IP as capital, but free-sharing can be commercialized. As such, this dispute is a conflict between capital and markets, the protection of property (capital) in the form of intangible content, and the promotion of 'pirate' markets in the circulation of goods and services in contravention of monopoly control over who can provide content.

Rupert Murdoch himself experimented with such a platform, offering free content to viewers as a means of generating advertising revenues from those keen to sell to such viewers. Murdoch bought and ran the 'MySpace' service, and it generated significant profits in the years before he sold it. Myspace began to falter and lose out to the rise of Facebook, which itself operated exactly the same idea of free content as a draw to an audience that advertisers pay to access. As noted in Chapter 3, the absence of an editorial nexus means advertiser-funded, free-access services do not produce the levels of control over content that were affected in older media forms. Indeed, free content linked to advertising reduced some of the inequality introduced by digital firewalls in the 1990s and beyond. However, live-streaming is not simply taking us back to the pre-digital era of free-to-air terrestrial sports broadcasting, because it retains the full range of content that the commercial digital revolution ushered in. As such, live-streaming is neither simply a return to an old mode of capitalism, nor is it being simply colonized by a newer mode of capitalism. Live-streaming does, however, give millions of fans the power to freely access content that was closed off to those unable to afford escalating subscription prices. As a form of pre-figurative economic counterpower, free-sharing is not entirely detached from money-making service providers, yet neither is it fundamentally colonized by such actors.

Sky's the Limit? The Limits of Power and Counterpower

The first and second digital revolutions in television sports broadcasting sit in uneasy opposition to one another – yet neither seems able to fully dislodge the other. On the one hand, Murdochized pay-to-view digital broadcasting, at least in its actual Murdoch-owned manifestations of Sky and Fox, became and remain highly profitable network enterprises, although not in the sense that their content is primarily 'networked' on the Internet itself (even as they sell Internet access alongside the very film and television content they seek to prevent users from sharing online). At the same time, free live-streaming service providers continue to flourish, despite the attempts of rights-holding broadcasters to stop them. Sky has ten million paying subscribers in the UK, a figure that has not declined since the advent of good-quality livestreams in the late 2000s. The EPL continues to sell rights to more than 200 territories worldwide. Yet, it is the combination of Sky's existing dominance and the ability of live-streamers to reroute broadcasts from any other of these 200-plus locations that has meant every attempt to copy Sky's commercial model in the UK has failed, a situation repeated now all over the world.

The UK example will be given for illustration. In 2007, the UK broadcasting regulator, Ofcom, ruled that the live domestic broadcasting rights to EPL matches should not be held only by one single broadcaster (Sky). The result was that the international digital sports broadcaster Setanta bid for – and was successful in gaining – rights to broadcast one of six 'bundles' of matches in the 2007–10 seasons. Anticipating the number of customers willing to pay for access to these matches (see Giulianotti and Robertson 2009), Setanta bid around three hundred million pounds for this three-year package; but, in 2009, their UK arm declared bankruptcy, as it had been unable to reach anything like the number of subscribers required to make back the cost of the rights the company had secured (Birmingham and David 2011). The Setanta rights for the remainder of the three years was bought up by another (US-based) digital broadcaster, ESPN (a subsidiary of the Disney Corporation). ESPN then continued to bid for and received rights bundles for the 2010–13 window. However, again due to the failure to recruit sufficient customers, ESPN withdrew from the bidding process for the 2013–16 round. Most rights in that round were bought up by Sky (as usual). The new player (required by Ofcom) this time was BT (formerly British Telecom). BT has itself also struggled to build a paying audience when only having a small proportion of games on offer, and when faced with the fact that Sky offers more. Unless viewers pay for *both* Sky and BT, they will be in a position, then, where they are more than likely to want to stream matches that their single supplier does not broadcast. As such, it is hard for BT to persuade existing Sky customers to switch, just as it is difficult persuading people who were either not watching live EPL matches before, or who were streaming them already, to start paying a new pay-to-view supplier with only a small bundle of matches on offer anyway.

Just as the dominant network power of broadcasters such as Sky is limited – in both its scope to overcome its challengers, and in its scope to spread as a business model when faced with the difficulties noted above – it is also the case that live-streamers are limited in the scope of their provision of an alternative. Live-streaming channels are able to reroute matches that are not being commercially shown domestically, but are being broadcast elsewhere, even when legal and commercial providers in home countries cannot. However, streaming channels can only (currently) stream matches that commercial actors, somewhere, do choose to broadcast in the first place. If a club is relegated from the EPL and its broadcast rights are no longer so commercially attractive (given that that team will play far fewer games – if any at all – against the 'big' clubs with the most 'international' fans), it is often the case that their matches will not be broadcast by any commercial digital service, and, as such, will not be available to reroute via streaming channels.

Sky's partnership with the EPL is the most advanced case of global network power, fusing cultural, political and economic networks. However, this global network of networks' programmers cannot control the switching of 'their' content that goes on beyond their networks. Counterpower arises when selling to anyone; anywhere, means it is impossible to prevent someone, somewhere, from rerouting that content and making it available freely to everyone, everywhere. Counterpower is, however, constrained precisely by the limits of power itself. Dominant pay-to-view business models do not show every match in every league, and what is not broadcast commercially cannot then be shared.

Conclusions: Power and Counterpower in Digital Networks

The transformation of television media (and live broadcasting, in particular), as a key driver in wider changes, is multidimensional and contradictory. In the 1990s, the first digital revolution in live sports broadcasting afforded the creation of a new hyper-commercialization of the sports–television nexus. This was worldwide, but driven first and furthest in the case of Association Football, with the EPL and Sky very much in the forefront. Academic researchers have documented the rise of a new hyper-commercial elite (King 1997b; Giulianotti and Robertson 2009); a new, more commercially exploitable, 'middle-class' audience (King 1997a; Giulianotti 2002); and a marginalized and disenfranchised 'traditional' fan base, priced out of their traditional modes of support (King 2002). This corresponds with Castells's account of the wider digital economy, where, as he described things, a core of elite (economic and technical) players was increasingly empowered at the expense of a geographically dispersed, interchangeable and marginalized mass of 'support labour'. Indeed, writers like Millward and Poulton (2014) parallel Castells's account with the situation of core players in sport and the marginalized 'support labour' of fans. They document how, in conditions where elite clubs and broadcasters have raised ticket and subscription prices beyond the reach of many 'traditional' fans, funding the wages of globally mobile elite players (on the pitch and off it), such (relatively poor and therefore marginalized) supporters use new media to articulate their political anger and cultural resistance. However, such expression of anger appeared to lack any serious ability to economically challenge the financial foundations of the new networked game. If fans wanted to watch matches, they had to pay, whether at the gate, or via digital television subscription services.

Yet, the second digital revolution, that of free online live-streaming of digital sports broadcasting, takes power away from the core of elite players within the commercial game – and hands choice back to those who were forced by the first digital revolution to either pay more, or see nothing. Live-streaming allows fans to make their own choices, and so enables a form of economic counterpower, in creating both an alternative means of reproducing content and distributing it, and a serious challenge to the dominant business model of pay-to-view access.

To end, it must be noted that power and counterpower are always incomplete and yet interconnected. In the case of live sports broadcasting, the extent of global commercial distribution is the very premise of global rerouting, even as the scope of what commercial providers choose not to broadcast is the limit on what sharers can reroute. Sky and the EPL have seen huge increases in their revenues since the creation of their business partnership in 1992. This huge influx of money has afforded a huge inflation in the cost of players within the EPL, and that has left half the league's clubs technically insolvent despite annual revenues running into the billions of pounds (Bose 2010). Only a few of the top clubs within the EPL are financially secure. This parallels the fact that, while Sky itself remains profitable, all attempts to emulate its success have failed. The edifice created by the first digital revolution, when media industries were flush with new money, remained eminently precarious despite the escalation in its revenues. The conditions of the sharing revolution are similarly uneven and contradictory. Services that enable sharing are themselves often commercial even while there is not the editorial nexus that exists in older print and broadcast media. Also, in the absence of alternative means of accessing content to broadcast in the first place, sharing, as a mode of counterpower, remains dependent upon, although not controlled by, mainstream networks. While dominant programmers cannot shut down alternative switchers, neither can today's alternative switchers generate their own content: the cat-and-mouse play of sellers and sharers continues. However, even while this is the case, those clubs in leagues that do not regularly have their matches aired live by commercial broadcasters *do* film matches; these matches could be streamed, and indeed some are. As such, some scope exists for new modes of non-commercial distribution beyond today's dependence upon dominant channels.

5

Open-Source Software and Proprietary Software

Introduction

This chapter will examine the relative creativity of corporate and open-source/hacker models for the development of innovative software. The copyright-based business model takes it for granted that the motivation for creativity and the conditions that allow creativity to be translated into workable innovation require strong protection for the rights of creators/innovators to own and control the sale of their intellectual property. However, intellectual property law over the past 150 years has developed in such a way as to enable the emergence of corporate research and development teams whose work can be owned by their employers, not by the actual researchers (May and Sell 2005). This corporate model of research and development (R&D), protected by current IP law, stands in opposition to a form of innovation that relies upon sharing ideas in the development of open-source software. Competition between these two models of creativity and innovation can be directly observed in the attempts by commercial developers to build forms of digital rights management (DRM), and attempts by open-source 'hacktivists' to break such systems of control. Every attempt to develop such DRM has failed. The emergence of peer-to-peer sharing (of music, film and television) has also shown how innovation has come despite, not because of, intellectual property restrictions. New forms of sharing software have evolved to bypass legal and technical efforts to shut them down, while IP-based business models have only trailed in the wake of such innovation. The open-source software movement further illustrates the power of non-proprietary models of innovation and regulation, as does 'Creative

Commons' licensing (within limits that will be documented below). The computer gaming industry powerfully illustrates this tension between proprietary and sharing cultures as well as between business models. Curiously, despite being far more dependent upon the sale of immaterial content (with no live concerts, cinema visits and sports attendances to fall back on if digital sales fall), the computer games industry remains far less dependent upon IP regulation than it does simply on being able to digitally innovate. Finally, this chapter will examine the Internet, the World Wide Web, Wikipedia, Facebook, Google, Apple and Microsoft as competing models of innovation – based as they are on very different conceptions of the relationship between user community sharing, expert community sharing and private ownership.

The Spirit of the Information Age: Hackers, Rebel Code and Play Struggle

Pekka Himanen (2001) sets out to disentangle the apparent contradiction within the hacker movement, between an advocacy of freedom of information, on the one hand, and a defence of privacy, on the other. On the surface, these two principles – one of sharing/disclosure and the other of privacy/closure – appear to be at odds with one another. Yet, what Himanen calls the 'net ethic', or Nethic (the moral code of hacker coders), brings the two together in a particular fashion that he refers to as 'the spirit of informationalism'. Where the industrial revolution was said to have had an 'elective affinity' with 'the Protestant work ethic' (Weber 1930), the spirit of informationalism seeks to break out of that model of deferred gratification, instrumental rationalization and disenchantment of the world. In an informational age of what Castells names 'self-programmable workers', hackers seek to take control of work in the name of collaborative and creative autonomy. Free speech and freeing corporate code go hand-in-hand with the need for privacy to defend net-citizens from both state and corporate regulation; and it is in this space of highly motivated, networked autonomy that hackers create code that outperforms the code generated in corporate silos still managed by the principles of the industrial revolution and its work ethic (see also Moody 2002 for a detailed account of how open-source software came to challenge corporate IP-based business models even within the mainstream software and hardware market – and not just in the domain of online sharing communities).

Johan Söderberg (2008) parallels the earliest forms of computing with those of today and yet contrasts the forms of resistance that arose in relation to each. In both England and France at the start of the nineteenth century, forms of automation were being introduced in the weaving industry. In France, Joseph-Marie Jacquard introduced punch card operated looms, while, in England, Charles Babbage set out the wider principles that could be transferred from such early mechanical computing to the deskilling of industrial production. Such alienating forms of deskilling and control over work have been central to the development of computing ever since.

However, while the nineteenth-century reaction of workers to the mechanization of weaving was to smash the machines, today's hackers seek to appropriate technology. Where yesterday's 'Luddites' were unable to resist the onset of industrialization, much as Manuel Castells's depiction of distributed and marginalized 'support labour' in today's network society (see Chapter 4), today's hackers do not seek to resist informationalism. Rather, they seek to liberate its potential to overcome the alienation of labour in capitalist society. Hackers embrace technology and work, but such work is a form of 'voluntarily-entered, collective labour activity' (Söderberg 2008: 2), motivated by aesthetics and play, as well as by mastery and freedom from the control of others. For Söderberg, the triumph of free-sharing movements online is a mode of 'dot.communism'. Söderberg cites Slavoj Žižek's parody of Lenin, that 'socialism = free access to the Internet + power to the Soviets' (Söderberg 2008: 4), and goes on to document the superiority of 'dot.communism' in terms of (1) the production of digital content, (2) the distribution of utility beyond scarcity and (3) the overcoming of the alienation caused by the subordination of play to work under capitalist principles of ownership and markets. The struggle of hackers to coproduce and share the future is what Söderberg calls 'play struggle' – a prefigurative fusion of politics, economics and culture that realizes, at least in part, an abolition of the social division of labour in the here and now, and shows the possibility of a fully liberated sharing-based society in the future.

The next four sections, on digital rights management, peer-to-peer software, non-profit organizations and open-source software, as well as on computer games, illustrate the power of shared coproduction relative to IP-regulated knowledge production. While the last of these sections, on computer games, illustrates the inaccuracy of the claim that IP is necessary or even a positive thing in relation to creativity in software creation, the subsequent section (on the seven most significant platforms within today's global network society) further illustrates the primacy of shared coproduction over corporate IP-controlled coding.

Digital Rights Management

The limited potential of enclosed teams of researchers who are employed to innovate, but who do not own or control the products they are paid to develop, is starkly demonstrated when set against the network communities of innovation that emerge when development is conducted through open-source sharing.

A curious contradiction recurred across the 2000s in relation to the response to infringement of IP-regulated dependent businesses. On the one hand, there were strong demands to pass tough new laws and to enforce existing laws more strictly. New legislation was passed by governments around the world in response to well-organized lobbying by content industry representatives who presented apocalyptical accounts of how infringement would undermine them and society more widely ('Piracy funds terrorism and will destroy our society and your future viewing enjoyment' – Federation Against Copyright Theft – Fact 2004; cited in David 2010: 97). Campaigns seeking to create a 'moral panic' around content copying (David and Whiteman 2015) asserted that it was essential that the law be used against sharers to prevent social and economic catastrophe. Yet, at the same time, the same lobbyists asserted a parallel narrative, which was that the threat of so-called 'piracy' could, or soon would, be dealt with by technical means. Better locks, it was suggested, would reduce the need for more police(wo)men; DRM software would act to police content by technical means, such that infringement would be prevented from occurring in the first place rather than prosecuted after the fact. Christopher May (2007) maps out the scope of such DRM, both in terms of 'hard' DRM (the building in of encryption code such that content can only be used in regulated ways by authorized users), and in terms of 'soft' DRM (the capacity to enact surveillance over content use to identify infringers so as to then apply legal sanctions against them). Lawrence Lessig (2002, 2004) identifies such 'code as law' – whereby technology, rather than legal deliberation, comes to determine what is and is not common culture and hence open to fair use. Lessig rightly presents this possibility for technical lock-down as a serious threat to a free society in which acts should be deemed permissible until found unlawful. The successful replacement of law by code would, Lessig argues, replace a free culture with a permission (or fee) culture.

While May and Lessig's concerns regarding what such a 'lock-down' approach to culture could represent are legitimate, it should be recalled that such a 'lock-down' has not been achieved, despite the best efforts of rights holders. It is one thing to warn of potential danger; but to also claim that the risk has been realized might, in fact, achieve the very thing such warnings were designed to warn against. William Bogard (1996) documents what he calls the 'simulation of surveillance', a condition where people are persuaded that they are always under surveillance when surveillance systems are in fact far weaker than they believe. Such a misconception is a much more powerful mode of control than the actual level of oversight affords. Regarding both hard and soft DRM, it is the 'machine's dream' (Bogard's phrase) that technology can effect mastery. It is not, in fact, true.

First, hard DRM does not work. Every attempt to create a form of encryption able to lock down content has failed. In the case of the compact disc, competing record companies simply failed to agree a common form of encryption. As a result, all CDs are unencrypted. Yet, even when encryption was agreed, such as in the cases of DVDs, Apple's iTunes Fairplay software, and for e-books, every version of encryption that has been released has immediately been cracked by open-source hackers (David 2010: 87–88). Open-source hackers, sharing tips and ideas, are far more effective at writing software than are closed teams in corporate silos. Similarly, the development of soft DRM, in the form of surveillance software, has been matched by anti-surveillance surveilling software designed to scan for surveillance trolls and to thereby avoid them (Banerjee et al. 2006).

Peer-to-Peer Software

The inability of proprietary models of innovation to compete with sharing-based models is also demonstrated in relation to the emergence of the MP3 digital compression format. While developed within the commercial sphere, the MP3 compression format became a standard foundation for music distribution because of the development of copyright-infringing peer-to-peer software, and in direct opposition to commercial copyright holders who resisted the development of any standard distribution format. The earlier quashing by record companies of the mini-disc and digital audio tape were examples of non-innovation in the defence of maintaining monopoly control over content. Record companies agreed amongst themselves not to release music on such formats and thereby stifled these innovations. The creation of file-sharing networks using MP3 compression formats prevented any repeat of such closure tactics, as material was being circulated outside record company control. It was this inability to prevent innovation that pressed record companies into dealing with iTunes (see Chapter 3 for related discussion). Again, it was hacker innovations, in unlocking iTunes 'Fairplay' encryption software, despite the attempts by Apple to out-programme their open-source hacker rivals, that saw Apple drop this attempt to restrict format shifting in 2008. Ongoing developments in peer-to-peer, torrent and streaming software have also shown the ability of sharing software to evade every legal and technical attempt to prevent sharing.

The first generation of file-sharing software, Napster, adopted a central-server-based model of exchange – such that communications between users seeking to share content, and to transfer MP3 music files containing that content, were passed through Napster's own central server. Shaun Fanning's innovative fusion of MP3 file compression, Internet transmission and his own program – which allowed the matching up of uploaders and downloaders for particular items – while revolutionary, had a fatal Achilles heel. Its central server model meant that it – Napster itself – was successfully held liable for the actions of those exchanging files through its central server. While this led to a successful legal challenge in 2001 and the closure of the service in 2002, new forms of sharing software arose that did not share Napster's vulnerability. First, fully peer-to-peer services developed. These were programmes where, once the software had been distributed, the service provider had no direct involvement in users' interactions, and so could not be prosecuted. Legal attacks on users who uploaded content were then undertaken. However, this legal attack was evaded with the development of torrent-based software, which allow a downloader to make a copy of a file from a torrent of uploads, taking only small fragments of the total from any one uploader; no single uploader, therefore, can be prosecuted as the source of any copy made. Subsequent targeting of downloaders saw the development of streaming services where those who wish to access content listen to a stream rather than make a copy. Legal targeting of torrent and streaming service providers have resulted in them distributing their servers across multiple jurisdictions to prevent successful blockage.

Networks of sharers and sharing network service providers have proven more than a match for those seeking to shut them down. Innovation has been key to this success. Such innovation has been the result of a combination of 'alternative business models' and 'alternatives to business models'. Some sharing services make money from advertising, so, while they promote 'sharing', they do so to create an audience whose eyeballs they can then sell on to other businesses. (Other services, meanwhile, and almost all users do not seek to sell information.) Importantly, attempts to criminalize sharing are a defence of one version of capitalism – based upon intellectual property rights monopoly control. Yet, what this defended against is actually a mixture of free-sharing and pirate capitalism. Sharing software has outflanked the IP-based version of capital protection, but is itself a curious fusion of profit-making (pirate markets beyond property rights) and free-sharing software writers and users. This tension in relation to 'sharing' as a crime against, and yet also working within, capitalism is a recurrent theme in this work.

Non-Profit Organizations in the Information Economy

Proprietary software companies and other content industry lobbies seek to present the world as divided between a private world of creative innovation, on the one hand, and, on the other, a commons that simply shares what has been created in the proprietary domain. This picture is simply false. The early days of computer programming were largely governed by norms of code sharing and collaboration. It was only later that emerging commercial software companies sought to claim ownership over their own adaptations of what had collectively emerged. This was, then, the point that non-profit organizations (NPOs) like the Free and Open-Source Software (FOSS) movement and the Free Software Foundation (FSF) emerged in an attempt to defend the open-source commons from being choked off by proprietary prohibitions against future collaborative innovation.

Jyn-An Lee (2015) explains how Richard Stallman created the first formal open-source licencing procedure in 1985 in order to document and assert the public nature of the operating system software – GNU – that he had made available two years earlier. He was concerned on two counts: first, about an assertion of copyright by AT&T (American Telephone & Telegraph) Inc. over the UNIX operating system, which had emerged from prior shared developments; and, second, concerning the prospect of his then-employer, MIT (Massachusetts Institute of Technology), asserting copyright over work being done within his Artificial Intelligence Laboratory. Stallman created Free and Open-Source Software licences and the

Free Software Foundation to ensure that any work based upon collaboration and past sharing remained in the public domain. Linux is the most popular operating system based on these principles. 'The ten fastest supercomputers in the world all run Linux' (Mason 2015: 122). Other licensing foundations, such as the Open-Source Initiative (OSI) and Creative Commons (CC), pursue similar goals, although with differing degrees of restriction of and control over commercial application. OSI requires those who build on prior work to keep their software open to view and adaptation, even while allowing developers to claim some control over how their particular code is used commercially. CC licences are very diverse and offer users a spectrum of options regarding how far a developer accepts future user freedom to develop their code. What all these organizations do is highlight the value of sharing the source code in the development of new software.

Lee sets out two major theoretical frameworks through which to understand the value of non-profit, sharing-based, advocacy organizations in relation to both the sharing economy, but also in relation to the general economy as well. First, following the work of Henry Hansmann (1980), Lee documents 'contract failure theory'. A double asymmetry exists between suppliers and users of a particular product or service – when (1) an informational asymmetry emerges, whereby the user cannot know the make up or quality of what they are being sold, and (2) monopoly control limits the availability of alternatives – the user's interest suffers relative to that of the supplier. Non-profit, open-source advocacy and licensing organizations address both these failures, failures that are particularly acute in otherwise IP-regulated sectors. Such NPOs prevent monopoly closure and enable information disclosure. They are also more trustworthy, to the extent that they are not invested in profiting from the combination of control and non-disclosure that arises under conditions of IP monopoly. Open-source frameworks enable access, collaboration and use of what would otherwise be hidden and restricted. Second, following the 'market failure theory' of Burton Weisbrod (1977), Lee suggests FOSS NPOs help overcome the undersupply of public goods by private sector providers. If perfect information is a requirement for rational consumer choice, and if private providers have no incentive to give away information that they could claim ownership over and sell, information goods need to be retained in the public domain – for the sake of maintaining markets themselves, in addition to serving the wider public interest in maintaining public knowledge and understanding.

The extent to which CC licences retain their foundations in the open-source sharing ethos of the FOSS movement is, however, brought into question by Ann Barron (2015). In recent years, many tens of millions of works have been released under CC licences rather than under copyright. Barron makes two observations. First, alongside the FOSS movement and the General Licensing Agreement (GLA) set out by Richard Stallman, and regulated by the Free Software Foundation, CC licensing of works to prevent them from being copyrighted is not the same as placing them directly into the public domain. There is no mechanism by which an 'author' can disown copyright control over something without first asserting that they have a right so to do. This renunciation, therefore, requires that the developer had something akin to ownership rights in the first place. Stallman sought to create a system of registration by which works drawing upon the common culture of shared and open-source production would not be enclosed by private rights; to do so, however, he adopted a mechanism that mirrored (at some level at least) the very thing it was designed to prevent. In order that nobody else can make a claim, the person taking out the licence must assert something similar to 'ownership', at least at the level of author rights recognition and in their assertion of rights to prevent future closure for commercial gain by others. Barron notes that what CC licensing has done (relative to open-source and 'copyleft' – which assert that a work is not copyright controlled, and that all works derived from that work must also remain open to free use, access and modification) is to extend significantly the discretion that can be exercised by the licensee when taking out such a licence. Where Stallman's 'open-source' GLA is a single licence stating that the work must remain accessible and that developments built on that code cannot be copyrighted either, a CC licence gives the person taking out the licence one of six templates. As such, rather than repudiating the 'all rights reserved' copyright doctrine in full, there is a choice as to 'some rights (being) reserved', even as others are disowned. Barron notes that this approach to 'sharing' is deeply individualistic and legalistic, and represents a significant compromising of hacker open-source culture with dominant business interests.

Computer Games

When, in the early years of the twenty-first century, record companies began to see sales crash after two decades of unprecedented expansion and profit, these losses were blamed on free-sharing. Record industry (and film) lobbies (BPI 2008) argued that their losses proved the need for stronger laws to protect their business model. It is ironic then that the computer games industry cites precisely the opposite reason to argue the need for stronger laws to protect their business. In recent years, the computer games industry has seen its sales increase rapidly – they are now greater than those of music and film (Chatfield 2010; BBC 2012). Its argument for increased protection is that, in being so successful, the computer games industry is a pillar of the economy in advanced societies – such as the United Kingdom, Japan and the United States. Yet, if the computer games industry has been so very successful, despite the 'threat' of free-sharing of its products, is it really the case that strong IP protection is needed?

At first glance, the case for a strong IP defence for computer games seems clear. Unlike in other sectors of the so-called 'creative industries' (O'Brien 2015) – such as music, film and sports broadcasting – the rise in free-sharing cannot be expected to boost the sector in other ways. Free music-sharing has increased the price and volume of live music ticket sales; cinema attendance is also boosted by free online viewing, and live sports event attendances have not suffered as a result of free-streaming. There is no parallel economy in computer gaming. It is an entirely digital economy, so surely its whole business model must be the most vulnerable to free-sharing. Yet this is not the case.

In fact, the computer games industry is – curiously – least reliant on either legal IP protection or technical DRM in maintaining its market in the face of readily available free copies. As Greg Lastowka (2015) observes, the history of computer games is an elliptical one in relation to IP. In its earliest manifestations, non-commercial programmers (in government or corporate research labs) created simple graphical copies of real world games (e.g., tennis) or generic narrative forms (e.g., space war). Neither the visual outcome nor the rules/narratives being replicated were open to copyright, and these games were not being sold either, so there was no profit to be protected. Subsequent arcade games created profitable markets in the sale of physical machines, but simple and generic forms and rules were hard to claim ownership over. The rise of the PC did, however, see an explosion of copying by end-users. The response was not to sue these end-users, but rather the development of new generations of console-based games. Whereas in the 1980s, PC gamers could swap and copy cassettes and, later, discs, users today can easily download copies of games to play on PCs, but are persuaded that the graphical quality afforded by dedicated consoles is worth paying for. Likewise, in offering users Massively Multiple Online Gaming (MMOG) spaces, online software providers persuade large numbers of users that their gameplay experience will be superior if they choose to use the proprietary service rather than the readily available free download alternatives. (These alternatives do not work with the official MMOG sites, but do work as standalone games.) Where the Internet as a distribution mechanism deeply troubled older distribution models in music, film and even digital television, the computer games industry has adapted to the Internet without the need to lock down content by legal means (Kamenetz 2013).

Again, where older content industries reacted to the digital revolution by seeking to better protect and sell their back catalogues – with the extension of copyright laws affording even longer terms to sell works made as far back as the start of the twentieth century – the computer games industry has responded in exactly the opposite fashion. In addition to releasing entirely new games, the industry routinely revises established best sellers – such as *FIFA World Cup*, *Grand Theft Auto*, and *Call of Duty* (CoD) – in updated forms. If these new versions are, in turn, successful, they will see multiple mutations and developments. The computer games industry, then, thrives by persuading users to pay for what they can easily get for free (appeal, not control) or in offering an endless supply of variations (first mover advantage, not monopoly control). Despite not liking its works being copied, the industry does not bother to lock down outdated content.

To close the elliptical cycle that has been the history of computer gaming, what started off as being too generic to copyright (simple graphics and simple rules/narratives) has morphed into a field that is becoming too complex to copyright. As games became sufficiently complex to claim 'originality' (in both code and narrative form), so it is that elements of this 'originality' are being claimed by users themselves. For a game to work as a game, it cannot simply follow a script. Users therefore have to co-create the gameplay experience and narrative amongst themselves. Increasingly, this now includes the possibility of 'user generated content' (Lastowka 2015) – digital artefacts and scripts not 'created' as such by the games' original creators, even while enabled by the games' more sophisticated programming. Originality increasingly comes to lie in gameplay (Kirkpatrick 2013), not in the game itself. Seeking to claim ownership over how users use their games would open games-makers to a regress in terms of claims made in relation to earlier source code and generic background coding. Fear of regress discourages overly dogmatic assertions of IP.

Platforms, Programmes and the Limits of Property

A brief survey of the dominant players in today's digital world offers a clear indication of the extent to which non-proprietary forms of shared knowledge production and distribution have driven development; this is despite the fact that some of these players have found ways of turning their origins in collaborative and shared production into profitable businesses. Such a survey also highlights a number of contradictions and challenges associated with free-sharing, in relation to not just private property but personal privacy as well.

The Internet

The Internet had its origins in publicly funded US military research. In part, the Advanced Research Projects Agency's Arpanet, which is what went on to become the Internet, was created to enable distributed communications in the event of a nuclear war, but was also funded to facilitate communication between geographically distributed scientists across the fields of military research that would enable just such a war. However, the depth and scope of militarily funded research was so large, and the project to create a distributed packet-switching network communications architecture so complex, that management of the Arpanet was delegated to a team of academic experts. What started out as the Network Working Group morphed into the Internet Engineering Task Force when the Internet itself emerged as a civilian platform (Abbate 1999). The task force remains responsible for maintaining and updating the protocols that manage addresses and distribution on the Internet. While this gives the task force significant potential power in ordering communication on the Internet – not just despite but precisely because of the Internet's distributed architecture, which requires a single common language to enable communication (Galloway 2004) – this is tempered by the fact that abuse of such power, through excluding certain domain names from the Internet and/or rendering certain addresses invisible in search engines, would fragment the Internet and thereby diminish its perceived universality. Abbate concludes: 'There seems to have been no corporate participation in the design of the Internet. Like its predecessor [the Arpanet], the Internet was designed, informally and with little fanfare, by a self-selected group of experts' (1999: 127).

The World Wide Web

If the Internet in large part arose from public-funded and academic-managed research in the United States, the story of the World Wide Web is a similar one, except that it arose from collaborative research across Europe. Tim Berners-Lee developed the Web as a platform to sit on the Internet, but which was user-friendly and allowed the creation of graphically naturalistic 'pages', simple search strategies and the ability to distribute digital content between users. Initially designed to assist in the sharing of research being conducted by the European Organization for Nuclear Research (CERN), the Web was launched in 1992. In 1994, Berners-Lee convened the World Wide Web Consortium (W3C) and established the standards and principles that govern web development. Key to these standards and principles is that all web distribution technology remains patent- and copyright-free, and is therefore free for all to access, use and develop. Since 1994, Berners-Lee has been active in maintaining the IP-free nature of the Web platform (Berners-Lee 2000), even while commercial actors have been active in using the platform to launch and run commercial sites. In this respect, commercial interests exist in a purely parasitical relationship to the underlying creative force of free-sharing.

Wikipedia

Wikis emerged on the Web in 1995, with the software being developed by Ward Cunningham a year earlier. Wikis are collaborative texts coproduced by a number of participants without, or with only limited, hierarchical management of construction. Wiki software is designed to facilitate shared production and distribution of content within the online world. By far the most famous example of a Wiki is Wikipedia, launched in 2001 by Jimmy Wales and Larry Sanger. Wikipedia is a user-managed wiki-based encyclopaedia, with millions of entries, hundreds of millions of users, and tens of thousands of active editors at any one time. While open to error in being co-constructed by so many, mainly amateur, editors, Wikipedia has proven to be radically and rapidly 'self-correcting', with error rates roughly equal to those of *Encyclopaedia Britannica*, but with the advantage of a much more rapid process of correction and updating (Giles 2005). Wikipedia is hosted by the Wikimedia Foundation, a non-profit organization dedicated to upholding the non-commercial, non-hierarchical principles of sharing information as the best means of increasing knowledge.

Facebook: Sharing as the 'end of privacy'

At a technology award ceremony in San Francisco in January 2010, Facebook founder Mark Zucherberg is reported to have claimed: 'People have really gotten comfortable not only sharing more information and different kinds, but more openly and with more people' (Barnett 2010). Zucherberg went on to claim that privacy was an outdated social norm, increasingly at odds with a culture of sharing. If true, if today's online distribution of all manner of personal information means personal privacy cannot be maintained, this does rather show the darker side of sharing. With more than one billion registered users, and with a business model based entirely on the willingness of its users to post (share) and search for personal information about one another, Facebook certainly appears to prove that, for many people, permanent, camera-ready, self-revelation has become an expected social practice. Nonetheless, Zuckerberg's claim must be treated with a degree of scepticism. Even if Facebook's users make active choices in sharing information about themselves on their profiles, they are not always fully aware of what Facebook is then doing with that data. Zuckerberg's comments must be seen in the context of criticism of his business's decision a month earlier (in December 2009) to fundamentally alter Facebook's privacy settings, increasing the scope for the company to commercialize personal information for sale to marketers and other businesses. As has been noted above in discussion of the free and open-source software/hacker movement, struggles over freedom of expression and freedom from surveillance do not mean simply choosing one over the other. Rather, the question to ask is: who do you believe should be free to speak, who should have privacy, from whom, and who would be free to watch whom?

The Googlization of everything

Google has arisen in recent years from amidst an array of similar service providers to become the Internet's predominant search engine. The service is free to use and its presentation of results to users implies a distinction between sponsored links (on the right-hand side of its results' screen) and those produced simply by means of Google's search algorithm (on the left-hand side). This distinction appears to suggest that those results shown on the left are free of bias, and, with the service being free to acquire, it appears the very definition of a freely shared informational environment.

However, Google's predominance, the scope for bias in its search algorithm (Kirkpatrick 2008) and its various personalization and localization algorithms (Vaidhyanathan 2012) mean Google can use its trusted status as a free, information-sharing service to disguise its primary commercial interest in selling user eyeballs to powerful economic actors and others. Google's 'spider bot' algorithm creates search results for specific search terms given by ranking pages with the keywords chosen by the user, according to how many other pages are linked to that page. This is seen as a neutral indicator of relevance – on the assumption that if many other pages have set up links to a particular page, this means that the page is seen as valid, trustworthy and/or useful by more people than a page to which nobody or only a few people have linked their page(s). However, this ranking calculus does mean that the pages of better-resourced and higher-profile actors will rank more highly in Google searches than will the pages of others. Similarly, Google operate policies to personalize and localize searches, not just in terms of user-defined needs, but also in terms of corporate advertising strategies and the laws of specific states. Underneath what appears to be a relatively flat system of free information-sharing, there operates an array of more hierarchical strategies of selection and persuasion.

Apple: Managing to profit within a sharing field

Steve Jobs and Steve Wozniak, the co-founders of Apple Computers, were famously part of the early computer hacker movement in late 1960s and early 1970s California – in particular, the Homebrew Computer Club in Palo Alto. While it was Wozniak who was mainly responsible for the technical development of the first Apple personal computer in 1976, it was Jobs who persuaded Wozniak that they should go into business selling such devices a year later. Although Apple has always sought to portray itself as more countercultural than its main rival Microsoft, its business strategy is anything but. For twenty years, Apple remained a niche computer manufacturer, making computers to run its proprietary operating system; unlike Microsoft, Apple did not license its software to others to run on their machines. Both Jobs and Wozniak left the company in 1985; Jobs returned in 1997. He then set about shifting Apple Computers, dropping the word 'computers' from the company title and moving the business model, from personal computers as previously understood, to a spectrum of digital devices: from iPods and iPlayers, to iPhones and a suite of lap-tops, the iPad and new generations of smart televisions, watches and the like. Apple has come predominantly to sell premium priced hardware that can be used to connect to and use the Internet, where most content then accessed and used is free. Even Apple's iTunes service was only made possible when record companies became willing to deal with a digital intermediary after all their efforts to prohibit free-sharing services had failed. Apple's own research suggests that 90 per cent of space on its iPods is filled with free downloads, not paid-for iTunes (Jobs 2007).

Apple had its origins in the freely sharing hobbyists of 1970s California. Today, it is the largest single company in the world by sales. Yet, since its post-1997 reorganization, its business has been built mainly on selling the hardware needed to access predominantly free content available online, and its main digital services were only made possible by the development of free file-sharing. Both now and in the past, then, Apple is a product of the sharing-based environments in which it operates; this has not, however, stopped it from becoming extremely successful at selling things at a very significant profit.

Microsoft: Attempting to control the field

Bill Gates also started out within the free-sharing software culture of the US 'Popular Electronics' culture of the early 1970s. However, having developed a version of BASIC to run on an Altair 8800 with collaborator and future Microsoft co-founder Paul Allen, Gates famously wrote his 'Open Letter to Hobbyists' in 1974, castigating the free-sharing community of hobbyists for not paying royalties for the copies of code they used and adapted.

Wozniak and Jobs's Apple I computer was sold as a piece of hardware (although this was only the computer board, not the monitor, box or keyboard), and the software (Apple basic) was given away for free. Gates and Allen's business model, in contrast, was to license their software to others who would then build the physical hardware on which it could run. For Microsoft, then, IP protection on software is their business model. To this extent, Microsoft has remained wedded to the creation of operating systems, mainly for personal computers but also for larger mainframe computers, and Microsoft has always been late in adapting to the *networked* nature of today's digital world. Microsoft software predominates on personal computers worldwide, but its late entry into the domains of Internet-based computing, web browsers, mobile devices and so forth has been further weakened by its reputation for seeking control over access and taking legal action against open-source opponents, and its failed attempt to bundle its operating system with its web browser (which would have compelled its software users to also use this web browser). However, just as was shown in Chapter 4 in relation to Sky/ Fox – where the business's 'first mover' advantage in largely creating the digital sports broadcaster market is, in part, reinforced by the inability of its competitors to secure a substantial paying audience in an age of free live-streaming alternatives – so Microsoft may have benefited from the unlicensed circulation of copies of its software in post-socialist and developing societies (May 2007). Free-sharing of the market leader's product undermined the scope for any commercial rivals to develop or survive.

Where Microsoft became the undisputed giant in the development of standalone personal computer software, it has been overshadowed by Apple in the age of mobile network communications – in large part, because Apple adjusted better to the digital-sharing space that is the Internet. While both remain highly profitable even in an age of free-sharing, they also highlight the significance of adapting to the new world of free content-sharing. The Internet, Web and Wikis (in particular Wikipedia) highlight the power of sharing-based software development and distribution. Facebook and Google highlight the scope for sharing to be manipulated and exploited. Apple and Microsoft, meanwhile, demonstrate how profitable a sharing world can be, even if at the same time showing how better adaptation to that world is more profitable than trying simply to control it.

Conclusions: Sharing, the Gift Economy, Play Struggle and Creativity

The failure of corporate digital rights management (DRM) when set against free-sharing-based hacker code highlights the fact that creativity is stifled by ownership, not motivated by it. This is all the more true given that it is corporations that own IP (in the work of the programmers they employ), not those individuals writing it. The evolution of file-sharing software further illustrates the more productive nature of open-source coding over corporate control. The commons is not only the best means of protecting the public sphere; it is also the best means of protecting the public from manipulation by those who would restrict information – information being the very base condition of rational decision-making, by citizens as well as consumers. However, the commons is not only the best defence against such potential abuses of information control; it is also the best means of stimulating creative production and the distribution of useful new code.

The spirit of informationalism, or 'play struggle', successfully challenges the Protestant ethic and its separation of work and play, its subordination of freedom to control, and of access to ownership. The creative play that sets information free while also generating it threatens to abolish scarcity, replacing it instead with a gift economy based on plenitude and sharing. The example of computer games as a business highlights that protectionism is only necessary in sectors based on old industrial conceptions of scarcity and control. In the fully digital economy, the best way to survive is to innovate rather than to cling on to yesterday's success. The history of the Internet, Web and Wikis illustrates the primacy of sharing to creativity in the digital age; this is true despite the fact that the plenitude which sharing creates has provided space for those who would pursue old models to parasitize the new – even while they falsely claim to be genuinely adding to the creative mix.

6

Publishing:
Academic, Journalistic and Trade

Introduction

This chapter addresses the significance of sharing to publishing: academic, journalistic and trade. The gift economy of free-sharing that underpins academic writing is based upon a peer exchange system that long preceded Internet-based modes of peer exchange and wikinomics. Digital networks enable such a sharing economy to leave behind a dependence upon commercial distributors whose role was based on the scarcity value of paper copies. Citizen witnessing and the scope of free online access to journalistic content promises/threatens to bypass the editorial/self-censuring nexus characteristic of 'traditional' print and broadcast media. Similarly, digital network sharing of fiction and trade non-fiction challenges the editorial control and commercial concentration characteristic of today's trade publishing industry.

The principle of peer review, at the heart of Merton's (1972/1942) notion of 'academic communism', has also become a source of heated argument in conflicts over who counts as a legitimate peer. The average Wikipedia science entry has four major errors, while the *Encyclopaedia Britannica* has three. However, Wikipedia can be instantly corrected (Anderson 2009), while the *Encyclopaedia Britannica* will carry its errors for years, until the next edition is published. In such conditions, the questions of what counts as an authority, who should be allowed to review whom, and of how knowledge should be produced, evaluated and used all become increasingly obviously at odds with commercial interests.

The current threats posed to the viability of mainstream print and broadcast journalism, when compared to new media sources of news and opinion, raise similar questions as to the relative merits of freely circulating media and commercial models of news and journalism. Claims regarding the balance between 'authority' and 'freedom' in the production of news reflect competing and 'interested' positions, not neutral and objective realities; and these 'positions' are themselves built on shifting foundations. Not only are such self-justifications by editors and journalists open to question, but the very existence of such roles as viable positions are also open to question.

This chapter will conclude with a discussion of fiction and popular non-fiction ('trade') publishing. Having undergone a fourfold process of commercial concentration in recent years, trade publishing has intensified a 'winner-takes-all' model of rewarding ever-smaller numbers of 'big books', selected according to ever-tightening processes of author, agent, editor, publisher and corporate self-regulation informed by dominant market definitions of value (platform, sales, 'sameness' and multimedia circularity – Thompson 2012). One per cent of authors earn welfare-benefit-equivalent earnings or above from publishing royalties, while around one-tenth of that number make the equivalent to average earnings or above. Most authors, even in this very small upper band, have to make ends meet by other means (Silbey 2015). As such, free-sharing offers a better way to engage with, and even make a living from, more direct interactions with audiences. However, to date, the sum of unpaid labour, shared by creative authors (as by academic authors and citizen journalists) but which becomes the saleable-content-IP controlled by publishers, remains a means of maintaining profit and so of not challenging the capitalist publishing model. The rise of the e-book and print-on-demand in publishing has not, to date, produced anything like a 'Napster moment' in publishing, even if this may one day come about.

Academic Publishing

Most academic publishing results in no payment made to the author. Academic journals do not pay the authors, it would be seen as a threat to the integrity of the claims being made by authors if they were to do so; in fact, some journals even charge for work to be published. While peer review processes exist in such a way as to avoid giving the impression that work is being published because payments have been made, such financial transactions remain 'suspicious', seen as potential modes of 'vanity' publishing, rather than respectable academic writing. In the case of academic books, the royalties system rewards only the most popular titles to any significant degree. Whether designated 'popular' or 'textbooks', such works that may sell in large numbers are not then deemed 'academic'. The reasons that academics publish have next to nothing to do with direct financial reward and is a clear illustration of what Robert Merton called 'academic communism': the requirement of academics to share their work with their peers in order to be given due recognition for their original insights. Academic principles concerning plagiarism are distinct from those of copyright and/or patent. Unpaid academic publishing encourages free use in exchange for recognition in the form of the appropriate citation of the works used.

As a model for creativity and innovation, science and academia in general are based upon sharing ideas. This is despite strong efforts to bend academic life towards an IP-based business model. However, changes in the production and distribution of academic works – in particular, the development of large online databases – and the requirement on academics to show increasing relevance and impact, make it increasingly difficult to defend a model of academic publishing based on the notion of IP protectionism, whether that be in respect of individual journal articles or books. Where universities increasingly negotiate online journal packages en bloc (such as with JSTOR) and where, at the same time, universities require, in the interests of 'impact', that academics make their published work available in an open-source format, the rationale for having commercial publishers publish journals for profit is challenged. In a global digital network society, the argument that commercial publishers can market and distribute journal articles better than academic networks and associations weakens. As such, the general principles of free-sharing, which, in fact, govern the writing, editing and peer reviewing of academic journals anyway, comes to challenge current conventions of payment and ownership in terms of control and distribution.

Publish or perish

The maxim 'publish or perish', as well as being the name of a software package designed to allow academics to check out how many people have cited their work (and also how many people have cited the works of their peers), is also a turn of phrase that paradoxically highlights why creativity assumes sharing. As Boldrin and Levine (2008) document, the most significant discoveries and inventions are almost always discovered by many people at the same time.

Whether it was powered flight, the theory of evolution, the structure of the atom or DNA, radio waves, or the steam or internal combustion engine, discovery comes from within a shared environment of innovation, not from individuals working in isolation. Creativity and innovation require sharing, which is why attempts to prevent sharing by means of intellectual monopolies are the antithesis of any functional academic and scientific system. In addition to 'standing on the shoulders of giants', scientists and academics share ideas with their current peers. Academics publish in order to share their ideas, not to get paid. However, this is not pure altruism. The maxim 'publish or perish' reflects the fact that credit for new discoveries and inventions goes to the first person to publish and disclose. While the patent system allows such primacy to be expressed in the form of ownership rights, academic publishing does not assert ownership over the ideas expressed, even if their particular expression may be subject to copyright. In essence, academics publish because being the first to give an idea away confers upon the sharer the status of 'discoverer' (not 'inventor').

Robert Merton's (1972/1942) 'academic communism' is a sharing-based economy that does not suspend competition. However, such an economy does not rely upon the principle of property; it is not a capitalist economy, even while extreme competition for status does lead to very powerful hierarchies akin to 'wealth'. Merton's 'Matthew Effect in science' (1968), where the best predictor of career success in science is the status of one's doctoral supervisor, highlights how status accumulation may come to parallel a form of 'property' (what Pierre Bourdieu – 1988 – would later describe as a form of 'cultural capital'). However, such status is still dependent upon successful gift-giving – in other words, being first to share an idea that is then cited by others. It is not enough, then, just to give things away. Status depends upon the number of people who subsequently take up the gift given, in terms of citing the work in their own publications – i.e., the gifts given must be deemed valuable. Status in academic life is therefore dependent upon both giving away the maximum overall value in gifts, and in having those gifts duly (and formally) accepted.

Academic journals: A very expensive gift economy

The academic gift economy may be 'communist', in sacrificing property as a gift to be given away in the hope of receiving 'discoverer' status, and also in gaining status respect as measured in citations given to such gifts. Yet this 'sharing' economy may or may not be at odds with highly profitable publishing strategies based on property rights in the form of copyright. For the most part, academic journals publish works freely offered by their authors. Researchers may be funded to carry out research, but journals do not pay researchers to publish the results of that research. Researchers submit papers for free, for the reasons outlined above: the need to share their work to acquire status, both as originators and in terms of the number of times such work is cited. Prospective journal articles (papers) are 'peer reviewed' by other academics who are themselves unpaid. Academic reviewers review work because they hope to read new ideas first, and because reviewing is deemed 'worthy' within an academic community based upon sharing. Being asked to review work is a mark of peer recognition, which itself exists in a hierarchy of such journal-based recognition: reviewing, joining editorial boards and eventually becoming editor of a journal. All these roles are primarily unpaid and undertaken as part of an economy of peer recognition that may or may not 'cash out' in other ways (such as institutional promotion). The academic editors of journals may or may not receive some payment to cover their expenses, and time taken from other duties, associated with their role; but, again, journal editing is largely done for recognition and not for money.

Nevertheless, the content of most academic journals is subject to copyright and, as holders of such copyrights, publishers can sell access to the journals and the articles they contain. Sales are mainly to academic libraries and individual academic subscribers. Unlike book publishing (academic and trade), academic journals are sold direct to academic libraries and individuals, and on a repeat basis, thereby eliminating both the margin taken by retailers and the risks associated with trying to sell particular books (actual sales of which are hard to predict). The free content and the secure market to libraries make academic journals highly profitable. That academics share their research – both by giving the content away for free and then by buying it back for libraries that will allow academics (and students) to freely access the content – is a situation that works very much to the benefit of publishers.

John Thompson (2005) outlines the shift in the academic journal market in recent decades. Between 1970 and the late 1990s, academic journal subscriptions in the United States and the United Kingdom increased in price by 13 per cent per year, meaning that journals increased in price by thirty times in that period. The increases have carried on apace since then (rising approximately 10,000 per cent between 1970 and 2016). This price increase is far greater than the rate of general inflation in the same period. As Thompson notes, it is not possible to read everything in an expanding academic field, and an academic's work is often judged on the basis of where it is published, not simply on the fact that it has been 'made available' somewhere. Many key journals have therefore become central markers of status, and 'anyone who is anyone' in a field will seek to publish in them. As a result, everyone in that field needs to have access to that journal, and the publisher that owns that journal (and via copyright over the content therein) can increase the journal's prices with near impunity, knowing that price elasticity – the change in sales volume that would follow an alteration in price – for such titles is very close to zero.

With free content, no retailer margins and a stable market, the field of academic journal publishing is very profitable. Expansion in the university sector since the 1960s has meant that, while increasing journal prices have squeezed university library budgets, overall journal budgets – and, hence, publisher profits – have remained high. Even as prices have rocketed, sales have not plummeted. As Thompson (2005: 99–102) documents, commercial publishers entered the academic journal market in the 1960s and bought up valuable titles, as well as whole journal publishing divisions and houses – thereby concentrating the field into a smaller and smaller number of dominant corporate hands. This concentration has further increased the bargaining power of publishers over universities in terms of the content that was, as has been mentioned, mainly given freely in the first place by academics working in those universities.

Faced with the spiralling cost of journal subscriptions, universities have sought to develop negotiating consortia – in part, built upon the shared, journal-searching databases that university researchers and libraries developed in the post-war era of expanding science research. Recent attempts by universities in the United Kingdom, the United States and the Netherlands to force the commercial journal publisher Elsevier to make a significant part of its content 'open access' (Jump 2015), without increasing its charges (either to libraries or to the authors of the works published), has been led by university principals, not just their librarians – a significant escalation in a longstanding conflict. These universities have threatened to require their staff not to serve as reviewers or editors for the company – which has radically increased prices and profits via digital distribution that radically reduces costs. This pressure from university leaders has been combined with grassroots campaigning by academics similarly angered by the company's profiteering from their freely provided content and editing labour. 'The Cost of Knowledge' (http://www.thecostof-knowledge.com/) campaign, which has organized a boycott of work for the company by academics, has more than 16,500 members. Bad publicity and the threat to the reputations of the company's flagship journals – as the perception is that key authors will take new work elsewhere – has forced the company to offer concessions, though the underlying issues are far from being resolved. While Elsevier has been the highest-profile target for academic disquiet over rising journal prices in an age where free academic labour combined with free digital distribution could set knowledge free, the issue is generic.

As such, universities and publishers face-off against one another, with consortia of universities seeking to bring down the overall cost of buying back the content, produced freely by their own staff, from publishers who also engage in various forms of aggregation in order to increase their bargaining position. Corporate concentration is one strategy, with more and more titles and imprints owned by fewer and fewer large corporations. Publishing consortia are another strategy, whereby publishers work together to strengthen their bargaining position. A third strategy is 'bundling', where publishers offer blocks of digital journal content, such that access to 'must have' journals is tied to a wider raft of other titles. Universities have responded by requiring their staff to provide their institution with 'pre-publication' copies of works that have been accepted for publication in journals so that this version of the content can be made available (online). This is via the university's portal in the first instance, but the content can also then be aggregated via university library consortia and collaborative research portals.

To date, 'sharing' in the academic journal field has, then, been a licence to print money for publishers. However, the creation by universities of ever-larger electronic modes of aggregation (searchable databases), combined with their take-up of strategies by which content that will appear in journals is enabled to circulate freely by other means, does challenge the currently dominant business model. Giving content away for free is profitable if such content is being given away freely to publishers who then assert exclusive copyright control – because the publisher is then able to prohibit subsequent free circulation to end-users (readers). If that prohibition is broken by various forms of free circulation, sharing becomes a serious challenge to the profitability of business as usual.

Wikinomics, 'Peer' review, metrics and assessment

The suicide of Aaron Swartz in 2013 represents an extreme outcome in the struggle between free-sharing of academic content and attempts to protect copyright control (Halbert 2014: 1–4). Swartz was arrested and accused of causing millions of dollars-worth of damage to academic publishers' profits by hacking into the electronic journal aggregation service JSTOR and de-encrypting hundreds of thousands of journal articles. At present, access to JSTOR requires the user to be an individual subscriber or belong to a subscribing organization (most typically, a university). Subscriptions are very, very expensive, at least relative to any individual seeking to subscribe. In de-encrypting a large number of journal articles, Swartz believed he was giving content back to the public who had, for the most part, already paid for it. The research that journals sought to own publication rights over was/is, in large part, publicly funded. Threatened with the prospect of 30 years in prison, Swartz killed himself.

The idea that academic publishing should be freely available, just as it is freely given and freely reviewed, is a form of 'peer review' that parallels what has, in other settings, been called 'wikinomics' (Tapscott and Williams 2008). It is often suggested that Wikipedia is the very antithesis of academic publishing, and yet, in many respects, it is very similar. Many academics fear that students rely too much on the peer-constructed entries provided by Wikipedia over and above the texts given 'authority' by dint of being published in academic journals (and books). Yet, the process by which authority is given in academic journals and books is 'peer review', not any other kind of 'higher' authority. While professors may offer their own selected reading lists to guide their students in what to read – at least as a first point of departure – it is hoped that students will not simply come to believe everything their teacher tells them, or only to read what the teacher has recommended. Instead, students should be encouraged to ask whether or not what they are reading is credible, not just to believe all of what an 'authority' tells them to read. The fact that the average Wikipedia entry – as noted earlier – contains no significantly greater number of errors than the average *Encyclopaedia Britannica* entry, while also being open to much quicker and more convenient revision (Anderson 2009), has salience in this respect. The principle of peer review, then, is simply ongoing with Wikipedia, even if it is essential for any user to ask who those peers are. Students have to learn what more established academics should already know. Everything needs to be cross-referenced and authority should not be taken for granted. If academic work carries some 'authority', this is due to reputable (usually university-employed) peers in the relevant field giving their input for free in the form of peer review. It should not be assumed that this authority comes from the publisher. As Thompson (2005) elaborates, recent cost-cutting measures in academic publishing have seen significant reductions in the time and money put into editing, copyediting and proofreading drafts, and with almost all of this work now outsourced in any case, it is even less credible to suggest that publishers themselves 'add' rigour to academic work.

Nevertheless, academics often use the status of particular publishers and places of publication as proxy signals for the level of academic rigour in the work contained, at least when assessing the merits of work they cannot themselves evaluate (for reasons of time and/or expertise). It is precisely for this reason that certain journals have become so very profitable. Academics have come to use journals to tell them what would be worth reading outside their own domain, not so much within it. If academics cannot read everything, then one might therefore suppose that commercial journal publishing is just a necessary cost to filter out the flood of things that are not worth paying attention to. Such a supposition, however, would be misguided on two counts. First of all, as argued above, the assumption that work in highly regarded journals will be more likely to be good than work published or distributed by other means is dependent upon the free peer reviewing of academics for those journals and not on their commercial control. That this quality control can command a price because it is under copyright control is not the same as saying this price is necessary to the production of 'quality' and hence is legitimate. The quality control affected by peer review is 'free', so is not causing necessary costs. Second, in an age of digital metrics, the question of whether an article is being cited widely can be independently verified, and academics do not need to simply assume that the best work will be that which is published by the most prestigious titles. The most successful academics use their peer networks to alert them to what is good to read as well as to what is new and of merit in their own area (Zeitlyn et al. 1999). Undergraduates ask their friends; so do professors. The difference between undergraduates and professors is not their technique, but rather their friendship networks. Professors tend to have better-read contacts, both in their exact field (Bourdieu 1988), and in adjacent fields (Granovetter 1973). Postgraduates (and management committees) use various technical proxies (citation indexes and bibliographic data-services).

Amongst established academics, 'place of publication' is really only significant when gauging the status of those outside one's own immediate field of expertise.

Cooperation and competition operate between and within networks: peer sharing and selling interlace. On the one hand, technical networks can act to distribute unencrypted journal articles. On the other hnd, they can also share peer reviews and recommendations that reduce publishers' distribution and marketing costs while increasing the distribution of copyrighted content that was written and reviewed for free. Sharing, as we have seen, is the foundation of what are currently very profitable academic publishing strategies; but such sharing, if it leaks out and cannot be controlled, may come to threaten such profitability. Current battles over 'open access' are illustrative. Publishers are keen that any such systems that will make research findings more accessible to wider communities of use will retain their right to set prices, even if that requires universities and government to pay publishers what they (publishers) claim they could have charged if they had kept control over access. On this basis, canal owners and pigeons should have a claim against the railways and the telephone service, respectively, for loss of earnings. University strategies to ensure that all work done by academics is made available (in pre-publication format at least), via university and research network web-portals, does see journals lose their monopoly position, without those bypassed being able to demand compensation for profits lost in the ending of their monopoly position.

Academic book publishing

Thompson (2005) distinguishes between academic monographs that disseminate the latest research findings to a mainly academic audience, and the forms of higher education publishing aimed at students (the 'textbook' market). The expansion of higher education provision in the last 50 years has seen increased library spending overall but not an increased spend per student. Larger student numbers have seen an increase in spending on textbooks (by students and libraries), but not on monographs. Libraries' budgets have been squeezed by increased journal prices (see above) and increased student numbers (leading to the need for more textbooks). As such, sales of monographs have fallen radically. In the 1970s, monograph print runs of 2,000–3,000 hardbacks were the average. This has fallen to 400–500, with 78–85 per cent of monographs never selling more than 750 copies (Thompson 2005: 95).

Only a very small number of academics make any money from writing textbooks; the majority of such works do not generate significant earning for their authors. This is because royalties are paid at only a very low percentage (around 5–10 per cent) of net sales, with a range of costs deducted even from this small amount. Those who write monographs cannot reasonably expect to earn anything from royalties – rates are even lower than those offered on textbooks. Royalties of 5 per cent (or nothing) are common, and on net sales (after deduction for the cost of indexing, some formatting, and image and other IP rights), there is no significant pecuniary incentive for academics to write monographs. As a result, the need to 'share' ideas to gain academic status is pretty much the sole incentive motivating authors of such works. Yet, in parallel with academic journal publication, content that is for the most part freely generated, with a view to sharing it, is then copyrighted by publishers for sale. While not as extreme as has been the case for journals, in recent years the price of monographs has also spiralled in the UK (and risen, although more slowly, in the United States), as publishers have sought to maintain overall profit levels on diminishing sales (Thompson 2005: 116–117). With prices escalating and with library purchases of monographs falling, the ability of other academics to access works (and, in reverse, the ability – of authors – to make their work accessible) is radically diminished. In a chilling fashion, authors produce 'outputs' simply to fulfil the requirement of their institutional five- (or six-) year research plan, but with little anticipation that any but a tiny number of readers will ever actually be able to access their content. By means of monopoly pricing, a form of censorship arises that many academics have come to accept as the necessary logic of their field.

Yet, the logic of sharing that motivates academics' willingness to write for next to no direct payment also creates scope for wider forms of free distribution that could challenge current publishing models. Google Books sought to offer the possibility of legal access to monographs currently out of print, or otherwise inaccessible, either in part (allowing readers to access selected pages/sequences of pages for free), or in full via new forms of print-on-demand publishing. This has been stifled for the present. However, the scope for freely available e-books circulating online in contravention of copyright is ongoing. Most academic monographs that are otherwise priced out of the market, for any but the most well-resourced libraries, are available online in illicit e-copy versions; and the choice of academics to put pre-publication copies of monographs online is another positive development, in terms of access to knowledge. That publishers seek to snuff out such moves suggests the threat that it poses to business as usual. At non-monopoly prices, Google Books offered to stimulate demand for previously inaccessible works and hence open up the 'long tail' of older works in a fashion similar to what Amazon has done for the market in currently available works (Anderson 2009). This is at odds with a business model (discussed below) that seeks to sell a narrow range of new 'big books'. Accessing the long tail benefits the overall culture. And as the music industry's success in closing down Napster simply encouraged more fully distributed forms of sharing, so clamping down on Google Books in part explains the profusion of illicit e-books.

Journalistic Publishing: The Editorial Nexus and Beyond?

In early 2015, the BBC and the *Guardian* newspaper in the United Kingdom both enthusiastically reported on the resignation of the journalist and commentator Peter Obourne from the *Daily Telegraph* newspaper. Obourne resigned, claiming that editorial policy at the *Daily Telegraph* had been dictated by the need to secure and please key advertising clients, citing in particular the HSBC banking group, whose numerous and significant infringements of UK banking regulations, and subsequent fines as well as other sanctions, were rarely reported in that title when compared to other titles not receiving significant advertising revenues from the bank.

The more cynical may conclude that this is merely the tip of the iceberg. Sociological studies of media organization and of media content (e.g., Curran and Seaton 2010) highlight how media ownership and its concentration, as well as the increasing role of advertising in the financing of newspapers, shapes content – both as business friendly and as focused around human interest rather than wider social organization (Habermas 1992/1962). Such control – by which ownership and finance shape content – is exercised through 'the editorial nexus'. Editors are appointed by owners and usually do not need day-to-day direction. Where Obourne's claims may be unusual lie in the suggestion that advertisers and marketing managers were said to have intervened explicitly in directing editors, when it is often assumed that an editor's position depends upon their ability not to need to be told on which side their bread is buttered.

However, Obourne's resignation does highlight the fact that journalists, to some extent at least, hold to, or at least claim to believe in, principles of journalistic integrity and professionalism that are at odds with the notion that they are simply 'hacks', paid to write advertising friendly copy in the interests of owners and advertisers (Allen 2013). That the *Daily Telegraph* is credited with being one of the United Kingdom's quality newspapers is to imply that it also holds to such principles of professionalism. Obourne's claims can be seen as a shocking revelation of corruption, even as his resignation can be seen as evidencing principles that resist such corruption. The same tension between self-congratulation and self-criticism is outlined by Jean Baudrillard in relation to the Watergate 'scandal' (1994: 14–15). Investigative journalism's occasional exposure of corruption becomes the warrant for business as usual, a news cycle that is fundamentally uncritical and subordinate to dominant interests. However, such control of investigative journalism – as merely an illusion of critique to persuade audiences to believe what is fundamentally propaganda – may not always be sustained.

Whether or not 'old media' journalism (here, print and broadcast forms of mass media newsmaking are being discussed together under this label) should be defended or abandoned has become central to debates over the significance of new forms of 'citizen journalism' – a free-sharing of 'on the spot' coverage from non-professional actors caught up in particular events, that is said either to supplement or replace traditional commercial/professional forms of news organizations and journalists.

The digital challenge

Stuart Allen (2006, 2013) notes that the current 'crisis' in journalistic news production is, for the most part, driven by attempts to reduce production costs. The process of collecting and reporting news is expensive by the very nature of its supposedly being 'new'. While some level of news gathering has always been 'outsourced' via news agencies, independent reporters and photographers, newspapers and broadcasters do require their own staff, both in-house and in the field.

James Curran and Jean Seaton (2010) document the proliferation of new media channels in recent decades. The upshot of such media pluralization has been that advertising revenues that were once concentrated in a small number of print and broadcast titles/channels are now spread far more thinly. Many new digital channels have very little interest in news content, while a small number of new digital channels (such as Fox, Sky and CNN) have specialized in news. Both types of new channel challenge traditional news-driven media organizations

– diverting advertising revenues and viewers (which again translates back into declining advertising revenues per channel). Digital technologies have radically reduced costs in print media. While this has saved money, digital publication has also afforded an explosion in lifestyle/niche magazine publishing (McRobbie and Thornton 1995). These new publications have eaten up a growing share of advertising revenues and diverted sales from newspapers (which has also reduced what advertisers pay established titles), so paralleling the crisis in broadcast news revenues.

Curran and Seaton (2010: 247) observe that declining budgets for news production are associated – not least in the minds of journalists and editors – with a reduction in the scope for 'investigative reporting'. Two things are worth noting here, however. First, the digital challenge arose primarily from commercial media competition, due to the proliferation of commercial channels and publications, not from the Internet and 'free' news distribution. Second, the claim that cuts have eaten into the capacity of journalists to engage in investigative reporting does rather assume that this was once a widespread practice, now being diminished. It should be recalled that the greater part of professional news reporting was and remains 'routine' news production – the practice of reporting the claims being made by dominant actors (politicians, business leaders, the police, stock markets, banks, other media commentators, celebrities, and so on). As such, 'free' citizen journalism is not responsible for killing professional journalism, and neither is most professional journalism the investigative heroism depicted in romantic accounts (whether in fiction or in the ideals of journalists themselves).

Between incorporation and outsourcing

Reduced news budgets bring into stark relief what are not fundamentally new pressures for journalists, those of incorporation and outsourcing. What Nick Davies (2008) refers to as 'churnalism' is the (supposed increasingly) self-referential character of news. For Davies, news is becoming a circular process of reporting on the reporting of comments about reports by established elites and other media commentators. This is compounded by the – again supposedly increased – reliance of journalists upon reports and press releases by those able to afford the production of such content. Without the funds to conduct their own research, journalists are only too pleased to be given reports compiled by others that can then be reported as news. All the better if the report has itself been produced by some kind of 'independent' research organization – even if this is more often than not simply a vested interest paying an 'outsourced' think tank, commercial research organization or university researcher keen to gain funding and willing to manufacture news. Given sufficiently well-defined parameters, such research will find what its funder was looking for. Results will be packaged in easily digestible form, and in such a way as to tell the funder's preferred account of events, and will then be circulated to journalists to be reported as news.

The claim that 'churnalism' is fundamentally new is, however, false. From Walter Lippmann (2009/1920) to the Glasgow Media Group's *Bad News* (1976), and from *Folk Devils and Moral Panics* (Cohen 1972) to *Policing the Crisis* (Hall et al. 1978), it has been recurrently observed that news production draws primarily upon existing hierarchies of power to define hierarchies of newsworthiness and to gain content. What has changed is the detail rather than the overall picture. Incorporation has altered in two ways. First, newspapers and commercial broadcast news channels are increasingly owned within global cross-media corporations, such that *infotainment*, linked to the full range of media production, is increasingly deemed 'news' (Castells 2009). Second, the production of expertise and evidence by interested lobbies is now more professionally packaged for rapid and pre-digested media circulation. What is deemed 'verified' is still based on assumptions concerning which authority should be trusted, even if the composition of those deemed authoritative has shifted. Novel or not, professional journalists, under pressure and under-funded, are always 'incorporated' and hence 'compromised' in their production of news, even if resistance and journalistic principle also exist.

It is in this context, then, of being faced with budget cuts and the perception of 'incorporation', that journalists are also threatened with their own replacement, through the 'outsourcing' of their role to 'citizen journalists'. Allen (2013) suggests that the Asian tsunami of 2004, where there was an absence of on-site journalists but a profusion of still and moving images captured on mobile phones by those caught up in events, brought into sharp relief the significance of new digital technologies in making every citizen a potential reporter/eye witness. Precisely because professional reporters go to where editors tell them the 'news' already is, and because such presumption as to what is already newsworthy carries the taint of incorporation and bias (press conferences, staged events, embedded reporting), journalists will not be located where genuinely unpredictable 'events' occur. In contrast, citizens with cameras on their phones *are* located (potentially) everywhere, without 'editorial' presumption as to what needs covering in advance. Against this backdrop, professional journalism loses its claim to bring 'news'. It is true, however, that the free distribution of citizen journalistic content may strengthen the commercial drive to reduce costs at the expense of paid reporters. Free content, when subject to editorial control over its use and interpretation, may simply reinforce the 'editorial nexus', at a reduced cost, and without the need to finesse the professional principles of those providing the copy.

Yet, outsourcing of this kind ultimately carries a significant risk to corporate news management. If the traditional 'fourth estate' (the 'free press' in its modern print and broadcast forms) comes to rely on new media sources (the 'fifth estate' – Dutton 2009), but simply does so to reduce cost, even while continuing to pursue editorial lines that reflect the incorporation of the fourth estate within other sets of dominant interests, this may further undermine the very 'trust' that underpins audience orientation to such sources in the first place. Why buy a newspaper or listen to the radio news if it is so deeply embedded with institutional bias, when key content may be better found via citizen journalistic sources online? The decline in newspaper sales, and, in particular, its decline amongst younger age groups, should alarm traditional newsmakers.

The case of Wikileaks (Beckett and Ball 2012) illustrates both sides of an argument over this very point. On the one hand, the capacity of a website like Wikileaks to bypass traditional media, when releasing evidence of perceived injustice and corruption, saw mainstream media running to keep up with what the new media 'whistle-blower' was revealing, in the hope of retaining their role as trusted sources of 'news'. However, at the same time, Wikileaks – in seeking to bring its most valued 'scoops' to the widest audience – chose to work with 'credible' existing newspapers.

Self-censorship

Another challenge for traditional mass media lies in maintaining the *credibility* of its editorial-nexus-based distribution model – a nexus by which news and commercial/political power are wedded – in the face of new media 'news' models that lack such editorial control. In a distributed new media age, the decisions of editors appear as forms of censorship. Editorial selection can no longer be presented as self-evident and natural. Worse still, perception of such selection as bias only encourages people's evasion of such restrictions by looking further afield online. In 2013, UK national newspapers were confronted with the dilemma of whether or not to publish images of a naked Prince Harry partying in Las Vegas. These images were widely available online. To some, the decision not to publish left newspapers looking outmoded. However, the decision to publish doctored images was deemed by others an infringement of privacy and an offence to public taste. Similarly, images of a topless Kate Middleton sunbathing caused editorial angst. Having been incorporated within global cross-media 'infotainment' empires, newspapers found themselves unable to keep *abreast* of the very downgrading of news of which they had hitherto assumed they were the champions and beneficiaries.

At the same time (in 2013), Twitter was widely circulating the names and personal details of various politicians, celebrities, sports personalities and journalists within the various estates of infotainment/churnalism who had secured 'super injunctions' against media coverage – not just of their private lives, but also against media coverage of the fact that they had secured earlier injunctions. A super injunction prohibits reporting of an earlier injunction. Super injunctions may have initially kept many in the dark. However, the fact that mainstream media were being gagged meant journalists and editors themselves were dependent – as was the population as a whole – upon the free online circulation of gossip/news for what might otherwise have been considered the job of journalism to report. A sense of journalistic purpose, let alone integrity, is hard to maintain in such conditions.

Citizen witness

On the question of 'free' sharing of news online, an interesting history is unfolded by Stuart Allen in his book *Citizen Witnessing* (2013). In 1963, the assassination of John F. Kennedy was filmed by Abraham Zapruder, a member of the public, even as many hundreds of professional reporters, photographers and film crews failed to capture the actual shooting. *Life* magazine paid Zapruder $150,000 to secure copyright on the film footage, which was subsequently withheld from public view for more than a decade. In 1991, in the early days of digital camcorders, but prior to the popular use of the Internet, the beating of Rodney King by Los Angeles police officers was captured on film by a local man, George Holliday. This footage was, after a few days, widely shown on television, widening the impact of such citizen witnesses, at least relative to the Zapruder case. The rise of the

World Wide Web and of digital film and camera functions on mobile phones escalated the capacity of non-professional citizen journalists to upload content as it happened from locations where they happen to be, rather than where journalists had been sent in anticipation of 'a story'. As noted above, Allen suggests the Asian tsunami of 2004 marked the coming of age of such 'citizen witnessing', but he also documents an array of cases since then where it is non-professional footage that captures the event, with professional news crews only able to cover the official post-event clean-up. What is of interest here is how such instant uploading of free content stands in marked distinction to the 'capture' of rights by *Life* magazine in the Zapruder example. The traditional idea of a 'scoop' has been replaced by a 'free-for-all' (King 2010), where access is no longer the determinant of attention. The question that consequently arises is exactly what does then determine attention? Can traditional news producers retain audiences in an age where they are neither first on the scene, nor able to claim scoops except in cases where that which is 'exclusively' possessed is only a contrived fabrication ('churnalistic' incorporation) and not 'new' news (in the sense of the unpredicted event)?

The free-sharing of citizen witness 'coverage' may simply help existing news organizations save money and hence stay 'in business' selling eyeballs to advertisers. However, such reliance on the outsourcing of 'eye witnesses', while cutting costs, also raises questions about why audiences should rely on the mediation of such professions, when the 'business as usual' of such mediators (editors) lacks neutrality.

The distinction between the 'public domain' (the space for free-sharing relative to the private domain of intellectual property) and the 'public interest' (a space for free exposure relative to the private domain of 'privacy') blurs in the domain of journalistic ethics. Images of John F. Kennedy's shooting were withheld by means of intellectual property rights but on supposed grounds of public decency. The more recent killing of Colonel Gadhafi of Libya (in 2011) was captured on the phones of the rebels who killed him, immediately circulated by the killers worldwide, and then 'splashed' on the front pages of newspapers. The killing of reporter Alison Parker and cameraman Alan Ward by a former (but recently sacked) TV station colleague in 2015, and the killer's live broadcast of his filming of the killings, adds a further twist to this dynamic. Free-sharing of such images online certainly limits the scope to censor such content, and it is beyond the remit of this work to address the ethics of sharing such content. The relationship between doing so and so-called 'cyber-terrorism' (Wall

2007; Yar 2013), where broadcasting murder and death is used as part of online propaganda, is another significant issue that is beyond the scope of this work. It may be the case that traditional journalism can reinvent itself as 'all the news that's fit to print' (Campbell 2006) in just such a 'free-for-all' (King 2010). Whether audiences will trust traditional mediators, in an age where less tied alternatives exist, remains to be seen. Whether such trust ever existed is another contentious issue (Cohen 1972). The emerging ecology of news is a shifting field of explicitly biased commercial newspapers and channels, public service broadcasters proclaiming 'balance' within state regulations, and an online 'free-for-all', with audiences increasingly mobile – not just between channels, but even across the former divide between being consumers and producers of content.

Trade Publishing: Capitalist Concentration

Thompson (2012) provides the most exhaustive account of the ongoing concentration of ownership and power within the field of trade (fiction and popular non-fiction) publishing in the English-speaking world. Concentration is effected by the combination of acquisition, multimedia integration, globalization and outsourcing. Concentration through acquisition is the first and most striking feature of trade publishing in the United Kingdom and the United States (that is, London and New York), which themselves dominate the English-speaking world, itself the dominant publishing field worldwide. Since the 1960s, older family- and founder-based publishing houses began to merge and be bought up to form larger houses, but it has been since the 1980s and 1990s that such concentration really took off – leading to a situation today where two-thirds of all trade sales are concentrated in the hands of five companies in the United Kingdom and eight in the United States. Although hundreds of publishing businesses exist, the number has fallen sharply, and the volume of sales achieved by smaller firms has shrunk, as sales by the majors take an increasing share. The larger publishing companies often retain the names of the smaller houses they acquire, so that the array of apparent 'publishers' – judged by what is written on book spines and on prelim pages – appears far greater than is in fact the case.

Acquisitions have been within increasingly integrated multimedia corporations, such that trade publishing becomes one part of an integrated business model. The integrated multimedia corporation will own a raft of companies controlling newspapers, television stations, radio stations, film production, distribution and screening companies, record companies, software and gaming firms, Internet distributors, as well as book publishing houses (Castells 2009). While Thompson urges caution regarding the idea that film tie-ins and TV spin-offs have either undone the integrity of publishing as a field, or saved it as a business model, he documents the rise of increasingly cross-platform strategies. Literary reviews in newspapers and other traditional outlets have declined markedly, while media-plugged literary prizes have boomed, celebrity endorsements have risen, and publishers struggle with one another to get their titles promoted by the likes of Oprah Winfrey's or Richard and Judy's TV bookclubs. Films, TV series and related TV and radio plugging become key to the business of blockbusters, while an existing media profile or a positive evaluation of a new author's potential for media pitching and plugging becomes central to getting a contract, and for determining its terms.

Thompson notes that four of the big five in the UK trade publishing field are also in the US top eight, something that was not the case thirty years ago. Publishing has become an increasingly global affair, or at least it has been increasingly profitable to publish worldwide since the 1980s (when in 1988 the United States fully signed up to the 1886 Berne Treaty – extending copyright to works physically printed outside the US), and even more so again after 1994/95, when the TRIPS agreement further enhanced the capacity of intellectual property owners to uphold their rights worldwide.

Outsourcing has also played its part in the concentration of trade publishing, at both ends of the production process. At the commissioning end, editors increasingly rely upon agents to supply them with new works for consideration, while at the other end of the production process, copyediting, proofreading and physical printing has been almost entirely outsourced – often to developing country locations. The latter has radically reduced costs, but the former (using agents) has – Thompson documents – increased costs for publishers dramatically. However, using agents to filter the 'slush pile' of prospective manuscripts produced by authors, and to represent authors with an existing reputation, has the effect of reducing publisher risk when choosing whom to publish. This has led to a further concentration in terms of what actually gets published by those larger publishers with the potential to promote and distribute widely. Successful agents will employ assistants to scan what comes into an agent's office, and to pass on only what the assistant comes to learn the agent is likely to think will sell (such that it can be pitched success-fully to an editor). Agents work on commission, and their reputation is built on the number of pitches they make that eventually sell well relative to those that lose money for the publisher. An agent cannot risk too often pitching works that may lower this reputation, as to do so would reduce the likelihood of editors taking their recom-mendations in the future. Reduced commissions would then limit that agent's ability to afford the assistants who allow them to filter so many prospective manuscripts looking for marketable works. The assistant and the agent learn what to look for 'in the field' as it cur-rently exists. Agents pitch to editors, who are themselves also versed in the art and necessity of selecting what they believe will sell, and which their publishing house will judge them on getting right (or not). The sales of the works that editors commission can be readily monitored by their publishing house, and this company will itself be monitored for sales success by the corporation that owns it within its stable of other publishing houses. At each level of filtering, risk is minimized – and any author seeking to get through this set of filters must also learn quickly to 'play the game' in what they submit and, following submission, to heed the advice they are given from those further up the chain. Agents and editors, Thompson observes, pride themselves on being active in moulding, not just filtering, content. In Thompson's study, publishers, editors, agents and authors learn that what is needed is 'platform' (an existing or marketable media profile), 'form' (past success), 'comparability' (the ability to fit new work into existing pigeon holes) and 'buzz' (the pre-existence of some kind of expectation within the media field about an author). The publishing field has become an increasingly closed space of commercial self-selection. While Thompson found that reference to 'literary' criteria remains in the talk of actors in the publishing field, their capacity to regulate the autonomy of the 'literary field' in Bourdieu's sense of the term (1993) does appear substantially diminished. Outsourcing simply forces everyone in the field to self-censor, as all are under the same pressure to pick hits to sell now.

As concentration has intensified in all the ways outlined above, publishing has become increasingly focused upon what Thompson refers to as 'big books'. In recent years, the volume of works sold has become increasingly concentrated in fewer titles, both within national markets and internationally. Thompson (2012: 398) gives the example of the United Kingdom, where the number of fictional works selling more than 200,000 copies in a given year doubled in the 2000s, while the number of books selling between 10,000 and 50,000 fell away sharply. The overall number of titles selling 10,000 copies or more dropped from around 600 to 450. As this figure (10,000) may be taken as a baseline for providing an author with something approaching the minimum wage/welfare benefit level earnings, it can be suggested that 450 authors therefore are making a 'living', however basic, from fiction in the UK. Added to this may be those authors who are writing trade non-fiction. However, almost all of these (at least those selling in significant numbers, according to Thompson) are celebrities whose books are either ghost-written biographies or tie-ins to existing TV or other media vehicles. As such, it is not the case that the current business model in publishing is incentivizing the creative process for anything more than a few hundred authors, in a field where the number of works published each year is at least 100 times that figure. A winner-takes-all, 'big books' strategy promotes repetition (in form and source) while offering next to no financial reward to those working outside existing expectations and platforms. The same pattern can be discerned elsewhere (see below).

The Long Tail and the Real Lives of Authors

Chris Anderson (2009) uses the concept of the long tail to explain how an online retailer like Amazon can make more money from selling small numbers of copies of each of the millions of lowest-selling books on its website than it does selling thousands of copies of each of its 1,000 most popular titles. This reverses the business sense that guides physical bookshops that have only limited shelf space. It is certainly true that Amazon has opened up a market for works at the low-sales end of the long tail, even though (as noted above) trade publishers still pin their hopes on a shrinking number of 'big books'. What is of more interest here regarding the long tail is that such sales highlight just how concentrated sales of books are today. Anderson (2009: 121) cites US book sales figures for 2004. Of 1.2 million titles recorded as having made sales, the top 12,000 titles sold, in total, approximately 150 million copies. The remaining 99.9 per cent of titles, however, sold more than 500 million copies *between them*. The top 1,200 titles sold more than 50,000 copies each per year (enough to give their authors something close to average wages or above). Yet only one-tenth of 1 per cent of titles (and hence authors) make these kind of earnings (the 1,200 titles may, of course, include multiple titles by single authors, thereby increasing individual earnings but reducing the number of authors in this 'fortunate' position of earning average wages or above). In the data Anderson presents, those selling more than 5,000 copies a year rises to 2 per cent of titles. If Thompson's figures for the UK suggest 1 per cent of titles sell more than 10,000 copies, then Anderson's 2 per cent selling more than 5,000 suggests some comparability between the United Kingdom and United States – with both suggesting that only a tiny percentage of authors make a living from the sale of their creative work.

How then do most authors get paid? Well, it might be noted that the majority simply do not get paid at all; and, of those who get anything, the vast majority do not receive anything approaching a living wage, let alone what could substitute for the wages they might otherwise earn given their level of ability. Jessica Silbey (2015) interviewed a range of authors and inventors. A recurrent finding in her interviews was that most authors have to make a living from things other than royalties-based authorship as such, although often this involved 'writing'. Journalism, ghost-writing and other forms of 'work for hire' (in marketing, advertising, editing, and so forth), rather than 'authorship' in exchange for copyright protected royalties, was typical. Teaching and tutoring at various levels was another common source of earnings to fund a life in letters. Most of those that gave up paid employment to focus on 'authorship' had to rely either on past earnings or on the earnings of family members to support them, and most had to accept a significant reduction in income when swapping paid work for royalties income. Even Thompson (2012), whose sample was skewed towards those who had to some extent been successful in making a living in the publishing field, found that most published authors with agents willing to represent them had to make ends meet through various forms of 'work for hire' (e.g., ghosting, journalism, marketing), talks, promotions or teaching. The suggestion that commercial publishing pays authors is rarely true, and, even when it is, what it pays is rarely significant and almost never enough to live on; it is most often only a superficial supplement to paid labour of some other (if related) kind.

Boldrin and Levine (2008) note that Shakespeare wrote prior to the existence of copyright and since copyright has existed there has been no new Shakespeare. Likewise, they point out, while Mozart and Beethoven could not claim copyright on their works in the German-speaking world, composers in England at the same time could. However, this did not prevent German classical composers from being far more significant and successful than their English contemporaries. Free circulation may in fact explain exactly why classical music flourished in German-speaking countries, as has Shakespeare worldwide. Reisel Liebler (2015) extends this view to the wider domain of fan fiction today. Free-sharing of authors' works, and freedom to play and innovate with originals, increases audience interest and engagement with works. The question remains, however, whether such interest can be turned into earnings, and if so by whom: authors or corporate intermediaries? If the latter is the case, then free-sharing may be just good marketing (Anderson 2010). If it is the former, however, free-sharing may challenge business as usual. Given that business as usual tends only to reward the established producers of 'big books', and those groomed by multiple layers of self-selection to emulate established formulae, while the vast majority of new and unestablished authors do not get paid, then the challenge of free circulation (the suspension of copyright in effect) does not threaten creativity. Rather, free-sharing threatens the profitability of the current winner-takes-all, 'big books', concentrated corporate model.

Is First Mover Advantage Enough?

What would be the effect of a suspension of copyright – i.e., the possibility of free-sharing? With the rise of print-on-demand and with projects like Google Books – which set out to digitally scan the works held in many of the world's largest libraries – the possibility exists for all works to become freely available. Google estimated (Thompson 2012: 365) that, with copyright extended to seventy years after the death of the author, only 20 per cent of known book titles are in the public domain (i.e., are out of copyright); a further 70 per cent of known titles are, meanwhile, in copyright but not currently in print. Therefore, only 10 per cent of known works are in copyright *and* in print. Publishers took legal action to prevent Google Books from proceeding with its plans, which had involved allowing limited access to content that would then link users to publishers or print-on-demand options for works currently out of print. Boldrin and Levine (2008: 104) argue that publishers are wise to fear such access to 'out-of-print works', as such a 'long tail' threatens to 'crowd out' sales of new 'big books', those on which their business model is currently focused. An even greater threat to publishers would come from currently out-of-print works falling out of copyright altogether. If such works were to be made available without copyright, not only would their appearance potentially crowd out new 'big books', but they would not even be any one publisher's to sell (being open for anyone to print or to be made available freely online). In response to this threat, publishers, as part of multimedia corporations, have been keen – and successful – in lobbying not just to maintain, but to extend, copyright terms. As Boldrin and Levine argue, extending copyright on works from fifty to seventy years after the death of the author cannot reasonably be said to promote the creativity of long-dead authors, but does extend the profitability of a small number of successful works (such as *Gone With the Wind* and titles featuring Mickey Mouse), even as it prevents the release of tens of thousands of other works that are 'owned' but whose owners do not continue to make the works available (the 70 per cent of all estimated books in existence).

Yet, while Boldrin and Levine argue that corporate publishing companies and the multimedia empires they belong to have good reason to lock down older content – retaining copyright but in most cases not keeping the work 'in print' – they also argue that publishing could be a 'profitable' business even in the absence of copyright. They argue that first mover advantage in a free market could make publishing creative works profitable, even if publishers had no monopoly control over subsequent distribution of the work. If true, a suspension of IP controls would not undermine 'capitalism', even if it would undermine a particular form of IP-protected capitalism where capital is protected by the suspension of markets. However, 'free' distribution based on instant and global sharing brings Boldrin and Levine's account of how a 'free' market could function in the absence of intellectual property monopolies into question. Moreover, free-sharing may challenge not only neoliberal monopoly capitalism (based on IP-based market suspension), but also free market capitalism as well. As most authors make a living in ways other than from royalties, it should be recalled that neither of these 'challenges' is to creativity as such, but rather to whether or not sharing represents a 'crime against capitalism'.

In publishing, first mover advantage is particularly acute. Sales of trade books are very heavily concentrated in the first weeks and months after release. Thompson (2012) suggests that the first six weeks see the majority of sales for the kinds of 'big books' from which publishers generate most profits. Boldrin and Levine (2008) cite evidence that may extend this to the first three months. But in either case, after only a very short time frame, the overall future sales value of most works falls away to an ever-diminishing level. While Amazon can profit from millions of such small sales, publishers – which have to print and warehouse such stock – cannot, and they remain afraid that digital versions or print-on-demand options for such older works would wrest control over sales from them and might also 'crowd out' their latest 'big books'. While the first mover to publish a work, and to have invested in preparing the work and having copies printed, may profit from early sales and may continue to profit from small future sales of existing stock, the cost incurred for a rival to bring out an alternative version of the same work after its sales have peaked, relative to the trickle of subsequent sales, will be, most likely, insufficiently attractive.

The argument in favour of intellectual monopolies such as copyright is that an imitator could reap the benefits of another person's prior invention without the investment required to produce that innovation. Once an innovation was made, it would be imitated; and prices for imitations could be set at a price below that which would cover the cost of the innovation's development. However, first mover advantage may mean that by the time imitators had determined what was commercially 'successful', the indicator of such success – sales – would have already peaked and fallen away. As the fixed cost of entering the field (i.e., having to get copies printed) is not zero, and because most profits have already been made, the temptation to enter the field will be, therefore, insufficient. Even if entry costs fell to zero, or next to nothing (such as by means of print-on-demand publishing), this fact would itself ultimately disincentivize entry, as any entrant would find that the resultant increase in levels of competition – introduced by virtue of such 'zero-cost' entry – would see prices, in turn, falling to next to nothing. Contrary to economy theories that seek to justify IP, Boldrin and Levine (2008: 159) argue that it is the very existence of artificial barriers to entry (such as IP) that inflates prices, and hence make illicit entry potentially profitable. This suggests that removing IP protection would not undermine scope to make a profit from printing and selling original content, at least not for the first mover. In the absence of intellectual property, the first mover may need to pay the author an upfront payment to be given first access to that content. For 'big books' this is – de facto – already the case (Thompson 2012), as publishers' advances for such works already exceed what royalty payments recoup in most cases. In effect, publishers buy the right to publish with a one-off payment that is repaid (to the publisher) from the overall value of net sales, even while the small percentage of such net sales that are owed to the author (in royalties) never amounts to enough to 'recoup' the advance they received before publication.

Boldrin and Levine highlight a paradox in what has become the orthodox economic argument for intellectual property protectionism. The standard model claims that high fixed costs of innovation cannot be recouped if innovations are not protected from free market imitation once an original creation is developed. They assert, however, that such unprotected conditions would themselves remove the incentive for 'parasitical' late entry. In conditions where new entrants could cut prices to marginal cost (the cost of producing items without the need to factor in past development costs), prices would plummet and, in such conditions, said new entrants would be unable to make a profit. It is only the existence of an artificially high profit margin, due to monopoly protection, that creates an incentive for illicit production of IP-protected goods, relative to simply selling other unprotected items. The first mover advantage that gives the initial innovator (such as a publisher) a profit on the sale of information-rich content cannot then be replicated by subsequent entrants in fully free market conditions.

However, there is a further catch that may bring Boldrin and Levine's account into doubt. There might be no profit incentive to enter a totally free market for the sale of content whose marginal cost is so close to zero, as such goods would not sustain a price if competition occurred; as such, a first mover may well not see market competition even in the absence of intellectual monopoly protection. However, the free circulation of copies of works using distribution channels with near zero marginal cost is not done 'for profit', and, rather, may be carried out by fans seeking to share with others their interest in particular works or by authors keen to share their work with an audience they cannot find through the current corporate filtering system. Some readers may be willing to pay a premium for a physical copy of the work, rather than just having free access to a digital copy, but even this market is fragile. The ease of access to digital content, and the rise of various means of 'print-on-demand' will challenge traditional publishing, and may well also represent a challenge to publishers, as distinct from printers, as a business at all.

One interesting possibility, noted by Boldrin and Levine (2008: 142–144), is complementary marketing, and the willingness of audiences to pay a premium for either the direct 'authorized' or 'signed' copy of an author's work, or for particular forms of supplementary materials. This may extend as far as the packaging of a work. In an age of free digital sharing and print-on-demand, it may be that authors can sell authorized and signed versions of works, just as they currently make money from teaching, speaking and touring to meet readers. Musicians today (as was always true) are mainly paid to perform. Even when recordings rarely pay, the distribution of recordings is good publicity for promoting live performances and for gaining other forms of lucrative direct engagement with paying audiences. Similarly, Charles Dickens made more money touring in the United States, where audiences flocked to hear him live after having read pirated versions of his stories (Pearl 2013), than he did from the sale of his better protected works at home. Publishers may, however, retain a role if the packaging of works remains something that audiences are willing to pay for, or if audiences are comfortable reading the same formulaic 'big books' by celebrity chefs and other brand name 'pot boilers'. If you want news that repeats your existing prejudices (fake news being anything but new), and novels that are anything but novel, business as usual may continue to satisfy, but, ultimately, you might not be part of a sustainable business demographic.

Conclusions: Recognition, Valuation and Innovation

Sharing occurs at a number of levels in the field of publishing. Authors (academic, journalistic and trade) share each other's ideas freely – whether this be through libraries or in the free submission of work to journals, or in scanning the online commentaries of other journalists (professional or otherwise). Content that is published is the result of shared exchange, and, to the extent that this is what produces the content that commercial publishers seek to sell, sharing is essential to any capitalist economy of publishing. Recent intensification of such exploitation of freely shared content, as documented in this chapter – whether in the pricing of academic journals, the concentration of meaningful payment in trade publishing to an ever-smaller set of authors with an ever-larger number getting next to nothing, and in the use of citizen-captured content to help reduce the cost of news production – suggests that 'sharing' is a very good way for capitalism to reduce labour costs and increase/maintain profits.

However, such sharing at the level of production of content can only remain a boost to capitalist publishing enterprises as long as such shared production does not spill over into a sharing of content at the level of distribution – i.e., distribution to those who would otherwise, and are currently, paying to access what publishers acquire (often for free). For all the supposed e-book breakthroughs, and with the potential (and in some cases the actuality) of online book repositories and print-on-demand services, the world of publishing has certainly not witnessed anything like a 'Napster moment'; to that extent, sharing at the level of production has not yet spilled over into sharing at the level of distribution in any fashion as challenging to profitability as was seen in recorded music. That is not to say that such a tipping point may not be reached, nor that – given the nature of commercial exploitation documented in this chapter, and the limited contribution of such commercial processes to the actual creation of new ideas – such a tipping point would not be highly desirable.

7

Genes, Genetically Modified Organisms, Patents and Agribusiness

Introduction

Disputes over the private ownership of genetic material – whether these be patents on genetically modified organisms or patents on techniques for the identification of existing, naturally occurring genes, both of which have been used to claim ownership over the use of such biological entities – have centred around resistance to privatization of what might otherwise be considered part of the biological commons. This chapter explores the relationship between such a biological commons and ideas of the public domain, shared culture and the ownership of inventions linked to or drawn from discoveries of existing processes in nature. It highlights parallels between scientific critiques of corporate-funded genetics research and critiques of global agribusiness that have emerged from farmers and food security activists in both the global South and the organic food movement in wealthier countries. This chapter also highlights the potential of sharing-based alternatives. Disputes in the realm of genetically modified organisms have highlighted tensions hinging upon claims that patent-oriented research either fosters creativity by providing incentives to development in the form of potential profits, or inhibits creativity by limiting natural biodiversity, fostering dependence upon agribusiness and limiting the scope for alternative forms of adaptation by farmers in different locations around the world.

The race to map the human genome saw conflict between the publicly funded Human Genome Project and Craig Ventor's venture-capitalist-funded attempt to patent particular genes. This race highlighted competing conceptions of how science should be carried out, how it should be funded and how scientific knowledge should be used: as common culture or as private property. Central to this tension was the fact that state- and charity-funded research produced a more systematic account of human genetics. Its corporate rival's ability to take publicly funded findings, while at the same time patent protecting its own additional findings to prevent these from being shared, led to a more superficial form of mapping – one that flagged up just enough markers so as to then enable an ownership claim, rather than seeking any comprehensive understanding. Such an approach relied upon the collective and shared work of others, and, as such, was only a supplementary form of research. In overall terms, innovation was primarily fostered by sharing. Protectionist forms of patent-oriented research were parasitical at best and, at worst, inhibited future innovation and utilization.

'The Genetic Commons': Human and Non-Human Nature

In the middle years of the twentieth century, it was the atomic bomb that – for C. Wright Mills (1959: 165–176) – symbolized the potential separation of truth and freedom. Modernity promised more freedom, in the form of democratic government, and more truth, in the form of scientific discovery. Modernity also held that the two would go together. The more we knew the world, the freer we would be; and the more democratic society was, the more science would flourish. For Zygmunt Bauman (1989), meanwhile, it was the Nazi Holocaust that highlighted most powerfully the error of assuming the necessary equation of science, technology and human progress. Both Mills (in 1959) and Bauman (in 1989) refer to this loss of faith as 'the postmodern' – although Mills did not endorse the outlook he nevertheless first named.

Modern Western science has always been bound up with the struggle to control nature, even as the Western culture in which modern science arose was 'humanist' – seeing 'man' as a free and rational agent in the world, able to 'transcend' nature in the very act of knowing and subordinating it. Michel Foucault's (2001/1996) 'death of man' claim suggested that the rational human actor was undone by the very attempt to apply human knowledge to human beings themselves. When the 'human sciences' put the scientific gaze to work explaining 'man', the human subject becomes just another object, stripped of autonomy, subjected to rational comprehension, and thereby opened up to 'disciplinary' and 'biopolitical' control.

Within the horizon of contemporary genetic science, and through its relationship to modern biotechnology, the capacity to own and control genes, and their modes of identification and expression, creates great power. However, to the extent that representations of genetics and biotechnology tend to falsely present genes as deterministic predictors of human behaviour and health (Anderson et al. 2004), fear about the scope of such sciences to 'control' human beings has been exaggerated. Nonetheless, abolishing the distinction between nature, human and non-human, on the one hand, and patentable invention on the other, has proved to be highly problematic. Both human and non-human nature are now presented as objects open to private ownership rather than being a common heritage of all humanity.

Culture: Heritage and Public Sphere

Biological nature, human and non-human, which pre-existed human knowledge of it, is treated as a common heritage. Similarly, knowledge that has arisen about nature, and which has modified nature over millennia, is treated as a common *cultural* heritage, when it cannot be reduced to any single person or even any single community of people. To the extent that such knowledge cannot be claimed as the creation of any particular named person, it is identified as part of the common culture, free to be shared by all. Such free access has, however, created powerful contradictions in the contemporary world. This is because traditional knowledge that has been taken to be free of any legal ownership rights has been used in the creation of new knowledge that *can* then be subject to patent claims.

Modifying a naturally occurring genetic sequence can lead to the creation of a new life form that does not occur 'naturally in nature'. Similarly, synthesizing a biological process or plant extract, whose properties are already known to offer beneficial effects by those within a traditional culture, into a new chemical product that did not exist before (in its 'purified' form) can be said to be 'creating' a 'new' drug. Such 'novelty' affords legal protection as intellectual property, despite its origins deriving – at least in part – from a common biological/cultural heritage. Traditional knowledge emerged as something outside the Western conception of private property; such knowledge continues to be treated as part of the public sphere. Products derived from such knowledge were, and largely remain, unprotected from subsequent incorporation as private (intellectual) property.

This has led some (Fowler 1994; Shiva 1997; Mooney 2000; and others) to demand that traditional knowledge be afforded a form of IP protection, precisely to protect it from subsequent IP control in a synthesized form, and/or to offer such traditional knowledge the kind of reward afforded by established forms of IP. This chapter will show how such attempts to protect shared knowledge from private control by means of imitating private control have proved to be deeply problematic.

Discovery and Invention: On Patents and the Public Domain

The development of private ownership in the realm of invention requires a public domain, and, in part, creates it – even as it then parcels out parts of what has been invented into a limited-duration domain of private protection. This is the domain of patent. Patents are legal protections granted for inventions. All invention builds on prior invention. The patent system offers limited protection precisely to enable future invention by preventing prior inventors from exercising undue control over all subsequent developments reliant on previous steps. Today, patents typically last for twenty years, although various devices can be used to extend duration (called 'evergreening').

What a patent requires:
Novelty, utility, non-obviousness and process

Within patent law, all prior knowledge (or prior art) is deemed part of the public domain, and after a patent's duration elapses, a protected invention itself passes into the public domain as well. Even during the span of a patent, the invention must also reside to some extent in the public domain. This is because, in order to register a patent, its novelty, its utility, its non-obviousness and its process must be declared to and approved by a patent office. The content of this application is made public so anyone can see what has been applied for and hence identify what the invention is or claims to be. Rivals can learn what the patent holder has done and how they have done it, even if they are legally prohibited from copying/using this inventive step without the permission of the rights holder. This creates a huge space for 'me too', copycat, reverse engineering to achieve the same end, if by slightly different means (Boldrin and Levine 2008) – a similarly huge domain of generic/infringing copying (Dutfield and Suthersanen 2005), and a huge potential for replication the minute the patent's protection actually expires. To this extent, the patent system relies upon, creates and fuels the public domain, even while, at the same time, it limits this domain.

Science as Method and Colonial Appropriation

In setting out to discover universal truths, Western science followed the paths of Western colonial discovery, in opening up, exploring and exploiting other lands and cultures. To the extent that geographical 'discovery' was, in fact, conquest, so too were the knowledge and resources of those 'discovered' appropriated in the name of science. Just as the emerging patent system in the West drew upon – even as it helped create – a public domain, so it was that the prior art of those people encountered and colonized was treated as unowned and so free to be appropriated and worked upon.

To the extent that traditional knowledge was said to exist as prior art, it was treated as part of the public domain. On the other hand, once such processes and products had been synthesized into Western scientific knowledge, the results could be patented – subject to a demonstration of utility, novelty, non-obviousness and mechanism. However, two limits can be observed. Firstly, non-obviousness and novelty are rare, as most innovation takes place in a shared environment of research and development. As Boldrin and Levine (2008) document, most great technical inventions and scientific discoveries arise in sets, with multiple groups and individuals arriving at much the same conclusions at much the same time; this is because the accumulation of prior art and knowledge, alongside the circulation of ideas within the technical and scientific communities, usually means that numerous actors converge upon solutions concurrently (more or less), rather than one person or group making it alone. Second, in the domain of biology, the notion of 'invention' (required for patent protection) has been hard to assert relative to simply 'discovery' (which cannot be patented). A scientific discovery, while it may make its discoverer 'famous', remains outside the domain of property rights. However, the distinction between discovery and invention has been radically undone in recent years. This undoing is cause and consequence of the rise of the contemporary genetics and biotechnology industries, and has led to suggestions that a new form of colonialism has arisen, of nature and the body, akin to the geographical conquests of earlier centuries where 'discovery' was said to warrant 'possession'.

'Reinventing' 'Nature': Undoing the Discovery/Intention Distinction via Genetically Modified Organisms

The distinction between discovery and invention in relation to knowledge of the natural world was commonly assumed to map the distinction between living things and 'man'-made objects. That distinction, however, has been systematically challenged in recent years, as genetic science and technology allow the creation of living things that did not previously exist in nature and so which can be said to be inventions rather than discoveries. As will be discussed below, the history of selective plant and animal breeding saw the extension of intellectual property rights over strains even prior to modern recombinant genetic modification; but it is the latter that has set issues of common genetic heritage and private property in starkest contrast in recent years.

The case of *Diamond v. Chakrabarty* (1980) has been much poured over in subsequent academic literature (Halbert 2005; Kramer 2015; Leong 2015; Rose and Rose 2012). Essentially, Chakrabarty genetically modified a bacterium such that it could digest oil and so be useful in clearing up spillages from tankers and rigs. Initially able to secure patents for both the creation process and the delivery mechanisms involved, a third patent, on the organism itself, was denied on grounds that a patent could not apply to a living organism. This refusal was reversed on appeal and the reversal was upheld by the US Supreme Court. The majority view was that the prohibition applied to natural discoveries, which, until then, it was assumed, included all living things. However, as the new bacterium was not 'natural', it could be treated as an invention, irrespective of whether or not it was alive.

This decision was a green light for an explosion of patent applications on genetically modified living things. These have come to include genetically modified seeds, genetically modified animals (the most famous of which was OncoMouse – a mouse with human cancer-inducing cells added into its genome and patented by Harvard researchers in 1988), and an array of human gene markers that are believed to predict a variety of cancers and other genetically linked illnesses. Again, in the case of human gene markers, it is not the gene as found in the human body that is open to being patented, but, rather, the process by which particular gene alleles (mutations) are identified. Nevertheless, patenting the marker creates a 'patent thicket', as subsequent work on the gene is dependent upon its identification and so requires the permission/payment of its identifying patent holder.

Patenting Human Gene Lines

In 1990, the Supreme Court in California dismissed John Moore's claim against the University of California at Los Angeles (UCLA). Moore's treatment for hairy cell leukaemia required surgery to remove tissue from his spleen. This tissue was, unbeknown to Moore, subsequently used to develop a cell line of T-lymphocytes in vitro. This became a valuable research resource and was itself sold by Moore's physician and UCLA to a commercial pharmaceutical company for millions of US dollars. Moore staked a property claim in his tissue. However, this was dismissed on the grounds that while they were in his body the cells had had no commercial value (and it was, in fact, in his interest that they be removed). As such, these cells' commercial value lay only in their being synthesized as a self-replicating cell line outside of the human body.

As Debbie Halbert (2005: 115–120) documents, the case hinged on the capacity of science and business to render Moore's tissue beyond his ownership and, as such, part of the commons, while also being able to claim that their own 'inventive step' – in rendering the tissue beyond its original state to one of artificial self-replication outside the human body – meant they could stake a property rights' claim in the cell line to the exclusion of Moore staking a claim for this tissue now it was outside his own body. Halbert (2005: 117) notes the conclusions of James Boyle regarding this case: 'Viewed through the lens of authorship, Moore's claim appeared to be a dangerous attempt to privatize the public domain and to inhibit research.' Of course, the scientists (authors) omit to reflect on their own privatizing act, and its legal limitation upon others to research using the rights holder's 'innovative step', at least without payment/permission.

Medical researchers depict human DNA and cells harvested from the body as 'shared' non-property, only to claim property rights over subsequent development of that 'raw material'. Moore failed to counter this property claim by failing to assert a prior property claim. Halbert's objection to IP claims in human genetic material, and cell lines, is that such IP claims open the door to a form of slavery over human beings as raw material in a technoscientific colonization of the body. Currently, rights over harvested human cells, cell lines and even DNA do not give ownership rights over their prior holders and producers. Michael Crichton's 2007 science fiction novel *Next* creates a fascinating, but imaginary, near-future scenario in which such enslaving rights would exist (and where bounty hunters pursue profitable cell carriers who are to be detained to have their cells forcibly harvested from them and to prevent other companies from accessing those carriers). However, while this story is frightening, its premise and plot device are both fictional. Human sources of what become valuable cell lines cannot be detained to prevent the re-sale of cells. Neither can such carriers be forcibly 'mined' for more DNA (see also Kazuo Ishiguro's 2005 novel *Never Let Me Go*). What is frightening about the extraction of and research into common human cells and DNA is not their use per se, but the privatization of owner-ship and the subsequent limitation of research and/or accessibility to treatments derived from such research.

Terminator Genes and Food Security

The extension of property rights into seeds did not begin with the new genetic technologies based on manipulating recombinant DNA. The new genetic biotechnologies, which started their development in the 1970s but which first saw patent protection in 1980, were pre-ceded by standalone (*sui generis*) intellectual property protection for seed breeders. This did not just provide protection to stock; it also gave control to seed breeders, even after sale, in that they were able to prohibit farmers from reselling, sharing or cross-breeding. The 1961 International Convention for the Protection of New Varieties of Plants created the International Union for the Protection of New Varieties of Plants (UPOV) to extend various national protection regimes worldwide. In many respects, seed protection laid the foun-dations for the global IP protection that came with the World Trade Organisation (WTO) and the Agreement on Trade-Related Aspects of Intellectual Property Rights (TRIPS) in the 1990s. WTO and TRIPS themselves subsequently extended the power of UPOV to prohibit seed sharing.

Recent developments have combined legal protection with tech-nical protection measures to further intensify ownership by plant-breeding agribusiness over seed even after it has been sold. Ownership rights over the DNA of a genetically modified plant is now enforce-able worldwide, and corporations like Monsanto actively enforce their right to prohibit farmers from storing, sharing, selling on or cross-breeding seed bought from them. Agribusiness corporations also actively engage in their right to inspect farms they have sold seed to, and to carry out inspections to see whether 'their' seed has crossed over into the crops of neighbouring farms. If they find this to be the case, it is then treated as theft. Attempts by organic farmers to reverse this account by suggesting that GM seed being blown into organic fields nearby constitutes 'contamination', rather than 'theft', have been rejected by US courts (Hauck 2014).

On the technical side, agribusinesses have sought to protect themselves from the 'threat' posed by farmers and seeds themselves – in terms of farmers shaping, sharing and cross-breeding, and in terms of seeds simply reproducing themselves with no regard for how this challenges the profitability of scarcity. Firms have done this by seeking to inhibit the capacity of seeds to replicate. What Monsanto calls 'sterile seed technology', critics have called 'terminator seeds' – seeds whose DNA has been altered to render them infertile (Hauck 2014). Such seed may be grown for one crop cycle, but farmers using this seed are required to return to the seed company for more stock year on year.

Alternatives and Critiques

In his discussion of the history of corn (maize), Richard Lewontin (1993: 53–57) notes that what preceded contemporary GM strategies to control seed was the use by seed breeders of hybrid crossing to produce seed that was itself not true breeding, in that any subsequent offspring did not carry the same qualities contained in the hybrid parent. Seed breeding companies were well aware that this gave them the upper hand relative to farmers, and they pursued the technique for this very reason. Lewontin goes on to note:

> The nature of the genes responsible for influencing corn yield is such that the alternative method of simply direct selection of high-yielding plants in each generation and the propagation of seed from those selected plants would work. By this method of selection, plant breeders could, in fact, produce varieties of corn that yield quite as much as modern hybrids. (1993: 56)

However, that there were lower profits in pursuing this less controllable technique meant that no commercial plant breeder would choose it over hybrid strategies.

This suggests the need for publicly funded agricultural science to promote the highest quality research without the bias towards profit-maximizing controls for breeders at the expense of growers. However, the very opposite outcome has taken place. Alongside the rise of commercial agribusiness, governments around the world have withdrawn from most agricultural research, leaving commercial imperatives to dominate the field. As such, at the current time, it is almost impossible to pursue a career in agricultural science without funding from commercial agribusiness; and such funding is not forthcoming to those that question the equation of corporate profitability and control with efficiency, safety and sustainability. This was most powerfully illustrated in the case of Arpad Pusztai, a UK-based GM researcher with a long career in working with agribusiness funding (see David 2005). When Pusztai announced provisional findings suggesting that implanting the genes that produce pest-resisting toxins in snowdrops into potatoes might not be safe, he was locked out of his laboratory and a Royal Society commission was hastily set up that debunked his findings. Every member of the commission had links to the food industry and all had careers dependent upon further research funding into the development of GM crops by that industry. Whether or not Pusztai's research was without fault is beside the point; all research is open to question (Woolgar 1988; Fuller 1997). In a field where all experts are dependent upon industry funding, impartial judgement becomes impossible (Levidow 2001; Heller 2002).

The Common Heritage of Humanity: Seeds, Plants and Farmers' Rights

Chidi Oguamanam (2015) documents the history of breeders' rights in relation to farmers' rights over the course of the last 200 years. While most of that time has witnessed the rise of the former (breeders' rights) through various forms of IP rights extensions over seeds and their uses, the last few decades have witnessed increased tension between efforts to further intensify corporate property rights allied to a particular model of scientific invention, and a counter-movement that validates the shared nature of traditional knowledge production, its value in maintaining and developing the common heritage of global biodiversity, and the rights of local and traditional farmers to share in the benefits of innovations based on their prior stewardship.

As noted above, in 1961, UPOV brought together various national *sui generis* IP protection regimes and extended such rights worldwide. Oguamanam (2015: 241) adds that the initial agreement was amended in 1972, 1978 and 1991, each time further reducing the so-called 'privileges' of farmers in terms of the extent to which they could replant, cross-breed and share seeds bought from breeders. Oguamanam explains that while hybridization (see above) was useful in creating corn (maize) that was high yield but not true breeding (hence requiring farmers to return for new stock each year), other seed crops (like soy beans, rice and oats) were less easy to control by such technical fixes. Hence, breeders resorted to the law via UPOV. While able to claim existing biodiversity as a freely accessible commons, breeders – by means of any scientifically documented 'innovative step' – could close off their 'creations' as private property, leading to the accusation of 'biopiracy' (Shiva 1997; Mooney 2000).

In opposition to UPOV and its extension of breeders' rights (something ever further entrenched in the initial drafting of the WTO's TRIPS agreement), Cary Fowler (1994) coined the term 'farmers' rights' (Dutfield 2015: 650). The 1992 United Nations Convention on Biological Diversity (CBD) upholds the sovereign right of states over genetic resources – a challenge to attempts to patent products derived from such resources. The Convention also recognizes the value of indigenous and local farming practices in the maintenance and development of biodiversity in those areas of the world not already dominated by agribusiness models of production. The UN's 2001 International Treaty on Plant Genetic Resources for Food and Agriculture goes further, requiring contracting parties to recognize 'the enormous contribution that the local and indigenous communities and farmers of all regions of the world, particularly in the centres of origin and crop diversity, have made and will continue to make for the conservation and development of plant genetic resources' (cited in Oguamanam 2015: 244).

The farmers' rights movement presses for recognition of:

- traditional modes of sharing-based innovation, in contrast to what Oguamanam calls the 'Eureka' moment of individualized genius assumed in Western models of scientific recognition and IP protection;
- a shared model of knowledge distribution; and
- a sharing-based model of sustainable food production going forward.

While farmers' rights have been depicted as simply a counter form of property rights – a demand for more property rights (for farmers over the seeds they use) to offset other rights (the rights of breeders from whom farmers buy) – this misses the significance of the challenge posed to IP by the farmers' rights movement. The movement proposes limits to dominant models of IP control, not to relocate ownership from breeders to another set of actors (farmers), but rather to temper property rights in seeds. The remedy to the imbalance between the traditional commons and corporate IP (such that the latter free-rides upon the former) is not to replace the commons with another level of IP to emulate corporate property rights. By extending the principle of shared biological diversity and development, farmers' rights protect the commons by extending its logic, rather than simply defensively mirroring the threat to it.

Traditional Knowledge Banks

Another assertion of common heritage against attempts to subordinate knowledge to private ownership has been the development of initiatives like the Traditional Knowledge Digital Project (or Library – hence TKDL) in India (Thomas 2015: 363–364), which was also briefly discussed in Chapter 2. The project has been a collaboration between Indian national- and regional-level government agencies and a number of traditional Indian medical and yoga associations, amongst others. The database contains a large number of textbooks documenting traditional medicine, 150,000 entries on particular traditional medical practices and treatments, and 1,500 yoga positions and techniques. The purpose of the database is to document existing knowledge as 'prior art'. In so doing, this content is shown to have been pre-existing and a part of a shared heritage, rather than the property of any individual or group. From a legal point of view, this demonstration of prior art is designed to fend off any patent or copyright claim that might be made on any such knowledge or technique.

As Thomas explains, the TKDL was created in India in the specific context of a large number of patent and copyright claims being made by Western companies and entrepreneurs for various products and techniques of Indian origin previously unknown in the West. These claims, when upheld in the courts of Western countries, had led to legal action against producers and users in India, and hence the Indian government's concern to put an end to such practices (see Darch 2015 for similar actions taken against South African rooibos tea growers prior to the introduction of a mark of Geographical Indication). The purpose of the TKDL was to provide evidence of 'prior art' so as to protect the shared Indian cultural heritage from appropriation. However, despite leading the global extension and harmonization of IP since the end of the Cold War, the US law regarding identification of 'prior art' only requires a demonstration that no prior art exists in the United States *itself* for an IP claim to be made that would then protect its holder from all others – within the United States or beyond (Halbert 2005: 148). Attempting to use the very rules of IP (requiring novelty) to defend the shared and open nature of common heritage against those that would privatize it is, therefore, limited by the fact that those who would extend the rule of IP worldwide do not themselves feel the need to follow such rules.

Biopiracy against Whom?

In the context of biomedicine, Graham Dutfield (2015) argues that too strong a reliance upon parallels with and revisions within intellectual property rights law offers a flawed defence to the world's poor, even those who might have some claim regarding the stewardship of 'traditional knowledge' that itself proves, subsequently, useful in the creation of new patents by pharmaceutical corporations. Daryll Povey's reconceptualization of indigenous peoples, as active creators of the 'anthropogenic cultural landscapes' in which the Earth's biodiversity largely resides (cited in Dutfield 2015: 650), repositions such communities as makers of 'Anthropocene' nature, rather than simply being part of 'wild' nature. In so doing, these people are said to have 'invented' the nature they steward just as much as modern genetic scientists might be said to invent – rather than discover – the genetic modifications and markers that are their stock-in-trade.

This framing led Pat Mooney (2000) to suggest that appropriation of traditional knowledge of indigenous peoples by pharmaceutical firms is just as much 'piracy' as is the appropriation of pharmaceutical firms' patents by the producers of unlicensed generics and counterfeits. The term 'biopiracy' that Mooney coined has been deployed to refer to new forms of colonialism, slavery and even rape of the global South, of the world's poor and of nature (Shiva 1997). Dutfield does not seek to defend the historical record of Western states and corporations in their exploitation of resources, knowledge and peoples in the global South. However, he suggests simply seeking to appropriate and invert the language of property rights and piracy has not proven very successful in addressing the substantive needs of the world's poor – indigenous, traditional or otherwise. There are a number of reasons for this.

First, the relationship between indigenous knowledge and the production of effective and profitable pharmaceutical products is weak. It is not the case that a patent taken out on a synthesized product based upon traditional knowledge of 'natural' products then prohibits the use of the original natural remedy. As such, if the original product is 'as good', there is no loss to those who can simply keep using it. However, this being said, it *is* the case that patents taken out on derivatives of traditional knowledge can enable those holding patents to seek protection from imports of original source produce, which can harm producers in developing countries. Halbert (2005: 146) reports the case of the Mexican yellow bean, a sample of which was taken to the United States. There, the bean was selectively bred to improve the uniformity of its yellowness and then patented under the name 'Enola beans'. The patent holder then demanded royalties on the sale of all such yellow beans made in or entering the United States, including those being imported from their original source in Mexico. Halbert (2005: 147) goes on to note that the number of similar cases of extraction, patent protection and then exclusion reaches into the thousands, although it should be noted that some such protection claims have been overturned (Darch 2015).

However – and this is a second reason why placing much faith in pursuing farmers' rights by mirroring patent protection is questionable – the fact that the US Patent Office was willing to offer patent protection in such cases, even as its 'prior art' search requirement only applies to searching within the United States, highlights US willingness to prioritize its own national corporate interest, exactly as it does when pressing for global respect for US corporate IP. Even if Mexican farmers were to assert a prior right to yellow beans as a form of farmers' right, this protection would not be upheld in the US anyway.

Third, the track record shows that where a traditional knowledge exists, it will usually be used by a number of communities, with competing claims to priority between, and leadership within, them. Most often, a new product, if marketable, will be significantly different in its effect and process from the original 'natural' product and its traditional use. As such, where a new drug 'works', it will be hard to claim that it derived fully from only one local product or knowledge. Contrariwise, to the extent that a synthesized drug is similar to its 'natural' source, the product is less likely to be profitable.

Fourth, many of the world's most valuable plants – coffee, tea, rice, soy, wheat, corn (maize), rubber, the potato – have been traded and circulated worldwide for centuries, making claims to origin impossible, at least in terms of legal protection such as with Geographical Indications (GIs). Even plants with less global reach, if known to have valuable properties, will have been circulated over time and so have no singular originator 'community'. While Dutfield highlights the success of the Peruvian potato park, which preserves many hundreds of varieties of this global food staple, the park makes no attempt to claim rights over the world's potatoes, but instead seeks to preserve the world's biodiversity in this product that Peru has shared with the world.

A fifth and final reason why extending property rights to traditional knowledge and local products fails to protect the poor is that such rights, when applied, tend to reinforce local elites or fuel disputes between such elite claimants, rather than 'trickling down' to the smallest and poorest producers (Darch 2015; Coombe et al. 2015).

Extending the logic of property rights, by extending the concept of piracy beyond pharmaceutical patent infringement to the expropriation of the traditional knowledge used by pharmaceutical companies in developing their drugs, has thus failed, on multiple counts, to protect the world's poorest people. Indigenous peoples and traditional farmers are far better off being able to share the results of pharmaceutical research (through generic drugs, as will be discussed in Chapter 8) than they are in attempting to prevent the sharing of their own traditional knowledge. Access to generic drugs (something pharmaceutical companies refer to as 'piracy') and reasserting rights to exchange, share and cross seed against plant breeders' rights (again, commonly defined as 'piracy') are better solutions to poverty and exclusion in developing countries than attempts to extend the very rights regimes that help impoverish the world's poorest people in the first place. It is for this reason, as pointed out by Oguamanam (2015), that farmers' rights must not be equated with just a mirror imaging of dominant conceptions of patent controls. Rather, farmers' rights represent a valuation of sharing as the basis for a more equitable, sustainable and effective mode of food production and science. As will be discussed below, while commercial agribusiness insist that patent is the best or only mode of incentivizing innovation and improvement, this is simply a convenient misconception for those who stand to gain from closing off alternatives and monopolizing the present.

When the World Intellectual Property Organization (WIPO) began promoting the idea of indigenous and traditional knowledge rights as a fundamental part of universal human rights in the 1990s, it might have looked like a victory for those seeking to defend the most socially marginalized communities from the threat of biopiracy (Halbert 2005: 143). However, in making such claims, WIPO was at the same time promoting its primary agenda of inserting intellectual property rights into the UN's Universal Declaration of Human Rights – something, which, if successful, would give the upholding of all IP claims, including the patent claims of global agribusiness, equal weight relative to the rights to life, food, shelter and healthcare. This would be to assert a moral equivalence between corporate property rights and the right to human life itself: a catastrophic outcome for the world's poor. The movement for farmers' rights and rights for indigenous peoples is part of a wider movement for global justice, including claims for access to medicine and for technology transfer to enable sustainability and development. These claims require challenging medical and other patent holders' rights to set prices, and the ability to share valuable knowledge rather than defend its status as private property. Such demands for global justice are fundamentally at odds with any claim that IP should be a fundamental and universal human right.

The Human Genome Project

The 'race' to 'complete' the sequencing of 'the' human genome, a race between the publicly funded Human Genome Organization (HUGO) and the privately funded Celera Genomics Corporation, highlights a range of significant issues regarding sharing relative to IP-based modes of genetic research. In this section, the complexity of these issues is set out in terms of three key dimensions: the ethics of sharing versus proprietary conceptions of the science of human genetics; the efficacy of research based on sharing versus that based on intellectual property rights; and the economics of sharing versus IP in terms of productivity and utility. In each case, the successful sequencing of the human genome demonstrates the superiority of the former.

Ethics: Property or shared heritage

John Sulston, director of the Cambridge Sanger Centre which led the British end of the Human Genome Project (HGP), suggests of himself: 'I'm not a good manager, but I do like partnerships; I assumed that we'd just share things and do everything together. And that's how it turned out' (Sulston and Ferry 2003: 64). While there was scientific competition between laboratories and teams within the publicly funded programme, the first principle of the programme was that all data would be shared. This was for two reasons. First, within both the HGP and the research projects that had preceded it (mapping and then sequencing the genomes of smaller organisms), sharing data was the only way to secure the trust of the whole research community whose shared efforts made completion possible. Second, the 'only reasonable way of dealing with the human genome sequence is to say that it belongs to all of us – it is the common heritage of humankind' (Sulston and Ferry 2003: 133). This 'etiquette of sharing' was formally set out as the Bermuda Principles in 1996, and became the abiding code of conduct for those engaged in the public programme of sequencing 'the heritage of humanity'.

Efficiency: Market forces vs public science

Sharing data was not only a core ethical principle. As noted above, one reason to share data is that it underpins the ability to sustain trust across a network of research groups, as opposed to the hierarchical structure of licensing that is required to coordinate research (or more often prohibit it) between proprietary rights holders and others. The free release of mapping information and then of the more systematic sequencing data allowed faster dissemination – and hence faster development.

It should not be assumed that commercial actors had no capacity to act or advantages to deploy. Craig Venter's Celera Genomics was set up in partnership with the sequencing instrument marker ABI, which was itself owned by the wider scientific instrument maker Perkin-Elmer. Perkin-Elmer put up the US$300 million, which enabled Celera to go into direct competition with the publicly funded HGP. As such, Venter had access to the latest versions of ABI sequencing machines, something that required the HUGO/HGP to rapidly buy up a stock of the latest equipment. If ABI had refused to sell HUGO/HGP their 3,700 level machines, Venter would have completed his sequence before the public research programme; but, with sales of over $1 billion, the machine manufacturer did not turn away willing customers. Capitalists are comfortable with competition as long as it remains profitable for them – even as they actively lobby for protectionism if that better suits their profit margins (see the next section).

However, even if ABI had used its IP rights to prohibit distribution of the fastest sequencers to the HUGO/HGP, it is unlikely that Celera would have produced a very accurate sequence. This was because Venter's method was to use 'expressed sequence tags' (ESTs) as simple gene markers to locate genes. This allowed fast throughput sequencing in what became known as the 'whole genome shotgun method' (Sulston and Ferry 2003: 128). This technique, which does away with the need for preliminary mapping, proved highly successful in sequencing bacteria. However, this was because most bacteria genomes only have 2 per cent repetition. Within the human genome, this rises to 50 per cent, rendering mapping essential for anything other than a very superficial draft. Such a superficial draft, Celera believed, would nonetheless suffice to identify the markers for 200–300 genes linked to particular diseases. If these ESTs were sufficient to put in patent applications on any subsequent use of those gene markers, irrespective of whether or not these markers were subsequently shown to be very vague, those patents would be good enough to mine the genome profitably as private property. When it came to sequencing, Celera simply used the more accurate HGP data, which was released into the public domain, to hang large parts of its more sketchy ESTs upon: '[W]ithout the public project there would not only have been no publically available draft human genome by 2000 – there would have been no draft genome at all' (Sulston and Ferry 2003: 270).

This act of 'free-riding' (Olson 1965), in which Celera was able to use HGP data even while avoiding sharing its own findings, meant Celera could issue press releases that implied that they were 'in front', or had produced more. Celera even tried to withhold some elements of its findings from the joint publication (in 2000), when the journals *Nature* and *Science* agreed to co-publish the results of HGP and Celera. The very principle that scientific research must be shared (made available for critical scrutiny) in peer-reviewed academic journals was threatened by Celera's attempts to retain information that might prove commercially valuable.

Economics: Protectionism or protection from protectionism

Right from the start of genomics research, ABI had tried to own the information produced using its sequencers. On the one hand, this has led to forms of 'defensive patenting' by companies, universities and others, which sought to patent in order to protect against the danger that, if they did not, someone else would. Having a near monopoly on sequencing technology put ABI in a strong position to control the field. It encrypted the software necessary to generate outputs from its machines. However, this code was rapidly broken by academic researchers, to allow scientists to work independently of the rules that their technology suppliers sought to impose upon them (Sulston and Ferry 2003: 94).

From the start, Craig Venter's ESTs were identified as a cheap and quick way of identifying just enough information to gain patent protection on genes identified by such a technique, even if this would not offer a full understanding of the gene marked. This offered commercial advantage to whoever staked such proprietary claims, but, at the same time, threatened to create an array of patent thickets – such that substantial research and development would become open to rent-seeking extortion by rights holders who had done nothing to actually turn markers into full comprehension, let alone turn comprehension into practical application.

The announcement in May 1998 that Celera Genomics was to create a 'catalogue of human variation', a database of single nucleotide polymorphisms (SNPs or snips), something that might then provide Celera with patentable rights over research into a wide range of minor human variations, led ten large pharmaceutical firms to create The SNP Consortium. This consortium was to create a free and publicly available database of such variations as a 'pre-competitive' move to avoid monopoly control down the line (Sulston and Ferry 2003: 224–226). As has been noted a number of times in this book, capitalists are not averse to suspending markets by means of IP monopolies when they are able to do so (see also Johns 2009). However, when threatened by the prospect of such protectionism being exercised to preclude them, they are sometimes willing to engage in 'pre-competitive' sharing to prevent this.

The willingness of capitalist firms and capitalist states to promote open access as 'pre-competitive' does not extend to suspending competition altogether. Pre-competitiveness implies a creation of conditions for future competition, not its permanent abolition. This explains why, despite campaigning for and exercising the principles of sharing in the development of the HGP, it was never the case that the project adopted fully 'open-source' or 'copyleft' principles, which would not only have protected the genome itself from IP claims, but would have prohibited any future IP claims based on work derived from it. The funders of the HGP were the US National Institute of Health and the UK Medical Research Council and the Wellcome Trust. They all supported shared public research, but are themselves constrained (by powerful commercial lobbies in the case of both states, and by their charter in the case of Wellcome) to fund work that will not prohibit business interests in the future. A curious irony lies in the fact that the Wellcome Trust's funding of the HGP was in large part possible (on the scale required) because the Trust was required to spend the fortune it had then just begun to acquire as a result of the super-profits derived from the Burroughs Wellcome patent for the AIDS inhibitor AZT. As will be seen in the next chapter, this drug was the product of largely publicly funded research, and its subsequent commercial control has sparked huge controversy over access to medicine.

Public Knowledge? deCode Genetics, the Public as Private and Vice Versa

Hilary Rose's ethnographic study of deCode Genetics in Iceland highlights a number of paradoxes around sharing, the public, the private and privacy (Rose and Rose 2012). Icelandic Harvard professor Kari Stefansson created the company deCode Genetics in 1998 by raising venture capital. The company sought to map the genome of the entire population of Iceland, which (being a relatively small and supposedly homogenous population) held out the prospect of enabling the identification of gene mutations associated with various medical conditions. Stefansson was able to persuade the Icelandic government to legislate in favour of automatic inclusion of citizens within the project (opting out had to be actively pursued).

In this context, a private company was given default access to citizens' genetic data, thus rendering what might be considered public knowledge a form of private property. On the other hand, critics observed that what might be considered patients' private data was being made public knowledge, even if, once public, any useful information gained could then be rendered private in the sense of being patented. The public duty of medical personnel was to their individual patients' best interests and that included their privacy, despite the claim by deCode that the wider 'public' good was being served by making all patients' information available for research. Claims that data-protection would ensure the anonymity of individual cases were shown to be rather more hope than secure fact.

In the end, deCode Genetics went bankrupt – in large part, because publicly funded genome research, and the weakness of deCode's claims to have invented rather than to have discovered what it found, limited its scope to patent. Nonetheless, Rose notes that the subsidiary company created at the time of deCode's liquidation did sell on its Icelandic database as just another asset (Rose and Rose 2012: 180–181). In another twist, genomics firms are now specifically targeting relatively poor Eastern European countries for future biobanks, as these countries tend to have relatively strong 'universal' healthcare systems, when compared to the United States at least. As such, these countries have relatively comprehensive information about the health of their citizens – a public resource that, when mapped against genetic information, may provide new sources of private profit in the development of genetic diagnostics and genetically specific therapies. Public goods, in creating scope for free-riders, have led some to call for the abolition of the public domain in the form of a complete 'privatization' of everything (Hardin 1968). Alternatively, the practical suspension of patents (whether by successful legal reform at the global level or in the making available of affordable generic drugs and seeds within the global South in defiance of Northern corporate demands) extends the logic of shared ownership, cancels out the free-riding upon the South by the North, avoids the thickets that inhibit research (see the section above on the HGP), and maximizes dissemination. The relative success of such an approach very much confirms the findings of Elinor Ostrom's research (1990), that forms of organized sharing can in fact overcome 'the tragedy of the commons' and create forms of resource allocation superior to markets and property rights.

The Eureka Myth

It is often asserted that any future genetic diagnostics and therapies will require private patent protection to incentivize investment in their development. Yet, as the cases of deCode and the HGP demonstrate, it is publicly funded science that has won out, outperforming private incentives. However, Jessica Silbey's (2015) research illustrates that it is not only publicly funded research that is driven by higher ideals, rather than profit. Her interviews with genomic researchers (amongst many others) in both public and private research contexts highlights that their primary motive is distribution and recognition; patents hamper both, in limiting 'experimental-use exceptions' (2015: 22) and in creating patent thickets that inhibit shared knowledge and development (2015: 258). As will be pointed out in Chapter 8, most research funding in pharmaceuticals comes from public and charitable sources, and what little funding does come from the private sector is inefficient and mainly applied to develop copycat, 'me too' drugs of limited value except in the case of evading other companies' IP. It is a myth that even if researchers are not profit-driven, their funding is. The shared nature of scientific knowledge production parallels that of traditional forms of learning (as suggested by Oguamanam 2015 – see above), in contrast with market- and IP-based conceptions of knowledge and its distortion of science. While Western science can be appropriated and distorted in the interests of corporate patenting and control, this is a distortion to be resisted, not a pathological necessity of science forcing its intrinsic association with strategies of appropriation and control. As Dutfield (2015), Darch (2015) and Coombe et al. (2015) all highlight, 'local' power struggles in the South can corrupt and distort claims for farmers' rights and traditional knowledge protection, just as Western science can be corrupted. What is important is to protect and promote the shared knowledge production and distribution that drive both (traditional farming practices and modern scientific knowledge production), and to build bridges between them.

Genetics and the Law

Suzanna Leong (2015: 675–680) documents that recent legal decisions return us to the very point at which the current patent gold rush regarding genetics began: the 1980 decision in relation to the invention/discovery distinction. The *Diamond vs. Chakrabarty* decision, in distinguishing naturally occurring life forms from genetically modified living organisms that did not previously occur in nature, opened up the possibility of patenting genetic code. However, the distinction between discovery and invention remained. Leong points out that while the genomics company Myriad Genetics was successful in defending the patent on its technique for isolating the gene mutations (BRCA1 and BRCA2) associated with breast cancer (both in the United States in 2011 and in Australia in 2013), the US Supreme Court did, in 2013, overturn the 2011 decision of the lower court – rejecting Myriad's claim that 'isolating' the faulty gene alleles constituted an invention. In the Australian court and in the lower US court, it had been accepted that 'isolation' meant creating separate strands of DNA and rDNA outside the cell in a fashion that does not occur in nature. The US Supreme Court's view was that this 'isolation' did not constitute the creation of something new, only a way of capturing a discovery. As such, the boundary between what can be owned and what is deemed the common genetic heritage of humanity remains contested.

Conclusions: Common Heritage
and Sharing Knowledge Production

Perhaps the most important conclusion to be drawn from this discussion of sharing and genetics is that the logic of sharing brings together campaigns for farmers' rights in the global South and opposition to the logic of IP control and to a profit-oriented model of knowledge production and control within Western science. Corporate IP control and resultant patent thickets are as much a threat to science as 'terminator genes', and other technical and legal controls, are to farmers. The binary opposition between North and South often lumps science in with capitalism and colonialism. Such associations have real historical and contemporary foundations, but remain distortions in need of undoing, rather than intrinsic features that make science 'the enemy' of farmers' rights. The struggle to free science from corporate interests needs to be aligned with struggles to free farmers (traditional and otherwise) from dependence upon IP protectionist agribusiness corporations.

The defence of farmers' rights, and that of scientists to research beyond the confines of private knowledge control requires that the subordination of 'common heritage' (free for all) to 'patent protection' (private ownership and control) be undone. This is best achieved by suspending the latter, rather than in further collapsing the former into private ownership. As the works of Dutfield, Halbert, Darch and Coombe et al. illustrate, extending IP over traditional knowledge and 'local' produce does not aid the poorest; and WIPO's attempt to make IP a fundamental and universal right (through the back door of a proprietary distortion of farmers' rights) would be a catastrophe for those seeking affordable and sustainable medical, sanitation, communication, energy and farming technologies.

Disputes over the discovery/invention distinction continue. However, while legitimate concerns should be raised about the creation of artificial life forms (with the most extreme cases being the ethical issues around human cloning and prospective eugenic genetic selection), the issue of discovery/invention can be considered something of a false dichotomy (David and Meredith 2016). No such absolute line can be drawn in reality to conform to the legal requirement to distinguish nature from human intervention. History has already woven nature and human action together. Also, philosophically, a myriad of interpretations of the distinction can and have arisen. In the context of this book, then, the issue is not the discovery/intention distinction itself that is important, but rather the idea that in making the distinction in language, it is then possible to define legitimate property rights on one side of the binary. Abandoning patent in favour of shared knowledge production and distribution would dissolve the need for any such legal fiction.

Acts of resistance to genetic IP strategies – modes of economic counterpower as it were – resistance in terms of asserting 'prior art' claims, and the producing and distributing of generic medicines, as well as in a range of campaigns and networks around saving, sharing and cross-breeding seed, have all received legal recognition to some extent, but also carry on in practical defiance of global IP protection and extension.

Sharing genetic heritage breaks down the separation between nature, traditional stewardship and modern science; it also challenges corporate distribution control and, perhaps, offers scope for a continued hope in modernity and its promise that truth and freedom can be combined for the good of all humanity. Sharing therefore strengthens science and democratic decision making, in the face of technocratic control – and beyond the stunted conception of choice offered by a market system sustained by an artificial and unnecessary scarcity, itself created by attempts to maintain the private ownership of knowledge.

8

Pharmaceutical Patents
and Generic Drugs

Introduction

Since the 1870s, companies in both the United States and in parts
of Europe have been able to claim legal ownership over innovations
developed by their employees as well as by others whose patents
they have bought. The 1880s saw the first attempt at a worldwide
regulatory framework for patent extension (the Paris Treaty of 1883).
However, this treaty remained relatively limited in scope until a
century later. This chapter will examine the attempt to protect and
extend ownership rights in information-rich biochemical formulae,
and the processes that derive from such formulae. Perhaps the most
controversial and high-profile case of such an attempt in recent years
was that of Western pharmaceutical companies seeking to prevent the
South African government from buying far cheaper 'generic' copies
of patented HIV-inhibiting drugs from India, but this is just the tip
of the iceberg. Western governments are selective in their indignation. These states actively defend the patent rights of 'their' corporations in developing countries, while being willing to suspend such
rights, or to impose arbitrary caps on payment for patented products,
when it is said to impact on their own 'national interest/security'.
Pharmaceutical companies claim that the only way to develop new
drugs is through their research and development departments, and
that a limited number of successes, relative to extensive investment,
require a high return on those drugs that are useful. Claims as to
drug development costs have been shown to be routinely exaggerated, while contributions made to the development of new drugs by
non-commercial bodies, such as charitable foundations, universities

and states, are routinely overlooked. Not only is the contribution of commercial risk-taking to innovation exaggerated, it can often have the opposite effect. Patent thickets constitute the opposite to 'the tragedy of the commons', creating rather the tragedy of private interests. Competing patent holders seek to lock down particular discoveries and innovations in the hope of future commercialization, only to inhibit the collaboration and connections required to make such breakthroughs possible. Forms of open-source pharmaceutical innovation offer the possibility of bypassing such innovation-inhibiting thickets, while limits on patent extension in time, space and practice rebalance the trade-off between private benefit and the common good in favour of the latter.

Ebola

The image that the commercial pharmaceutical industry likes to present of itself is one in which private incentives lead to high-risk investments in speculative new products. As viewed through this lens, many such investments will never generate a profit; the few products that do succeed, it is argued, must finance the losses on the rest, and only monopoly profits on these rare successes can reward such risky enterprise and so incentivize further investment into similarly uncertain research in the future. As this chapter will make clear, this image is very far from being correct. The case of the Ebola outbreak in West Africa in 2014–15 is simply one case in point – a case this chapter will show offers a far more accurate image of so-called 'BigPharma' than the more flattering image they seek to present of themselves. Because Ebola has primarily impacted upon the very poorest people in a number of the very poorest countries in the world, research into a vaccine against it has not been a priority for private pharmaceutical companies. To profit-maximizing businesses, the poor never represented a credible source of future wealth generation. It is also true that governments in wealthy countries had similarly failed to make research into a cure for the disease a priority until the most recent outbreak saw cases move out from West Africa. Global migration, and the movement of health and aid workers, between West Africa and the United States, Western Europe and Japan, saw infected patients being diagnosed in rich countries. Non-containment, then, raised the possibility of infection spreading in affluent countries. Once the spectre arose of an Ebola 'epidemic' in rich areas of the world, state health agencies in those countries began fast-tracking research and clinical trials into an Ebola vaccine. Non-commercial bodies organized a prospective distribution mechanism by which the vaccine – once available – could be mass-produced and administered (*Guardian* 2014). While private pharmaceutical firms were to make up a part of this fast-tracking of trials, production and distribution process, they did so only when guarantees of profit were provided by non-commercial actors. As this chapter will demonstrate, private pharmaceutical firms are risk-averse, profit-maximizing monopolists that play only a very limited role in innovation. They engage with the innovation process only to the extent that non-commercial actors do most of the research and provide sufficient securities for private players to participate and then profit from such results as do arise.

AZT: A History of Control

It might be suggested that the example above is unrepresentative, as it is of a very acute health emergency, where it might reasonably be expected that the state would step in to fast-track research, clinical trials, manufacture and delivery. This is doubly untrue. First, Ebola has been a serious threat to health for many decades, and the failure by corporations and states to prioritize it is financial, not simply a matter of it only recently becoming urgent. (Of course, Western states and pharmaceutical companies are equally guilty of not prioritizing the disease when it did not appear to threaten people they consider important – whether that means wealthy in the case of pharmaceutical companies, or citizens of their countries in the case of Western governments.) Second, the case of Ebola vaccine research is *not* unusual in the relationship between commercial and non-commercial investment. The case of AZT – the first significant antiretroviral drug successfully deployed in the containment of the human immunodeficiency virus (HIV) that causes the acquired immune deficiency syndrome (AIDS) – similarly illustrates that while innovation and risk are the justifications given for monopoly profits on successful medications, such innovations are primarily funded publicly.

The creation of a second-order patent (decades after the fact) on AZT is what David and Halbert (2015: 72) refer to as the kind of 'appropriative practices' that characterizes today's commercial pharmaceutical business model. AZT was developed in the 1960s by researchers funded by the US National Cancer Institute. The drug was first applied therapeutically as an antiretroviral in cancer patients whose treatment regimens (such as chemotherapy) had compromised their immune systems. However, by the mid-1980s, the drug became an 'orphan'. The 1980 US Bayh-Dole Act allowed government-funded research to be patented for the first time, initially by the university or other body doing the state-funded research, but later by private firms that could then buy out the rights from the original research bodies. AZT became the property of Burroughs Wellcome. The drug – which was very cheap to make as the research had already been paid for, from public funds, long in the past – generated vast profits, becoming the foundation for the 'cocktail' of medication that has formed the basis for HIV inhibition since then.

After AZT, the next significant antiretroviral drug was Didanosine, originally emerging in the work of researchers at Brigham Young University in the 1960s and then developed as an HIV-inhibiting antiretroviral by researchers at the US National Cancer Institute in 1991, with funding from the National Institute of Health (NIH). The NIH then gave an exclusive licence (an effective but truncated patent) to a private company (Bristol-Myers Squibb Co.), which, as with AZT, proved highly profitable. Further primary research led by universities and state-funded institutes followed, with clinical trials 'pharmed out', as it were, to private firms to profit from only when the product began to look hopeful. Boldrin and Levine (2008: 227) note that the current 'cocktail' of HIV-inhibiting medication – of which AZT is a foundation – was itself developed by the university professor Dr David Ho, not by any single private corporation. Ho developed what is variously referred to as 'highly active antiretroviral therapy' (HAART), 'combination antiretroviral therapy' or simply 'the cocktail' – doing so with support from various states, the Gates charitable foundation, his own various university and hospital research departments, and from the US National Institute of Allergy and Infectious Diseases (itself funded largely by the NIH); this is even while – as is typical – private firms such as Merck and Co. have joined in at later stages. The other drugs that have made up this (shifting) cocktail are also interesting illustrations of the same tale – of mixed funding leading to private profits through variations of the same kind of 'appropriative practices'.

In the case of Ebola, private firms have claimed a role in the background research process, a process that – they argue – was essential to draw upon when an emergency arose, and where it was the state that needed to 'step in' to fast-track outcomes. In the case of AZT, meanwhile, it was the public sector that carried out all the early development and it has been private companies that have 'stepped in' to sell the product. In each case, however, private firms position themselves as key players in a mixed economy of research, development and distribution – suggesting, although differently in the two cases, that they are best able to deliver either the base research or its safe, effective and cost-efficient release to human patients (via clinical trials and then for sale). It is interesting to note that, in both instances, private firms claim that the part they play is the part that warrants the lion's share of any future earnings. Both claims *could* be true. It might simply be the case that in different cases the skills and expertise of the private sector are needed in different dimensions of the process of delivering medicines to meet human need. However, as this chapter will evidence, these claims are not in fact true. Private pharmaceutical firms are neither the most effective contributors to the production of new knowledge, nor are they the most efficient actors at delivering clinical trials or distribution of approved products to patients. On both sides of the coin, a patent-free form of shared research and development by non-commercial actors would (and, when tried, does) supply far better outcomes to a far greater number – and at a far lower price.

Bold Claims

As Andrew Kirton (2015) elaborates in relation to the music industry, the claims of the pharmaceutical industry to require large profit margins and long periods of protection on successful products to recover the cost of earlier investments (on both the successes and the many failures) are 'wildly' exaggerated. The most succinct and authoritative critique of the evidence behind claims made by pharmaceutical lobbyists and researchers paid by such lobbyists is made by Donald Light and Rebecca Warburton (2005), who set out the headline finding of researchers analysing data supplied by the pharmaceutical industry to the Tufts Centre for the Study of Drug Development, 'a research centre that receives significant unrestricted grants from pharmaceutical companies'. This data had been said (by the Tufts Centre) to show 'that it costs $802 million on average (in 2000 dollars) to research and develop a self-originated new chemical entity, including failures and cost of capital' (Light and Warburton 2005: 1030). This figure is not just the cost of developing a new drug, but the cost of all the research that did not result in anything workable. Given that uncertainty is a part of any good research, this is perfectly reasonable and does not form part of Light and Warburton's critique. The 'hits' do have to pay for the 'misses'. Their critique is different, and has six dimensions.

First, the research is based on confidential reports submitted by companies themselves drawing on their claims regarding costs. Confidentiality means that widely divergent methods and time frames may be included, and that no possibility exists to verify them. Second, in addition to simply the random error that might arise from confidential data that cannot be verified externally or even compared internally, there is also strong pressure towards upward estimation bias, as participants have a vested interest in the results being as large as possible. Confidentiality ensures that such upward estimation bias is not tempered by any transparency pressure to be either honest or consistent. Third, there is a likelihood of systematic sampling bias – with ten out of a frame of twenty-four large firms choosing to participate – creating a possibility that those with the highest costs in any given sampling period will volunteer to participate, while those with lower costs in that period will decline to take part. Once companies were in the sample (by self-selection), products within their portfolios were selected at random, but this does not prevent sample bias if what is found is then said to be representative of costs in all companies – and not just those that took part. Fourth, the industry-funded research was restricted to the cost of developing entirely novel chemical entities 'in-house'. Only one-third of 'new drugs' registered by the (US) Food and Drug Administration in the period covered by the research contained a new molecular entity, and only two-thirds of the products of the companies surveyed were produced 'in-house' ('self-contained'). Self-contained (in-house) development of entirely novel chemicals therefore only represents a limited number (22 per cent) of new drugs. As 'in-house' development and producing an entirely novel entity both significantly escalate the overall cost of a drug's development, results based on the combination of these two factors are highly atypical, in both cost and incidence. New drugs that are not based on an entirely new chemical entity are almost four times cheaper to develop; and, of course, sharing knowledge between companies and between public and private sector actors also radically reduces development costs.

Light and Warburton's fifth and sixth points of criticism are that such figures produced by industry-funded research do not take account of either state subsidies or significant tax deductions and credits. Both of these elements combined will greatly reduce the 'real' cost relative to the headline figures being cited. As will be seen below, the combination of subsidies and tax incentives cut 'real' costs by two-thirds; and given that the first four criticisms indicate that head-line figures are already exaggerated many times over by various forms of calculation and selection bias, the true cost of private pharmaceutical company drug development may bear very little resemblance to that presented by those funded by the sector to help justify their subsequent prices and profit margins.

Light and Warburton thus conclude that claims of high development costs, used to justify high protection to secure high prices that then afford high levels of investment, are grossly exaggerated. Nonetheless, their critique only suggests that the warrant for strong protection against the free-sharing of pharmaceutical research findings is overstated, and that protection and profit margins need not be as high as they currently are. In what follows, it is shown why such protection and monopoly pricing has no justification *at all* (not just that their current scale and duration simply need reigning in).

Who Pays and What Gets Bought?

Michele Boldrin and David Levine (2008: 212) start out from the same headline figure as that of the aforementioned Tufts Centre (of just over $800 million) as being the supposed cost of developing a new drug. They cite cases of up to a billion dollars being written off when an end-product is found to have no market value. Yet such amounts, they go on to demonstrate, are deeply misleading.

First, Boldrin and Levine (2008: 227) show, most research in the pharmaceutical sector does not come from private companies. They cite US data from different years to highlight the same general ratio, but parallel this to the situation in other industrialized nations. Over half of all research and development money comes from the central government (mainly from the NIH in the US), while another 10 per cent comes from the government in the form of grants to university research laboratories. On top of this, there are tax credits available for private firms to claim back some of the cost of their own investments. Overall, only around one-third of research and development in the pharmaceutical sector comes from private investment.

Second, most of the research carried out in the private sector can be characterized as redundant adaptation to the patent system itself, rather than any valuable contribution to new knowledge and effective treatment incentivized by the promise of monopoly rent (via patent controls). Because patents exist on the most effective new products, firms that do not hold patents on such drugs invest mainly in attempts to find new ways of simply mimicking their effects. These are referred to as 'me too', or 'copycat', drugs. Such products add no value to the sum of human health, but do potentially add to the profit margins of companies that can then compete with existing patent holders where otherwise patents would mean they could not. Competition here is only in providing copies of existing treatments (by marginally different means), rather than by genuinely original new products. Boldrin and Levine (2008: 231) cite research suggesting that of all new drug approvals in a given year, less than a quarter contain any new chemical agent. Indeed, some 'new' approvals are simply existing patent holders 'evergreening' their product (modifying it slightly to extend the patent); most are 'me too'/'copycat' drugs.

The array of 'me too' drugs then creates pressure on all companies to market their own product to persuade doctors and patients to take one product over another. As averse to genuine markets as pharmaceutical companies are, such 'competition' more often than not takes the form of 'bribing' doctors – often dressed up as 'post-clinical trials'. This amounts to offering initially discounted costs to doctors in the hope that, after the initial 'incentive', these doctors will prescribe the new product (at a high price) to patients. While this has led in recent years to a string of high-profile legal cases in which companies have been required to pay hundreds of millions of dollars in fines for what has been declared 'bribery' (Boldrin and Levine 2008: 234; Qi 2015), companies themselves account for such activity as research and development costs. The term 'post-clinical trial' covers a multitude of sins (literally and often legally). Fines become a routine business expense (within research and development budgets). Companies are thereby factoring even the cost of criminal prosecutions and civil penalties into their estimated research and development costs.

For all the above reasons, Boldrin and Levine argue that patent-protected private pharmaceutical firms offer no 'value for money' relative to state-, charity- and university-funded research. Public funds develop more and develop better (genuinely novel rather than mainly copycats) products. Even the claim that commercial firms better provide the final – and supposedly costly – clinical trials is found to be problematic. Boldrin and Levine discovered such trials were between two and four times more expensive when conducted privately than when they are carried out by non-commercial actors. That private firms have a vested interest in the outcome of clinical trials on products they will then have rights over means that commercial trials are not only more expensive, but also that their results are less trustworthy.

Patent and Medical Innovation

Boldrin and Levine (2008: 218–227) set out to examine what a world without patents would mean for medical- and health-related research and development. They first contrast the United States and the United Kingdom with continental Europe in the period between 1850 and 1980. This was a time when the former pair had strong patent protection on pharmaceutical innovations while the latter did not. If patents are a strong force for encouraging innovation, we would expect to see more pharmaceutical innovations in the United States and United Kingdom than in France, Italy, Germany, Switzerland, the Netherlands, and so on. The opposite is, in fact, the case. The reason 1980 was chosen as the break-off point was because it was then that a number of West European countries tightened up their patent laws to be more in line with the United States and the United Kingdom. Since the TRIPS agreement in 1995, this harmonization around tighter IP regulation has intensified even further. Has that meant greater levels of pharmaceutical innovation? Boldrin and Levine show this not to be the case, but rather simply that the cost of such research has rocketed (even if the reasons that the pharmaceutical industry typically give for this increase are not entirely credible given all that has been outlined above). Monopoly rents and profits have certainly risen even as innovation has tended to dry up – except in relation to innovative start-ups and university-/government-funded laboratories, whose results are bought up by private firms if they prove to have profitable potential.

Another way to gauge the relative merits of patent versus free access to knowledge as a foundation for innovation is to identify the sum of key innovations and to then see how many of these were patent-based and how many were not. Boldrin and Levine (2008: 228–230) compile and cite three such listings. Of the top fifteen 'milestones' in medical innovation, as selected by contributors and editors of the *British Medical Journal*, only two were covered by patent – and there is no particular reason to believe that these (the contraceptive pill and chlorpromazine) could not have been developed by non-proprietary means. Of the top ten public health innovations of all time, selected in 1999 by the US Centre for Disease Control and Prevention, none had been patented (nor had been funded with a view to patenting). Looking at purely chemical and biologically based medical innovations, a study by *Chemical and Engineering News* found that of the top forty-six best-selling pharmaceutical innovations at its time of composition (2005), patents had nothing to do with twenty of these cases. Meanwhile, four cases were developed by chance and then patented; two were developed by university researchers before the Bayh-Dole Act allowed university research to be patented, but which were patented after the 1980 legislative change; and a number of others were developed simultaneously by different research teams, leading to protracted legal battles over patent. Patent did not 'cause' the products development in these latter cases. Rather, patent impeded collaboration, innovation and dissemination. As such, most currently best-selling drugs were not patent-based, while some were, in fact, inhibited by patent battles. Of those that are/were patented, many were simply profitable 'me too' drugs with no public benefit. Overall, patent has almost nothing to do with the most valuable innovations as calculated in terms of human benefit. Patents do start to make inroads when the measure being used is sales. Yet, even there, the claim that patent-protected monopolies are the core driver of business-based research is highly exaggerated. Similarly, the claim that business-based research is the core driver of pharmaceutical innovation is itself also false.

One Way Street: The Case of Anthrax and National Security

Intellectual property rights can be said to be balanced rights – but then again, all rights contain scope to be set against other rights, in practice, if not always in principle. The question of whether or not rights are inalienable or tradeable is longstanding. Ian Brown (2015) documents the various conflicting rights that are potentially infringed by a strong defence of IP rights, while Halbert (2005) and Álvarez (2015) illustrate how the infringement of IP is the only realistic way many of the world's poorest people are able to fulfil basic rights to access either health or education.

Pharmaceutical companies are well aware of the fact that poor people who cannot afford the patent-protected prices of their medicines will not respect the niceties of IP law if the result of doing so is death or severe illness. As such, Western pharmaceutical firms argue that it is the role of governments in both the global South and in the North to make provision of 'their' medicines available to those who cannot afford them – but to do so in a way that ensures that these medicines are still bought at a price set by their patent holders. Western states have been keen to back their own nationally domiciled pharmaceutical companies in legal disputes with governments in the global South (as will be detailed more below) – although these firms have not always been so keen to reciprocate when it comes to domiciling their profits and hence pay tax.

While Western governments have been very keen to support pharmaceutical firms in taking legal action against the governments of countries in the global South that have sanctioned the production of generic drugs that infringe patents but make medicines affordable to those in poor countries, they (Western governments) have also been perfectly willing to suspend patents, or at least threaten to do so, if it is deemed to be in their 'national interest'. Graham Dutfield (2008) notes how the US government threatened to suspend the patents on vaccines that would need to be deployed in the event of an outbreak of anthrax. In the years after the terrorist attacks in the United States on 11 September 2001, the threat of a dirty bomb being used in a large urban area was deemed a credible threat, and contingency measures were set in place. One part of this was to ensure a sufficient supply of vaccine doses to treat victims of an anthrax-based attack. The US government demanded, on grounds of national security, that patent holders delivered a specified volume of vaccine shots at a specified price, or else the patents would be revoked on grounds that the companies concerned would be 'profiteering' during wartime. The same threats to suspend patents and the same accusations of immoral profiteering have been levelled against Western companies in relation to the AIDS epidemic in Africa, but such threats and accusations are not accepted by Western governments – which continue to support the pursuit of protection and profit abroad, and, it must be said, most of the time at home as well. Rights remain inalienable or become tradeable mainly depending upon which is the most powerful actor in any given situation, not because of any intrinsic (let alone universal) valuation of human need or entitlement.

Generic Medicines

Salvador Millaleo and Hugo Cadenas (2015) outline the relationship between patent and generic drug production in Chile, and highlight parallels with other South American countries in their relationship with the United States of America. As a part of the requirements for its membership of the World Trade Organisation, Chile, like all other states, was required to sign up to the TRIPS agreement and to sign into domestic legislation the TRIPS extension of IP protection to all foreign patents, trademarks and copyrights. Like other countries of the global South, Chile was given time to adapt to these conditions; it was allowed five years to comply, between signing the treaty in 1995 and implementing it in 2000.

Unlike its largest neighbours, Argentina and Brazil, which have resisted the imposition of US-led enforcement of tougher international IP regulation, Chile has signed into domestic law its acceptance of US-dominated Free Trade Agreement (FTA) rules that require respect for foreign (mainly US) patents over pharmaceutical manufacture and sale. However, the Chilean government and courts have taken a different view from that of US courts (and legislators) regarding whether or not a drug can be given authorization to be sold if it does not have 'linkage' to its current patent holder – where one exists. Chile rejects US claims that the FTA agreement requires this, claiming that authorization can be based on health efficacy, not only evidence of patent-holder consent.

This divergence of interpretations has led to the development of two parallel pharmaceutical sectors in Chile: one 'international' sector, producing patent-compliant drugs under licence to mainly US firms; and a generics sector making drugs that are either out of patent or which are in breach of existing patents. Both sectors can exist in parallel, Millaleo and Cadenas argue, because Chile is a society caught between a traditional form of hierarchal, and a modern form of functional, division of labour. A minority of the society experience a standard of living on a par with richer Northern/Western societies, while the majority experience extreme forms of poverty and exclusion. Those at the top can afford, and often do choose, to purchase IP-compliant branded products, while the rest of the population can only afford generic alternatives. While IP-compliant firms – and their mainly US patent holding partners – claim to experience unfair competition, the existence of a robust market for generics is essential, Millaleo and Cadenas suggest, to meeting real health needs, and does not appear to have eliminated the market for IP-compliant drugs amongst those who can afford them.

Faking Fakes: The Attempt to Present Generics as Counterfeits

Many countries, particularly but not exclusively in the global South, engage in the manufacture of generic medicines. If the patent on a particular drug has expired, the practice of manufacturing generic copies is not controversial. However, for drugs that are still in patent, and because an increasing number of drugs are open to patent due to changes in legislation allowing publicly funded and university research outcomes to be patented, much controversy exists. Brazil, India and Thailand have particularly large generic pharmaceutical sectors, and are especially challenging to Western pharmaceutical interests. China has also been very productive in this field, but has in recent years become more keen to accommodate itself with the Western interpretation of WTO TRIPS rules that deem generic versions of drugs currently in patent as criminal 'piracy'. Not only do these developing countries supply their own domestic markets with generic medicines at prices well below those demanded by patent monopoly-holding suppliers of the same drugs; they also export medicines to other developing countries seeking to uphold the right to healthcare of their citizens. This is presented as 'international piracy' by BigPharma lobbyists.

As will be pointed out below, there has been controversy over the term 'piracy' insofar as TRIPS rules have been interpreted differently by different actors. Patent holders seek to assert the view that infringing patents is always piracy. Developing states and generic pharmaceutical companies claim that TRIPS rules allow for compulsory licensing (an effective suspension of patents) where this enables a state to deal with a health emergency. Publicly at least, the view of developing countries has prevailed on this issue, with generics not being deemed 'piracy', at least in a number of high-profile cases – such as over HIV/AIDS-inhibiting antiretroviral drugs. However, behind the scenes, Western pharmaceutical lobbies continue to resist what they see as theft (May and Halbert 2005).

Parallel to claims regarding generic medicines as 'piracy', there has been a second strategy of delegitimation undertaken by Western states and IP holders. This is to seek to equate generic medicines with 'counterfeit' medicines, under the label of 'fake' medicines (Sen 2012). This is doubly erroneous. First, counterfeiting refers to the infringement of a trademark – such as would be achieved with false packaging, branding and labels. This is not the same as 'piracy', which is the commercial infringement of copyright or patented 'content' (not the packaging). By their nature, 'generic' medicines do not copy the labelling, but are made as alternatives to the patent holder's branded product and are sold as such. 'Counterfeit' medicines are sold in falsified packaging to appear as if they were the product of another (IP-holding) firm, whereas state-sponsored generics are not 'falsified' in such a fashion. Falsification of packaging most often goes along with a falsification of content – such that the pills or treatments contained in such fake packaging are not actually the same chemical products as is being claimed. This falsifying activity is 'fraud' (not being an actual *copy* of what it *pretends* to be), not 'piracy' as such (which would be an unlicensed *copy*). This 'fraud' regarding content is not even the same crime as the 'counterfeiting' of packaging – although counterfeiting and fraud go together in the faking of medicines by organized criminal networks. A patent-infringing generic medicine does, in contrast, actually copy the content of the patented medicine. This is why it is an infringement of patent. State-sponsored generics are designed to reduce the price of medicines, not to artificially inflate prices either by patents or by counterfeit packaging. Counterfeiters trade on the inflated prices that can be achieved where patents are in operation, and upon the labelling used by patent holders for which many customers are prepared to pay more.

As such, it is not patent-infringing generics that actually create the problem of counterfeit medicines. The criminal practice of using trusted brand names to create false packaging for content that is not what it claims to be (the fusing of counterfeiting and fraud) is motivated precisely by the legal monopoly pricing created by patents. Generic medicines constitute patent infringement exactly because they are physically the same as what they copy (unlike many counterfeit products). In reducing the price of the real chemical products, generics make genuine medicine cheaper and undercut the market for counterfeits. To reiterate, counterfeits are a problem created by the patent (and trademark) system. Generics, insofar as they address the problem of monopoly pricing created by patents, also go a long way to dealing with the problem of counterfeit capitalism (Rojek 2015). Far from generics being the 'friendly' face of counterfeiting, and of both being best lumped together under the label of 'fakes', it is the 'profiteering' of both IP holders and counterfeiters that should be compared to each other.

Most useful pharmaceutical research is publicly funded. Most of what is privately funded is only for 'me too/copycat' drugs or 'post-clinical trials' that often amount to little more than bribery. Neither offers social benefit but merely play around the thickets created by the IP system to boost profits. What little actually useful research that is done privately costs between two and four times what it would have cost if it had been done publicly. As such, the claim that patents need defending against generics on grounds of future investment is as false as the claim that generics are the same as counterfeits.

HIV in South Africa, Brazil and Elsewhere

Debbie Halbert (2005) provides a detailed account of the conflict between the South African government and Western pharmaceutical firms (and their state backers) over the 1997 South African Medicines and Related Substances Control Act Amendments – commonly referred to as the South African Medicines Act. This act set out the view that countries signed up to TRIPS did have the right to order compulsory licences for patented medicines, or to parallel import such medicines from markets where those drugs were available at a cheaper price than were being offered by patent holders in the country concerned – although if, and only if, this was to deal with a genuine health emergency.

The South African government believed that HIV/AIDS was just such an emergency. Halbert documents the scale of the HIV/AIDS crisis at the time when the legislation was passed, with 22 million people in sub-Saharan Africa estimated to have been infected, 4.6 million people in the state of South Africa itself. Each month, 20,000 people were dying of AIDS, infection rates were threatening the survival of whole communities, and the number of children either infected or left orphaned was spiralling upwards. The South African government believed it had an obligation to treat the victims. The annual cost for the cocktail of patented medication deemed most effective at limiting the condition was set by patent holders at US$12,000 per patient. The South African government could not afford the cost (at least at the monopoly controlled prices). However, the view that TRIPS allowed states to enact compulsory licensing/parallel importation meant that cheaper generic drugs from Brazil, India or Thailand could make an effective and affordable treatment policy possible.

The reaction of patent-holding pharmaceutical companies was a predictable condemnation of what they claimed was an invitation to state-sponsored 'piracy' of their intellectual property. Thus began a legal, diplomatic and political conflict that saw Western pharmaceutical firms and their 'home' states demanding respect for intellectual property rights. These actors were arrayed against a set of developing nations and a range of campaign groups, both of which were demanding access to medicine as a basic human right. Halbert details this conflict, the upshot of which was, foremost, a success for campaigners in reversing the discourse on victims in the world of medicines. While IP holders have been very successful in lobbying (of Western politicians at least) that they (the IP holders) are the primary victims in need of protection in a world of infringing IP pirates (see David and Whiteman 2015), groups like ACT UP, the Treatment Access Campaign (TAC), MSF, Oxfam and HealthGAP reversed the moral gaze, such that those with HIV/AIDS became seen as the victims of profiteering corporations willing to put profit before life itself.

In 2000, the legal action brought by Western pharmaceutical companies in the South African courts was dropped, for fear that a public trial would require these corporations to explain how such a large amount of research funded by governments, universities and charities had come to be privately patented in the first place (see discussion of AZT and subsequent developments above). In May 2000, US Democrat President Bill Clinton ended US unilateral pressure on South Africa to cease what the US government had, until then, claimed was a violation of TRIPS. A year later, the new Republican administration under George W. Bush agreed to continue the policy of non-confrontation (in public at least), providing more state funds to pay US firms to supply IP-compliant medicines, rather than endorsing generics as a solution. However, these funds would only supply thousands of patients at the prices IP holders still demanded, so generics – which cost many tens of times less to buy – remained the only credible solution on any serious scale.

In September 2001, Brazil pushed ahead with the threat to make and export its own HIV-inhibiting generics, and was able to thereby force a deal with one IP holder, Roche; the Nigerian government, meanwhile, in the same month went ahead with the importation of generic antiretroviral drugs from India. Developing countries were working towards solving their own problems, and the case of Brazil, where the strategy of domestically producing generic medicines was extremely successful in reducing infection and increasing life expectancy, was threatening to make TRIPS redundant. As a result, in December 2001, what is known as the Doha Declaration (after the Doha round of TRIPS negotiations) was agreed. This declaration recognized the right of countries to issue compulsory licences, but did not mention parallel importation. As a concession to a reality that had already 'pulled the rug out' from under Western states and corporations, rather than any kind of substantive advance, the declaration sought to reign in the 'threat of a good example'. Compulsory licensing assumes the capacity to make your own generics, whereas parallel importation simply means buying items from a country where the patent holder is selling at a cheaper price, or where another manufacturer is making cheaper generics.

It is interesting to note that it was the South African case that received the greater level of publicity, while it is very much the Brazilian example that offers the most hope. The South African case – as Halbert documents – saw a reframing of moral discourses such that the patient, not the patent holder, became defined as the primary victim; but much of this discourse still acted to frame the West – its states and its corporations – as villains only to the extent that they did not do more to help the helpless. The Brazilian case illustrates that it is far better for a developing society to shake off the binary of victim and saviour in relation to wealthier nations, and simply get on with solving its own problems for itself.

Conclusions:
Sharing Knowledge and Improving Human Health

As medical emergencies like the 2014–15 Ebola outbreak in West Africa and beyond highlight, it is public and charitably funded research that is best able to deal rapidly in fast-tracking and distributing medical developments. What the case of HIV/AIDs antiretroviral drug research shows is that the same is true for the long-term development from blue-skies to practical medication. Whether in the short or the longer term, medical research is best performed by non-commercial science. The sharing of knowledge, not its subsequent private control, creates most and distributes it best.

As Light and Warburton (2005) show, the claims made by private firms regarding the cost of their research and development 'investment' is grossly overstated; and Boldrin and Levine (2008) go on to demonstrate that even when these inflated figures are cut down to size, what is being produced by commercial pharmaceutical firms is rarely the most useful content anyway. Patents inflate prices and reduce innovation. Most commercial research aims to develop patent-adaptive 'copycat' drugs, not genuinely original chemical products; and the cost of clinical trials – which is often where private firms claim they make their biggest contributions – are themselves between two and four times more expensive than if the same work had been done publicly. With a large part of what else private firms 'invest' being 'post-clinical trials' that amount to a spectrum from 'marketing' to downright 'bribery', it is necessary to conclude that a publicly funded scientific research programme based on principles of shared investigation and free access to results would be, and is, by far the cheapest and most effective way for societies to fund research and tackle disease (at least at the level of medically based intervention).

Indeed, developed states are only too willing, it seems, to follow this line of thinking – at least to the extent that they currently meet most of the cost of most of the worthwhile research that actually takes place, and to the extent that they agree to suspend patents when sharing (in the form of compulsory licensing) is seen to be in their national security interest. Pharmaceutical firms, too, are themselves very willing indeed to promote the efficacy and efficiency of publicly funded science when it means they get so much quality research paid for by others. They are, however, equally keen to ensure that, once the benefits of shared science are produced, they are able to claim ownership of such developments 'down the line'. This requires patents to protect future profits, but these patents did not produce the products on which the profits will then be drawn. These patents need enforcement at home and abroad – again, to ensure profits, not to ensure the future of scientific research and development itself.

It is interesting, therefore, that a curious symbiosis arises to the extent that most research and development of value is funded by advanced Western states, and is then reproduced in generic form by less developed state-backed generics companies in the global South. Just as advanced states underpin the profitability of Western pharmaceutical firms in a form of sharing (giving away vast sums in research funding, that is), so it is that states like Brazil, India and Thailand do the same (by protecting their own national drug manufacturers when they 'share' in the knowledge that has been created). That the latter's 'sharing' of patented knowledge upsets Western states and patent-holding pharmaceutical firms should not be confused with evidence that such patent infringement is itself a threat to innovation. Just as sharing knowledge is in fact the key to valuable scientific innovation, so it is that sharing the products of knowledge, in terms of making available generics at the lowest possible price, is no threat to future research – even as it is the best way to maximize the utility of such products that scientific endeavour can deliver. What such a mode of economic counterpower represents is a threat to the dominant network of pharmaceutical business interests, itself interlinked within a network of economic, cultural and political networks threatened by the possibility of free-sharing more widely.

9
Conclusions:
Sharing – Crime against Capitalism

Introduction

Free-sharing is criminalized under capitalism: it is a 'crime against capitalism'. This is not because free-sharing is a parasitical drain upon the work of others, but precisely because it is a more efficient, effective and incentivizing mode of economic production and distribution than capitalism. This has been documented in detail throughout this book, and is summarized in Table 9.1.

The computer (Hal 9000 etc., the Terminator etc.) is not the enemy. 'In reality, the network has allowed humans to rebel' (Mason 2015: 24). Mason (2015: 112) cites Peter Drucker: 'That knowledge has become the resource, rather than a resource, is what makes our society "post-capitalist".' Informational goods can be digitally copied without loss or corruption, and increasingly without marginal cost. 'Economists call this "non-rivalry". A simpler word for it would be "shareable"' (Mason 2015: 118). The first principle of capitalist economics, scarcity, is dissolved. 'Today, the main contradiction in modern capitalism is between the possibility of free, abundant socially produced goods, and a system of monopolies, banks and governments struggling to maintain control over power and information. That is, everything is pervaded by a fight between network and hierarchy' (2015: 144). It is in the nature of the network society that control over content is fundamentally lost. For Mason, the modern age was ushered in by the printing press and science, as well as a flood of looted gold from the Americas, even as the Black Death finished off feudalism's material and ideological foundations. For him, the digital network combined, with a flood of free information, will usher in a post-capitalist future, even as 'energy depletion,

Table 9.1 The superiority of free-sharing

	Efficiency	Efficacy	Incentive
Music	Better publicity and distribution	Everything, everywhere, for all	Eliminating opportunity costs
Software	Greater productivity at reduced cost	Informed choice, affording better development	Peer recognition, and 'hacker ethic' of 'play struggle'
Sports live-streaming	One platform for all content	More choice and wider access	Fan control, not hyper-commercialisation
Trade publishing	Cost falls for readers and writers	A very long tail indeed	New author/fan interaction, over 'big book' pumping
Journalistic publishing	Free content as it happens	On the spot, without editorial filters	Citizen witnessing
Academic science	Freeing what is freely given	Open access to all	Peer recognition within gift economy
Pharmaceuticals	Blue sky is open, public science is cheaper	Quality/access beyond thickets, interests and 'me too'	Most innovative research is public/charity funded

climate change, ageing population and migration' (2015: 243) will be its 'great plague'. Mason and other 'left accelerationists' argue that global networks offer the possibility of 'subversive universals' (Srnicek and Williams 2015), a reclaiming of modernity and 'the future' as a progressive and egalitarian possibility in an age when such optimism is in short supply. Srnicek and Williams (2015: 78) put forward the notion of 'synthetic freedom'. It has often been said that free speech is not free beer. While negative freedom, as liberty, is to be valued, it may also represent the freedom to starve. Positive freedom, the freedom from want and the freedom to achieve, has often been separate from simply the absence of constraint. Sharing in the digital age represents such 'synthetic freedom', the fusion of both positive and negative freedom.

In the following discussion, the evidence set out in the preceding chapters, showing how the free-sharing of non-rivalrous informational content is (1) more *efficient* than property and market arrangements, (2) more *effective* in terms of the quantity and quality of that being made available and (3) better able to create *incentives* for innovation, will be brought together into one overall synthesis. Today, across multiple intersecting domains is witnessed the 'triumph of the commons', even as an ongoing criminalization of sharing – in the attempt to maintain scarcity – continues to manifest 'the tragedy of the anti-commons'. However, attempts to 'recolonize' the free-sharing domain through advertising are limited both by the lack of an editorial nexus in new media, and by the rise of ad-blocker software; meanwhile, free content as promotion for live and public events does see performers better paid. There is money to be made offering expertise, filtering services and ease of access; but there seems no ready likelihood that audiences will accept any wholesale commercial appropriation of the digital commons.

The Efficiency of Sharing

Today, we are witnessing the emergence of what Jeremy Rifkin (2014) calls 'the zero marginal cost society'. Online sharing of informational content reduces the cost of each additional copy to as close to zero as can no longer be calculated. Digital sharing is more efficient than market- and property-based arrangements. The case of recorded music has in recent years most clearly manifested the rise of this zero marginal cost society, with the traditional recording company business model becoming increasingly outdated and inefficient – a manifestation of pre-digital production and distribution methods.

With production, manufacture, distribution, and marketing now being open to digital-sharing alternatives, signing a record deal is not, now, the only option. In conditions of debt bondage, rights management (the fifth dimension of the traditional record company's 'offering' to artists) comes to represent less and less of an attractive proposition, at least when other means of attracting a paying audience are now available. Free-sharing offers scope to attract a paying live audience without the need to run up a large debt in the process. Few artists get paid for recordings, and even those who do regret it when royalties do not recoup costs. As such, freely circulated copies of artists' work attract a larger audience at no expense to the artist themselves. Reduced opportunity costs to fans means artists' live performance earnings actually increase.

Free-sharing is also more efficient in delivering 'news'. The Internet is often blamed for 'the crises' in print and broadcast journalism, but this accusation is unfounded. In reality, the challenge of the Internet to traditional print and broadcast media is as a more efficient substitute, not as a degradation of its established quality. The Internet's challenge as a substitute comes in the form of 'citizen journalism' (Allen 2013). Witnesses, participants, as well as the perpetrators of events now broadcast their 'news'. Such actors, and not professional journalists, also broadcast their news *first*. Reporters, photographers and other news staff have been made redundant because they cannot capture such images, and certainly cannot compete at the level of cost with direct, freely uploading, participants at events. However cheap, cost cutting by means of outsourcing supply of content to free online suppliers also weakens the rationale for using 'old' print and broadcast media suppliers in the first place.

Free-sharing of scientific knowledge underpins research and affords more efficient delivery of medicines. Two-thirds of pharmaceutical research and development funding comes from non-commercial sources. Most commercial pharmaceutical research money is spent not on primary research at all, but on clinical and post-clinical trials. In the private sector, clinical trials cost between two and four times what the same trials cost when conducted publicly (Boldrin and Levine 2008: 231). Shared, publicly funded research does most, costs least and avoids waste. Once the primacy of public science in the production of pharmaceutical knowledge is recognized, the claim that sharing results freely would undermine the production of new medicines is debunked. Similarly, scientific research is most efficiently produced in conditions of non-proprietary sharing.

Research and development in corporate silos, such as in software or pharmaceuticals, is not the efficient production system it claims to be. Another demonstration of the relative inferiority of silo-based (privately owned) corporate research and development, relative to free-sharing-based creative production, is digital rights management (DRM) software and the computer hackers who break such DRM. Free and open-source software, as well as code-sharing hackers, are more efficient than commercial programmers. Ironically, hackers feel greater 'ownership' over what they coproduce for nothing and give away for free, than do employees paid to produce but whose work is taken from them by their employer.

In terms of production and allocation efficiency, free-sharing out-performs proprietary models in software – as it does also in news and scientific research. Digital copying and circulating of recorded music, live and recorded visual content, and trade and academic publishing too, via free-sharing networks, are far more efficient than traditional physical modes of production and distribution, or dedicated (narrow) commercial broadcast/downloading channels and services that are limited by property-based access restrictions on what is available and who is able to access it.

The Efficacy of Sharing: Fostering Quality and Access

Free-sharing is fundamental to the achievement of the 'common knowledge' that itself enables fair access, informed choice and quality of outcomes. The creation of property rights in information, a pre-condition for selling such information (and hence of markets), does, in the first instance, produce fundamental forms of asymmetry between suppliers and prospective users – summarized in Henry Hansmann's (1980) 'contract failure theory'. Where information is IP-protected, prospective users are denied the free and perfect information required to make optimal selection decisions. Without reasonable knowledge, there can be no reasonable choice. Furthermore, monopoly over informational goods restricts the supply of alternatives, disadvantaging end-users both in terms of immediate prices and, further, in stifling future improvements induced by open cooperation (or competition). Such 'market failure' (Weisbrod 1977) is best solved by the free circulation of information as a 'public good'. Free-sharing of information, in maximizing 'informational efficiency', also leads to optimal efficacy in terms of the quality and availability of outcomes.

Jyn-An Lee (2015) documents the development of non-profit organizations dedicated to the promotion and protection of open-access in the production of informational goods – such as the Free and Open-Source Software (FOSS) movement, the Free Software Foundation (FSF), Creative Commons (CC), Copy Left, The Wikimedia Foundation and the World Wide Web Consortium (W3C). It is not just that open-source software, which is freely available to use and modify without payment or permission, outperforms proprietary code making (Moody 2002); 'common knowledge' as 'shared culture' and 'public good' is the foundation for future works, the means of ensuring user choice – and informed choice at that.

Free-sharing is also essential in the creation of the 'common standards' by which interaction is achieved and transaction costs kept to a minimum via sharing, both of content and format (the MP3 file). Without free-sharing driving forward a common standard, record companies would not have made a deal with iTunes, so even Apple's proprietary service owes its existence to free-sharing's creation of a common standard. The same is also true of today's legal streaming services (Spotify and Beats, for example). Such services seek to tame illegal free-copying by simply copying it – making free access legal only after it became ubiquitous.

Equally, the Internet and World Wide Web (Galloway 2004) are examples of common standards being developed through shared protocols devised by non-commercial expert working groups. The development of digital sports television in the 1990s occurred prior to Internet bandwidth being sufficient to allow users to livestream visual content. Satellite and cable providers used legal monopolies and technical limits to buy up and control access to ever wider domains of formally free-to-air 'terrestrial' sports broadcasting. This was then sold back to fans at ever increasing prices (Millward 2011). Rights revenue escalation has fuelled chronic player salary inflation, leaving around half of clubs in elite leagues technically insolvent, despite the flow of additional money (Bose 2010). At the same time, player inflation does not improve 'play' as it is the same players who simply command more money. Hyper-commercialization may even damage sports if the same super-rich teams can afford to buy up all the best players. It is in this context, alongside increased Internet broadband speeds, that web-based live-streaming channels have risen in popularity; they have cut through legal and technical controls to allow fans access to all matches, in all sports in all leagues (at least if they are being broadcast somewhere) through one platform – and for nothing. Even matches embargoed for paying viewers in home countries at kick-off time are accessible to live-streamers (re-routing content from other jurisdictions). The common platform created by live-streaming channels, alongside the common standards developed by free-sharers in music, the Internet and on the Web, has undone monopoly closure, and so increased transactional efficiency in gaining maximum access and utility (that is, efficacy).

The 'editorial' defence of traditional broadcast and print journalism, that professional and expert newsmakers can do a better job of selecting and packaging events, becomes problematic when such editorial selection has become synonymous with editorial 'bias' in favour of advertiser and proprietor interests (Habermas 1992/1962), and when titles and channels find themselves continually 'behind the curve' (relative to the Internet) in revealing 'scoops'. It is hard to defend 'quality' news production against direct Internet citizen journalism when there is so little quality in evidence. This is compounded by the recurrent use of citizen-uploaded content in commercial media coverage anyway.

Global IP harmonization has seen trade publishing increasingly concentrate ownership into fewer hands and sales into fewer 'big books'. Digital free-sharing offers to liberate reading from such formulaic and cross-media tied-in pot-boilers and repeaters, and instead open up 'the very long tail' of literary creation. The same is true in science, where monopoly control reduces efficacy (quality and overall utility), relative to free-access to both data and publications.

Innovation tends to come from publicly funded 'blue skies' science. While distribution via IP-infringing generic drug manufacture is beyond the scope of free-sharing as such, the free-sharing of scientific knowledge that allows such affordable access to medicine is important. Freely shared knowledge, the foundation of scientific research (Merton 1972/1942), is more efficient and effective in production; and as generic medicines also undermine the market for 'fake' (counterfeit) medicines (a market created by patent monopoly pricing), IP-infringing free-sharing increases efficacy in terms of quality and overall utility (Sen 2012).

The Incentive Structures of Sharing

If creations are freely given away, can there be any incentive to create them in the first place? The answer is yes. In addition, the reduction of opportunity costs incurred by fans (no longer having to balance the cost of recordings against that for concert tickets) means more money being spent on live performance.

The relationship between IP protection (the obverse of free-sharing) and creator exploitation can be seen across the full spectrum of so-called 'creative industries' (O'Brien 2015). Intensified regulation of IP since TRIPS has run alongside the deregulation of employment conditions for those working in the cultural sector. The rise of educational debt, unpaid internships, and temporary/part-time contracts goes hand-in-hand with the non-employment-based contracts exemplified by royalty 'payments' (non-payments, in most cases). IP does not protect or incentivize those working in the 'creative industries'. Rather, it serves the holders of corporate brands, trademarks, copyrights and patents who, while seeking maximum protection and reward for themselves, have pressed for minimum protection and reward for those whose creativity they exploit.

The incentive structure in science is to give knowledge away in order to receive credit as discoverer/innovator (Merton 1972/1942). Charles Darwin's race to publish 'his' theory of evolution arose because if Alfred Wallace had published his parallel account of natural selection first, the epithet 'his' would have gone to Wallace. Scientists are incentivized to publish their results without payment to gain recognition as scientists. The private 'free-riding' (Olson 1965) upon the publicly funded Human Genome Project, by venture-capital-funded genome companies, as discussed in Chapter 7, is only the most high-profile, recent illustration of the problem of commercialized incentives disrupting the free circulation of scientific discovery (Sulston and Ferry 2009). Fortunately, superior public science pre-empted a large number of potential 'patent thickets' by placing knowledge in the public domain, thereby bankrupting many private gene prospectors (Rose and Rose 2012: 183–216).

Academic journal prices rose 10,000 per cent between 1970 and 2016, rising at an average of 13 per cent a year. Free contributions by authors are reviewed free of charge by other academics, and also edited in most cases without payment. The struggle within digital networks between new modes of free and open access and new forms of closure is ongoing (David 1996; Vaidhyanathan 2012).

Since the United States signed the Berne Treaty in 1988, and after TRIPS, global IP protectionism has incentivized the rise of 'big books' (celebrity cookbooks, pot-boilers and repeaters). Horizontal and vertical integration of publishing houses within global cross-media corporations, the outsourcing of new-content-finding to agents who must deliver works that fit the 'big book' frame, and a diminishing market share to those who do not have 'profile' (media presence), 'track record' (past sales), 'comps' (similarity to existing works) or 'fit' (a media marketable 'personality'/'life') means that only a few hundred 'established' and/or corporate-media-'friendly' authors make a living from copyright royalties (Thompson 2012). The majority of 'authors' earn most from work for hire – as journalists, teachers, public speakers, ghost writers – not from royalties. The free distribution of their written work is good publicity for what most of them actually make a living from (Silbey 2015; Liebler 2015). Free-sharing of creative content is also the wellspring for new works, and this is itself a pressing justification for libraries, of freely accessible copies of work – whether housed in stone and paper or circulated via digital networks (Vaidhyanathan 2004). T. S. Eliot suggested that: 'Immature poets imitate, mature poets steal.' Eliot, however, was not the first to say this. He took the line from Mark Twain. Twain was also no slouch when it came to taking good ideas when he found them (Vaidhyanathan 2003). Prior to joining the Berne Treaty in 1988, Twain's United States did not respect the copyright of foreign authors. This explains why Charles Dickens earned more money from speaking tours in America than he did from selling books in his own (copyright-respecting) England (Pearl 2013), paralleling Krueger's (2004) findings regarding music and live performance today.

The willingness to coproduce code for the sake of recognition within a community of creative hackers routinely overcomes silo-based research carried out by 'code-monkeys' and 'micro-serfs' (Coupland 1995), employed to 'create' code, but who are alienated from what they produce. This incentive structure is what Pekka Himanen (2001) calls 'the hacker ethic and the spirit of informationalism', and Johan Söderberg (2008) calls 'play struggle'. IP-rights-fuelled sports star wage inflation has not increased the incentive to 'play' sport, nor necessarily improved 'play'; the incentive of fans to support such 'play' is better served by the shared sense of ownership they hold, in contrast to the hyper-commercial incentives of external investors. Challenging professional journalism citizen witnessing promotes unedited exposure (pleasant or otherwise) in the face of powerful filters and censoring processes.

Sharing's Challenge to the Tragedy of the Anti-Commons

'The tragedy of the anti-commons' occurs in the creation of scarcity itself by means of inefficient forms of distribution based on property rights and market mechanisms, as seen in the inferiority of commercial distribution relative to free-sharing-based access models in music and news, pre- and post-clinical trials, contract failure and market failure in informational goods, a shrinking number of formulaic 'big books', and the commodification of news.

Copyright in recorded music fails to reward artists. The extension of IP protection for global brands, trademarks and copyright holders has gone hand-in-hand with the undermining of earnings, security and incentives for most working in these 'creative industries' – and the outsourced sweatshops that also underpin them. Patenting in scientific research threatens to stifle innovation and limit access to new knowledge-based products, just as copyright control over academic journal articles has enabled chronic 'price gouging' and placed new knowledge beyond most people's reach.

'The tragedy of the commons' myth suggests that property and markets are 'necessary evils', limiting over-use and resource exhaustion, while facilitating efficiency, efficacy and incentives to increase overall utility. As this book has shown, in relation to informational goods, scarcity is the product of market- and property-based restrictions. 'The tragedy of the anti-commons' is that scarcity is only necessary to sustain markets and property rights. Property rights and markets are *not* necessary evils. In truth, 'the tragedy of the anti-commons' lies in the non-necessity of scarcity.

Sharing and the Triumph of the Commons?

Elinor Ostrom's (1990) work on common pool resources, the sharing of rivalrous scarce goods within small-scale communities using non-property based forms of self-regulation, debunks metaphorical overextension of Garrett Hardin's (1968) 'tragedy of the commons' thesis. Similarly, Ostrom's study of free-sharing of non-rivalrous informational goods (Hess and Ostrom 2011) highlights the significance of free-sharing in overcoming 'the tragedy of the anti-commons' (the attempt to lock down research outcomes within various forms of IP control) in large-scale (now global) academic knowledge production communities governed by non-property-based principles of sharing in return for due recognition. In *Sharing: Crime against Capitalism*, I demonstrate the validity of Ostrom's findings within science far beyond just the sphere of academic knowledge sharing, showing the inefficiency caused by patent thickets, 'me too'/copycat pharmaceuticals, conflicts of interest, cost escalations associated with commercially administered clinical trials, secrecy in scientific research (driven by profit motives), and silo-based software coding.

In relation to informational goods, free-sharing undoes 'the tragedy of the anti-commons'. Sharing fosters greater *efficiency* in production and distribution, and, via increased informational and transactional efficiency, higher *efficacy* in terms of utility (quality and overall access), while offering superior *incentives* for creativity and innovation. This is amply demonstrated in the cases of music, journalism, broadcasting, academic and trade publishing, computer programming and scientific/medical research.

In many ways, free-sharing – in reducing costs, increasing quality and widening distribution – creates golden opportunities for innovative businesses. Yet, post-scarcity challenges traditional market- and property-based business models aiming to sell content that is otherwise freely available. Post-scarcity is also a challenge for alternative business models based on selling advertising linked to free content. Advertising revenue is increasingly concentrated in new free-content filtering services (Google, YouTube, Facebook and Spotify), and so is ever more thinly spread elsewhere, as content availability proliferates. Ad-blocker services also diminish viewing levels and, hence, click-through-generated advertising revenues. Old media formats – newspapers, television and academic journals – feed on free content, but are also challenged by new-media channels that provide access to the same content faster, cheaper and more conveniently.

Google, Facebook, YouTube and Spotify exemplify the new breed of free-content access and filtering services. On the one hand, these companies manifest the triumph of free-access over markets and property rights in relation to informational content. On the other, these businesses have found it possible to make money (although in the case of Spotify, not yet a profit). Interestingly, these services replace ownership and selling with forms of accessing and filtering content. They offer management of post-scarcity, not a means for allocating scarce content. What remains scarce is time; and it is time-saving filters, not scarce content allocation, that is valued in these companies. Legitimate concerns exist regarding the potential for distortion in Google's search algorithm (Vaidhyanathan 2012; and Malcomson 2015). However, even Google does not edit content in the traditional 'old' media sense. There is no editorial nexus selecting content to 'fit' market and proprietary interests. While sharing maximizes efficiency in production and allocation, and efficacy in terms of informational and transactional costs, and offers incentive to creative workers, profit can still be made in selling time-saving services. Time remains scarce even as, and perhaps more so because, information becomes less scarce.

Struggles over access remain. Open access in academic publishing is a major concern within universities and beyond. Access to medicine via generic pharmaceuticals is an even more pressing issue, as is access to patented technology essential for sustainable development in the global South (Rimmer 2015). Global media corporations continue to prosecute live-streaming service providers, albeit largely unsuccessfully (David et al. 2017). The law seeks to uphold markets and property rights in informational goods, the latter (property rights) fabricating the scarcity necessary to maintain the former (markets). Whether a post-scarcity economy, one based on free-sharing of informational goods (which will come increasingly to include things fabricated on 3D printers – from medicine to handbags), will continue to be 'capitalist' remains to be seen.

Global Network Capitalism

Conflict over intellectual property intensifies inherent tensions within capitalism between markets and property. What was always a tension becomes a full-blown contradiction when property rights apply not just to individual items but to entire categories, such as is the case with intellectual property. Neoliberalism advances strong global IP regulation even when this enables dominant players to become monopolies (Crouch 2011). In simultaneously promoting global property regulation and labour market deregulation, neoliberalism expands the gap between the retail price and production cost of IP-rich products. Such monopoly conditions create inflated prices that are attractive to IP-infringing pirate capitalists (Rojek 2015). This is a conflict between different modes of capitalism. As each suspends one supposedly essential feature of 'capitalism' (markets or property rights) to profit by the other, this conflict within 'capitalism' does go very deep.

Colin Crouch distinguishes between today's neoliberalism and *ordo-liberalism*. Ordo-liberalism uses regulation to limit the emergence of monopolies to preserve market competition. Crouch offers the example of manufacturing in Germany. The same process can be seen, however, in relation to generic medicines in the policies pursued by developing countries (such as India, South Africa, Chile and Brazil). Suspending patents, and allowing generic manufacture, reduces monopoly prices and drives down the motivation for profiteering counterfeiters. Allowing patented knowledge to be shared by other manufacturers is, again, only an example of enabling capitalist market competition to challenge neoliberal monopoly capitalism. Another example of 'ordo-liberal' market maintenance can be seen in Rupert Murdoch's (after his Fox Network acquired broadcasting rights) pressing for a draft system of selection in American Football's NFL, so that losing teams got first pick of available players in the next season. The draft was designed to prevent the same teams from always winning, a criticism made of English football's EPL, where additional revenues (from Murdoch's Sky collaboration) has seen just such a concentration of money and top players within elite clubs, potentially reducing competition.

Global digital networks allow informational goods to flow beyond just pirate capitalists. Informational content can flow everywhere, to everyone, and for next to nothing. Generic drugs undo the profits of both lawful monopoly patent holders and pirate counterfeiters. Similarly, digital networks undo the monopoly control of publishers, broadcasters, record companies, software businesses and the like. Yet, in the case of copyrighted content, end-users do not need a commercial intermediary to produce the end copy: they can make copies for themselves. While end-users often use commercial hardware, software and networks to access content, they do not have to pay directly for the content. They can share and copy between themselves.

Trademark holders have largely outsourced the production of branded goods to deregulated labour markets in order to reduce cost and thereby increase profit margins. Outsourcing also increases the scope for counterfeit copies. In similar fashion, copyright industries undertook to digitize their production and distribution to increase profits, only to find this made it easier for end-users to bypass them. Again, unlike knock-off handbags and dresses, purely informational content, like music, film, live sports, and software, can be copied for nothing and by anyone with a networked computer. While global network capitalism is riven by its own internal contradictions, a more fundamental contradiction is that between capitalism itself (whether IP monopolist or free-market privateer/pirate) and modes of free-sharing that suspend both property rights and markets.

Power and Counterpower in the Global Network Society

Network power (according to Castells 2009) hinges on the ability to programme and switch. Programming relates to content and switching refers to the ability to link content. As such, network power involves the production of content and its distribution, along with this distribution's control. Power within a network of networks requires not only the ability to make and broadcast content; it also requires the ability to control who has access to that content, whether that be through cross-network deals or in terms of end-user access. However, while Castells offers a valuable account of such communication power within the network society, his account of economic counterpower remains underdeveloped.

For dominant networks of networks to remain powerful, they must constrain various forms of counterpower, attempts to re-programme and counter-switch distribution. Castells offers much detail (2009, 2012) concerning various political and cultural movements that have arisen, in recent years, to question the status quo – in particular, the 'Occupy' movement in North America and elsewhere, the 'Arab Spring' across North Africa and the Middle East, and 'Indignados' (the Indignation Movement) in Spain. He documents how new network affordances allow for political and cultural protest and identity formation through alternative channels of communication (see also Sancho 2014; as well as Guertin and Beuttner 2014).

Yet, while Castells variously mentions digital sharing as a challenge to the logic of dominant business models, this is never developed into an account of economic counterpower in the way he more explicitly deals with the rise of forms of political and cultural counterpower. Given the extent to which Castells's earlier work focused upon the economic uptake of network affordances, and his later attempts to show the integrated nature of economic, political and cultural networks as essential for the understanding and maintenance of power within the network society, it is essential to examine the scope for economic counterpower. It is suggested here that 'sharing' represents just such a mode of economic counterpower, and that it is both viable as an alternative form of economic production and distribution, and significant as a challenge to dominant forms of scarcity-based capitalist economics. Libraries, museums and archives offer one illustration of such a mode of economic counterpower, as does the sharing of music online. Given the centrality of Rupert Murduch's News Corporation to Castells's theorizing of network power, and its centrality to the development of digital sports broadcasting, the challenge of sharing as a mode of economic counterpower is significant because recorded music, film and television, digital sports broadcasting, computer software and publishing are all central to Castells's account of power – but not of counterpower. While Castells has had little to say about genetics or pharmaceuticals, the scope of economic counterpower based on sharing in these domains further illustrates the value of developing his theory of counterpower beyond his own account.

Only a Return – to Advertiser Funding?

The first digital revolution in television (led by live sports broadcasting) took previously free-to-air terrestrial television content and put it behind a firewall that required payment to access. The second digital revolution, whereby streaming services have allowed users to view content freely, does, it might be thought, simply return viewers to where they were a generation ago. In the past, free-to-air terrestrial broadcasting was funded either by advertising or by licence fees. Today, streaming channels are advertiser-funded. Is streaming, then, merely a 'counter-revolution', returning viewers to yesterday's business as usual? In the case of music, the first digital revolution replaced one mode of paid-for content with another (the CD replacing vinyl records and tapes). As such, advertiser-funded digital music services (legal and infringing) may seem only to take music to where commercial television was a generation ago.

Print and broadcast journalism display similar parallels and divergences. The first digital revolution in broadcasting enabled new subscription services. In print journalism, meanwhile, the digital revolution allowed free online access to what was previously only available if paid for (buying a newspaper or magazine). In both cases, 'sharing' news digitally can be a commercial enterprise via advertising revenues. Nevertheless, the digital revolution challenges even that which it has made possible; and free-sharing of news, both in terms of citizen journalism and in the breaching of firewall-protected subscription services, challenges 'business as usual' and creates the expectation that news should be free (both in price and in the suspension of editorial control).

Another substantial challenge to the suggestion that free-sharing is merely a return to yesterday's business as usual is the shift in the relationship between the menu and the meal. Where once the recording was the meal and the live show was a loss-making exercise to promote record sales, now the recording publicizes live performance. While free recorded content acts to promote live concert ticket sales, the free menu for the meal to be paid for does, as a very elaborate(d) form of advertising, also constitute a meal in itself (not just a snippet or taster in the traditional sense of a promotional sample). The appetiser is in itself an 'all you can eat' free lunch. In respect of feature films, meanwhile, free film downloading has increased cinema attendance; for those who cannot afford or access the cinema, however, the film can still be watched in full and for free online. As such, free-downloads and streams fulfil the function of both product and promotion in one.

To the extent that audiences get free access and performers also get better paid, the shift from monopoly control to free access is more than just a shift from one form of capitalism to another. While capitalism remains, the position of performers and audiences, relative to the 'capital' acting as a bridge between them, has changed. Direct producers and end-users are relatively empowered. Sharing is, then, a new and viable form of economic counterpower. Bypassing commercial media intermediaries offers creators and users much more for much less.

The Rise of 'Live': Unmediated Mediation

Free-sharing revalues performance relative to 'capital'. The case of music is the most obvious example, where musicians are better paid from live performance, not only relative to record sales, *but also precisely because record sales are falling*. However, the increased availability of recorded and live-mediated content everywhere shifts economic power to direct performance in many other fields too. In relation to sport, for instance, escalating digital subscription fees has fuelled elite-player inflation, but free-sharing revalues fan engagement. As Castells suggests, the first digital revolution escalated the power of (concentrated) 'elite players' relative to the (marginalized) 'support labour' who were distributed across the whole global network society. This experience was certainly replicated in sport, where traditional fans were increasingly marginaliszed in global digitally marketed and hyper-commercialized clubs and leagues. That streaming has enabled marginalized fans to assert some degree of economic counterpower, relative to 'elite players' (on and off the pitch), gives such fans a capacity to challenge dominant arrangements within 'their' game – something that was denied them in the initial stages of digitisation.

Unmediated media – whether in terms of direct engagement between performers and audiences, between writers and readers, or between citizen journalists and other interested citizens – all increase the capacity for cultural engagement, for shared creativity and for finding direct forms of rewarding creativity. Hacker communities have amply demonstrated the superiority of alternative forms of non-proprietary knowledge production, through encouraging participatory programming and sharing ideas. Similarly, science is premised upon knowledge-sharing. Innovation is best facilitated by direct producers exchanging findings freely between themselves, rather than having knowledge locked down in either copyright- or patent-restricted forms. Merton's 'academic communism' underpins science and works better through the free circulation of formally copyright-protected papers and patented inventions than it does through commercial transactions or formal technology transfer agreements.

Contrary to the claim that free-sharing would lead to a 'tragedy of the commons', unmediated media (in the sense of unregulated access and interaction) has led to new forms of reward and recognition, and the reinvention of traditional modes of valuation – such as actually paying musicians (which record companies rarely did) and other performers via live event ticket sales; peer respect in hacker communities and in science, leading to various forms of material and symbolic reward; and in direct exchange (financial and otherwise) between readers and writers.

The Criminalization or the Colonization of Free-Sharing?

Digital sharing was first identified as a threat to the copyright industries in the mid-1990s, with the revised WIPO Copyright Treaty explicitly noting the novel significance of consumer CD burners. From the late 1990s, an ongoing legal cat-and-mouse battle commenced between copyright holders and online file-sharers. Each legal strategy led to the development of new and more distributed forms of sharing, removing whatever nexus in the exchange process the latest legal strategy was targeting. Technical strategies to defend copyright by means of hard and soft digital rights management have proven equally ineffective in preventing sharing, and have only promoted the development of new modes of hacking hard DRM (i.e., encryption) and of distribution to frustrate soft DRM (i.e., surveillance). To this extent, the criminalization of sharing has been ongoing, but, at the same time, it has also been largely unsuccessful.

The failure to enforce copyright in the face of free-sharing infringement means that free-sharing remains an ongoing 'crime against capitalism'. Failure to prevent such crimes against capitalism is, in part, the result of pirate capitalist enterprises entering the field to profit from the distribution of free content. These are not the traditional pirate counterfeiters, selling physical copies of infringing content, but rather commercial actors generating advertising revenues from the sites to which viewers orient in order to access infringing content.

Other, non-piratical capitalist enterprises have been established to lawfully enable streaming of free content, with advertising funding payments to rights holders (Spotify, Beats and so on). Other lawful network enterprises have successfully generated advertising revenues by drawing users to free search and content providing services (Google and YouTube), and free social networking services where users provide valuable content for nothing (Facebook). These legal providers of free access to content might be seen as evidencing the possibility of post-scarcity capitalism, a colonization of free-sharing within the logic of profit-making (what Chon 2015 calls 'cognitive capitalism'). These businesses make content free but make money from offering access, storage and editing services (their servers being physical machines doing this work in conjunction with physical networks that users are also paying to use). Just as free-sharing revalues live performance (labour), so businesses like Facebook and Google revalue physical capital in the sense of hardware. They do not 'sell' access to their software via copyright either. Rather, they use their own software to undertake searches for and deliver content to users – users for whom it is time, not content, that is scarce. While businesses such as Google and Facebook can flourish in a network ecology based on free-sharing, they don't have the capacity to 'colonize' that network in terms of locking down content in either the proprietorial or editorial senses of that term.

A recurrent danger that can arise from the freely available distribution of certain kinds of digital content is flooding. The availability of free live-streaming makes it hard for commercial competition to eat into the existing market share that Rupert Murdoch's Sky network built up when it had full market and technical monopoly control. Loss of technical control, such as is manifested by live-streaming, has not meant a loss of market dominance, and may have even reinforced it as new commercial players cannot compete with either the existing power, nor a free alternative. As such, a certain form of what Castells calls 'Murdochization' may be sustained even by its own challenger. When counterfeit copies of Microsoft software flooded the developing (and large parts of the developed) world, a similar form of 'Murdochization' might be said to explain why, even in the face of free alternatives, and perhaps even by means of them, Microsoft still dominates the commercial software market in personal computer software. The power of Google and Facebook also lies in their ability to use free access as a means to create and sustain monopolistic positions. Freely shared programmes and platforms can facilitate power, not only counterpower. While free-sharing does challenge capitalism as a system of profit based on property rights, as content can be accessed without payment, some continue to profit, either by continuing to sell access to established users of pre-sharing technologies, or by selling eye-balls to advertisers.

A Gift Economy?

A post-scarcity society, beyond the control of property, law and political power, resembles 'pre-scarcity' societies (Sahlins 1974) – siliconage economics partially reinventing stone-age economics. However, economic anthropologists do not agree on whether non-monetary exchange systems do, or do not, manifest utility-maximizing rational choice behaviour; and social scientists generally cannot agree how far honour, obligation and tradition challenge, or simply manifest differently, utilitarian calculation in 'total services' and 'free markets' (Hann and Hart 2011). While all agreed that 'economic' action is 'embedded' (Polanyi 2001/1944), rescuing a fictional Robinson Crusoe from a mythical island does not predict/explain whether sharing or selling work best, when, or even whether, they are always different or contradictory. Giving always has strings attached (Mauss 1990). What varies lies in whether repayment of debt is direct or indirect, specific or in general, material or symbolic.

This book judges sharing by utilitarian standards: incentive, efficiency and efficacy. Sharing outperforms capitalism by its own standards, but the meaning of a sharing economy remains unclear. 'Sharing' refers to two very distinct forms of gift-giving, as distinct from direct (market) exchange. Economic anthropology helps us clarify these. *Reciprocation* involves the circulation of gifts within a circle of equals. The paradigmatic case is the cycle of Kula gift-giving between the clans of the Trobriand Islands (Malinowski 2002/1922). This circulation of value parallels freely given contributions made by hackers, open-source coders, scientists, musicians, authors and other creative workers within their own communities of coproduction. Without an expectation of direct reward, contributions enable honour and the fulfilment of generalized obligations amongst peers. *Redistribution*-based gift-giving occurs when the 'big man' gives away (or destroys) his 'wealth' and thereby acquires status. For Mauss (1990), 'Potlatch' festivals only become redistributive if their routine function in reciprocation breaks down when there is too much surplus to be repaid. Specific obligations may be cancelled out, but a generalized social obligation and connection is created. Beyond the co-creation of informational goods within a community of reciprocal exchange relations, the free copying of games, software, books, music, articles, scientific and pharmaceutical data, etc., flows out as a form of generalized redistribution to the whole of society. Tomorrow's co-creators are nourished by today's redistribution, and free access creates the fans who both pay for and co-create live performance, just as fan fiction and user-generated content blur the distinction between peer reciprocation and generalized redistribution.

The Kula ring always saw some 'truck and barter' on the side, just as obligatory betting on a kin member's bird in a Balinese cock fight never precluded side betting based on purely instrumental calculations of likely success (Geertz 1972). Freely circulating informational goods increase ticket sales and promote other earning streams; while citations for unpaid articles (and books – fingers crossed) help on promotion panels. However, reciprocal gift 'objects' in pre-monetary societies often included women (Lévi-Strauss 1971), and the development of redistributive gift ceremonies out of purely reciprocal arrangements also mapped the emergence of *tribute* societies based on class hierarchies (Wolf 1982). Pre-capitalist societies should not be romanticized as being more egalitarian than they were. A gift economy based on reciprocation and/or redistribution does not preclude hierarchy based on status even while threatening property. Digital reciprocation better affords innovation, efficiency and efficacy than property rights and markets, even while digital redistribution challenges scarcity. Defenders of property rights and markets claim unregulated 'negative' reciprocity, taking without giving – i.e., theft (Polanyi 2001/1944), will undermine creativity and productivity by parasitizing reciprocal coproduction. This book suggests otherwise. Incentive and access expand, but not all inequalities are suspended.

Sharing: A Crime Against Capitalism

Free-sharing networks challenge capitalism, both as a system of market exchange and as a property-based system for regulating scarcity. The rising significance of non-rivalrous goods within global network capitalism, from purely informational content to physical goods whose primary economic value lies in their informational content, is the key to profitability in the twenty-first century, but also the root of the biggest challenge to such profitability continuing in the long term. The contradictions of globalization, of networks and of capitalism itself fuel this tension between increased scope for profit and increasing scope for free distribution. As this book has shown, free-sharing is more efficient and effective than markets and/or property-based arrangements – and better incentivizes innovation. As such, the potential for a 'triumph of the commons' is very much evident, and it is an expanding potential as the domain of non-rivalrous goods expands with new and faster modes of digital distribution and with the rise of the 3D printer revolution. Maintaining scarcity through property, and in particular through intellectual property, is required to sustain markets and, hence, prices and profit. The artificial manufacture of scarcity is 'the tragedy of the anti-commons'. Free-sharing of informational content can promote the sale of other, more tangible (and hence rivalrous), 'things', from live performances and cinema tickets to the use of expert filtering services. Free-sharing may act as advertising, or as a means to draw attention to sites funded by advertising. This is another route for continued profit-making. However, ad-blockers present a serious challenge to this potential and so offer up a new dimension to the struggle between free-sharing and profit-making, as users of free content-providing services also seek to access that content free of commercial interruptions.

The recorded music industry has been revolutionized. Free access abounds – legal and infringing. Live sports coverage witnesses a stand-off between commercial and free-sharing-based digital revolutions. Publishing (journalistic, academic and trade) experiences similar struggles between paid-for and free access alternatives, as do the domains of software, science in general, and pharmaceutical research in particular. Manual Castells's account of the rise of the network society places emphasis upon the rise of elite players within the global digital field, enabled and empowered by the affordances of distributed network technologies. In this book, *Sharing: Crime against Capitalism*, I have shown how the same networks also afford new forms of economic counterpower. New forces of production (what Castells calls a new mode of development) have not just afforded the rise of a new mode of global digital capitalism and communication power. Digital networks have also been used and developed to create a new, global, digital mode of production and distribution: that of free-sharing. This new mode of economic counterpower interlinks with new and old forms of cultural and political counterpower. As such, free-sharing of informational content today does represent a crime against capitalism – because free-sharing prefigures a way of life beyond capitalism.

References

Abbate, J. (1999) *Inventing the Internet*. MIT Press, Cambridge MA.

Albini, S. (1994) The problem with music, *Maximum Rock and Roll*, 133. http://www.arancidamoeba.com/mrr/problemwithmusic.html.

Allen, S. (2006) *Online News: Journalism and the Internet*. Open University Press, Maidenhead.z

Allen, S. (2013) *Citizen Witnessing: Revisioning Journalism in Times of Crisis*. Polity, Cambridge.

Álvarez, L. (2015) Author and cultural rights: The Cuban case. In David, M. and Halbert, D. (eds.), *The Sage Handbook of Intellectual Property*. Sage, London, pp. 279–299.

Anderson, A., Petersen, A. and David, M. (2004) Source–media relations in science journalism. In Allen, S. (ed.), *Journalism: Critical Issues*. Open University Press, Milton Keynes, pp. 188–198.

Anderson, B. (1983) *Imagined Communities*. Verso, London.

Anderson, C. (2009) *The (Longer) Long Tail*. Random House, New York.

Anderson, C. (2010) *Free*. Random House, New York.

Banerjee, A., Faloutsos, M. and Bhuyan, L. N. (2006) P2P: Is Big Brother watching you? Technical Report. http://www1.cs.ucr.edu/store/techreports/UCR-CS-2006-06201.pdf.

Barnett, E. (2010) Facebook's Mark Zuckerberg says privacy is no longer a 'social norm'. *Daily Telegraph*, Technology section. http://www.telegraph.co.uk/technology/facebook/6966628/Facebooks-Mark-Zuckerberg-says-privacy-is-no-longer-a-social-norm.html.

Barnett, S. (1990) *Games and Sets*. British Film Institute, London.

Barron, A. (2015) Intellectual property and the 'open' (information) society. In David, M. and Halbert, D. (eds.), *The Sage Handbook of Intellectual Property*. Sage, London, pp. 5–27.

Baudrillard, J. (1994) *Simulacra and Simulation*. University of Michigan Press, Ann Arbor.

Bauman, Z. (1989) *Modernity and the Holocaust*. Polity, Cambridge.

BBC (2012) Game sales surpassed video in UK, says report. *BBC Online* (Technology Section), 22 March. http://www.bbc.co.uk/news/technology-17458205.

Beckett, C. and Ball, J. (2012) *Wikileaks: News in the Networked Era*. Polity, Cambridge.

Bell, D. (1976) *The Coming of Post-Industrial Society: A Venture in Social Forecasting*. Basic Books, New York.

Berners-Lee, T. (2000) *Weaving the Web: The Original Design and Ultimate Destiny of the World Wide Web*. Harper Collins, San Francisco.

Bernstein, B. (1970). Education cannot compensate for society. *New Society*, 15(387): 344–347.

Birmingham, J. and David, M. (2011) Live-streaming: Will football fans continue to be more law abiding than music fans? *Sport in Society*, 14(1): 69-81.

Bogard, W. (1996) *The Simulation of Surveillance: Hypercontrol in Telematic Societies*. Cambridge University Press, Cambridge.

Boldrin, M. and Levine, D. K. (2008) *Against Intellectual Monopoly*. Cambridge University Press, Cambridge.

Boliver, V. (2010) Expansion, differentiation, and the persistence of social class inequalities in British higher education. *Higher Education*, 61(3): 229–242.

Boliver, V. (2013) How fair is access to more prestigious UK Universities? *British Journal of Sociology*, 64(2): 344–364.

Bose, M. (2010) The deflating world of English football. *Spectator*, 20 February, pp. 14–15.

Bourdieu, P. (1988) *Homo Academicus*. Stanford University Press, Stanford.

Bourdieu, P. (1992) *Language and Symbolic Power*. Polity, Cambridge.

Bourdieu, P. (1993) *The Field of Cultural Production: Essays on Art and Literature*. Polity, Cambridge.

Braverman, H. (1974) *Labour and Monopoly Capital: The Degradation of Work in the Twentieth Century*. Monthly Review Press, New York.

BPI (2008) *More than the Music: The UK Recorded Music Business and Our Society*. BPI, London.

Brown, I. (2015) Copyright technologies and clashing rights. In David, M. and Halbert, D. (eds.) *The Sage Handbook of Intellectual Property*. Sage, London, pp. 567–585.

Brown, P. (2000) The globalization of positional competition. *Sociology*, 34(4): 633–653.

Buskirk, E. V. (2007) *Comscore: 2 out of 5 Downloaders Paid for Radiohead's 'In Rainbows' (Average Price: $6)*. http://blog.wired.com/music/2007/11/comscore-2-outmusic.html.

Byatt, A. S. (1997) *Unruly Times: Wordsworth and Coleridge in Their Time*. Vintage, London.

Campbell, W. J. (2006) *The Year That Defined American Journalism: 1897 and the Clash of Paradigms*. Routledge, New York.

Castells, M. (1996) *The Rise of the Network Society. The Information Age: Economy, Society and Culture, Volume 1.* Blackwell, Oxford.

Castells, M. (2009) *Communication Power.* Oxford University Press, Oxford.

Castells, M. (2012) *Networks of Outrage and Hope: Social Movements in the Internet Age.* Polity, Cambridge.

Chatfield. T. (2010) *Fun Inc.: Why Games are the 21st Century's Most Serious Business.* Virgin Books, London.

Chon, M. (2015) Slow logo: brand citizenship in global value networks. In David, M. and Halbert, D. (eds.), *The Sage Handbook of Intellectual Property.* Sage, London, pp. 171–188.

Cohen, S. (1972) *Folk Devils and Moral Panics.* Paladin, St Albans.

Coombe, R., Ives, S. and Huizenga, D. (2015) The social imaginary of geographical indicators in contested environments. In David, M. and Halbert, D. (eds.) *The Sage Handbook of Intellectual Property.* Sage, London, pp. 224–237.

Coupland, D. (1995) *Microserfs.* Flamingo, London.

Crichton, M. (2007) *Next.* Harper Torch, New York.

Crompton, M. (1997) *Women and Work in Modern Britain.* Oxford University Press, Oxford.

Crouch, C. (2011) *The Strange Non-Death of Neo-Liberalism.* Polity, Cambridge.

Curran, J. and Seaton, J. (2010) *Power Without Responsibility.* Routledge, Abingdon.

Darch, C. (2015) Politics, law and discourse. In David, M. and Halbert, D. (eds.) *The Sage Handbook of Intellectual Property.* Sage, London, pp. 631–648.

David, M. (1996) Information: Culture or capital? *Radical Philosophy,* 79: 56.

David, M. (1998) Knowledge, information and power. In Kalekin-Fishman, D. (ed.), *Designs for Alienation: Exploring Diverse Realities.* SoPhi Press, Jyvaskyla, pp. 199–213.

David, M. (2001) Lost in cider-space. *Systemica,* 13(1–6): 91–109.

David, M. (2005) *Science in Society.* London: Palgrave.

David, M. (2006) Romanticism, creativity and copyright: Visions and nightmares. *European Journal of Social Theory,* 9(3): 425–433.

David, M. (2010) *Peer to Peer and the Music Industry.* Sage, London.

David, M. (2013) Cultural, legal, technical and economic perspectives on copyright online: The case of the music industry. In Dutton, B. (ed.) *The Oxford Handbook of Internet Studies.* Oxford University Press, Oxford, pp. 464–485.

David, M. (2016) The legacy of Napster. In Whelan, A. and Nowak, R. (eds.), *Networked Music Cultures: Contemporary Approaches, Emerging Issues.* Palgrave, Basingstoke, pp. 49–65.

David, M. and Halbert, D. (2015) *Owning the World of Ideas.* Sage, London.

David, M. and Kirkhope, J. (2004) New digital technologies: Privacy/

property, globalization and law. *Perspectives on Global Development and Technology*, 3(4): 437–449.

David, M. and Kirkhope, J. (2006) The impossibility of technical security: intellectual property and the paradox of informational capitalism. In Lacy, M. and Witkin, P. (eds.), *Global Politics in an Information Age*. Manchester University Press, Manchester, pp. 80–95.

David, M. and Meredith, D. (2016) Book review symposium: Steve Fuller and Veronika Lipinska, *The Proactionary Imperative: A Foundation for Transhumanism*. *Sociology*, 50(3): 614–616.

David, M. and Millward, P. (eds.) (2014) *Researching Society Online*. Sage, London.

David, M. and Whiteman, N. (2015) 'Piracy' or parody. In David, M. and Halbert, D. (eds.), *The Sage Handbook of Intellectual Property*. Sage, London, pp. 451–469.

David, M., Kirton, A. and Millward, P. (2015) Sports television broadcasting and the challenge of live-streaming. In David, M. and Halbert, D. (eds.), *The Sage Handbook of Intellectual Property*. Sage, London, pp. 435–450.

Davies, N. (2008) *Flat Earth News*. Chatto and Windus, London.

Dredge, S. (2013) Thom Yorke calls Spotify 'the last desperate fart of a dying corpse'. *Guardian*, 7 October. http://www.theguardian.com/tech nology/2013/oct/07/spotify-thom-yorke-dying-corpse.

Dutfield, G. (2008) Delivering drugs to the poor: Will the TRIPS Amendment help? *American Journal of Law and Medicine*, 34: 107–124.

Dutfield, G. (2015) Traditional knowledge pharma and patents. In David, M. and Halbert, D. (eds.), *The Sage Handbook of Intellectual Property*. Sage, London, pp. 649–664.

Dutfield, G. and Suthersanan, U. (2005) DNA music: intellectual property and the law of unintended consequences. *Science Studies*, 18(1): 5–29.

Dutton, W. H. (2009) The fifth estate emerging through the network of networks. *Prometheus*, 27(1): 1–15.

Dutton, W., Blank, G. and Groselj, D. (2013) Cultures of the internet: The internet in Britain. *Oxford Internet Institute Report 2013*. Oxford Internet Institute, Oxford.

England, L. (2015) Apple has a playbook for killing free music, and it was written by Steve Jobs. *Business Insider UK*. http://uk.businessinsider.com/how-steve-jobs-killed-free-music-2015-5.

Foucault, M. (2001/1996) *The Order of Things*. Routledge, Abingdon.

Fowler, C. (1994) *Unnatural Selection: Technology, Politics and Plant Evolution*. Gordon and Breach, Yverdon.

Fuller, S. (1997) *Science*. Open University Press, Milton Keynes.

Galloway, A. (2004) *Protocol: How Control Exists After Decentralization*. MIT Press, Cambridge, MA.

Geertz, C. (1972) Deep play: Notes on the Balinese cockfight. *Daedalus*, 134(4): 56–86.

Ghosh, S. (2015) The idea of international intellectual property. In David, M. and Halbert, D. (eds.), *The Sage Handbook of Intellectual Property*. Sage, London, pp. 52–71.

Giles, J. (2005) Internet encyclopaedias go head to head. *Nature*, 438 (December): 900–901.

Giulianotti, R. (2002) Supporters, followers, fans and flaneurs: A taxonomy of spectator identities in FOOTBAEDS.LL. *Journal of Sport and Social Issues*, 26(1): 25–46.

Giulianotti, R. and Robertson, R. (2009) *Globalization and Football*. Sage, London.

Glasgow Media Group (1976) *Bad News*. Routledge, Abingdon.

Gouldner, A. (1976) *The Dialectic of Ideology and Technology*. Macmillan, London.

Granovetter, M. S. (1973) The strength of weak ties. *American Journal of Sociology*, 78(6): 1360–1389.

Guardian (2014) WHO aims for Ebola serum in weeks and vaccine tests in Africa by January, 22 October. http://www.theguardian.com/world/2014/oct/22/ebola-serum-in-weeks-and-west-africa-vaccine-tests-by-january-says-who.

Guertin, C. and Beuttner, A. (2014) Introduction: 'We are the uninvited'. *Convergence*, 20(4): 377–386.

Habermas, J. (1992/1962) *The Structural Transformation of the Public Sphere*. Polity, Cambridge.

Halbert, D. (2005) *Resisting Intellectual Property*. Routledge, Abingdon.

Halbert, D. (2014) *The State of Copyright*. Routledge, New York.

Hall, S., Critcher, C., Jefferson, T., Clarke, J. and Roberts, B. (1978) *Policing the Crisis*. Macmillan, London.

Halsey, A., Heath, A. and Ridge, J. (1980) *Origins and Destinations*. Clarendon Press, Oxford.

Hann, C. and Hart, K. (2011) *Economic Anthropology*. Polity, Cambridge.

Hansmann, H. (1980) The role of nonprofit enterprise. *Yale Law Journal*, 89(5): 835–901.

Hardin, G. (1968) The tragedy of the commons. *Science*, 162(3859): 1243–1248.

Heller, C. (2002) From scientific risk to paysan savoir-faire: Peasant expertise in the French and global debate over GM crops. *Science as Culture*, 11(1): 5–38.

Heller, M. (1998) The Tragedy of the Anticommons. *Harvard Law Review*, 111: 621–688.

Heller, M (2008) *The Gridlock Economy*. Basic Books, New York.

Hauck, D. (2014) Supreme Court hands Monsanto victory over farmers on GMO seed patents, ability to sue. *RT USA*. https://www.rt.com/usa/monsanto-patents-sue-farmers-547/.

Hediger, V. (2005) The original is always lost. In de Valck, M. and Hagener,

M. (eds.), *Cinephilia. Movies, Love and Memory*. Amsterdam University Press, Amsterdam, pp. 135-49.

Hern, A. (2015) Why the term 'sharing economy' needs to die. *Guardian Online*, 5 October. http://www.theguardian.com/technology/2015/oct/05/why-the-term-sharing-economy-needs-to-die.

Hess, C. and Ostrom, E. (eds.) (2011) *Understanding Knowledge as a Commons*. MIT Press, Cambridge MA.

Heylin, C. (2015) *It's One for the Money*. Constable, London.

Heyne, P. (2008) Efficiency. In Henderson, D. R. (ed.) *Concise Encyclopedia of Economics* (2nd ed.). Indianapolis: Library of Economics and Liberty. http://www.econlib.org/library/Enc/Efficiency.html.

Himanen, P. (2001) *The Hacker Ethic and the Spirit of the Information Age*. Secker and Warburg, London.

Hobbes, T. (1991) *Leviathan*. Cambridge University Press, Cambridge.

Holmes, B. (2003) The emperor's sword: Art under WIPO. http://world-information.org/wio/readme/992007035/1078488424.

Hull, G. (2004) *The Recording Industry*. Routledge, London.

Ishiguro, K. (2005) *Never Let Me Go*. Faber and Faber, London.

Jobs, S. (2007) Thoughts on Music, posted 6 February. http://www.apple.com/hotnews/thoughtsonmusic/.

Johns, A. (2009) *Piracy: The Intellectual Property Wars from Gutenberg to Gates*. University of Chicago Press, London.

Jump, P. (2015) Elsevier journal editors 'may be asked to resign' in open access row. *Times Higher Education*, 3 July. https://www.timeshighereducation.com/news/elsevier-journal-editors-may-be-asked-resign-open-access-row.

Kamenetz, A. (2013) Why video games succeed where the movie and music industries fail. *Fast Company*. http://www.fastcompany.com/3021008/why-video-games-succeed-where-the-movie-and-music-industries-fail.

King, A. (1997a) The lads: masculinity and the new consumption of football. *Sociology*, 31(2): 329–346.

King, A. (1997b) New directors, customers and fans: the transformation of English football in the 1990s. *Sociology of Sport Journal*, 14(3): 224–240.

King, A. (2002) *The End of the Terraces*. Leicester University Press, Leicester.

King, E. (2010) *Free for All: The Internet's Transformation of Journalism*. Northwestern University Press, Evanston.

Kirkpatrick, G. (2008) *Technology and Social Power*. Routledge, Abingdon.

Kirkpatrick, G. (2013) *Computer Games and the Social Imaginary*. Polity, Cambridge.

Kirton, A. (2015) Music, technology and copyright: the making and shaking of a global industry. In David, M. and Halbert, D. (eds.), *The Sage Handbook of Intellectual Property*. Sage, London, pp. 586–606.

Kirton, A. and David, M. (2013) The challenge of unauthorised online streaming to the English Premier League and television broadcasters. In

Huchins, B. and Rowe, D. (eds.), *Digital Media Sport: Technology, Power and Identity in the Network Society.* Routledge, London, pp. 81–96.

Kittler, F. (1997) *Literature, Media, Information Systems: Critical Voices in Art, Theory & Culture.* Routledge, London.

Kramer, W. (2015) Outer space, alien life and intellectual property protocols. In David, M. and Halbert, D. (eds.), *The Sage Handbook of Intellectual Property.* Sage, London, pp. 708–726.

Krueger, A. (2004) The economics of real superstars: the market for rock concerts in the material world. Lunchtime speech, 12 April. www.irs.princeton.edu.

Krueger, A. and Connolly, M. (2006) Rockonomics: The economics of popular music. In Ginsberg, V. and Throsby, D. (eds.), *Handbook of the Economics of Art and Culture.* North-Holland, Amsterdam, pp. 667–720.

Lastowka, G. (2015) Copyright law and video games. In David, M. and Halbert, D. (eds.), *The Sage Handbook of Intellectual Property.* Sage, London, pp. 495–514.

Lee, J. (2015) Non-profits in the commons economy. In David, M. and Halbert, D. (eds.), *The Sage Handbook of Intellectual Property.* Sage, London, pp. 335–354.

Leong, S. (2015) Patentable 'invention', difference and harmonization. In David, M. and Halbert, D. (eds.), *The Sage Handbook of Intellectual Property.* Sage, London, pp. 665–684.

Lessig, L. (2002) *The Future of Ideas.* Vintage, New York.

Lessig, L. (2004) *Free Culture.* Penguin, New York.

Lévi-Strauss, C. (1971) *The Elementary Forms of Kinship.* Beacon Press, Boston.

Levidow, L. (2001) Utilitarian bioethics? Market fetishism in the GM crops debate. *New Genetics and Society,* 20(1): 75–84.

Lewontin, R. C. (1993) *The Doctrine of DNA: Biology as Ideology,* Penguin, London.

Liebler, R. (2015) Copyright and ownership of fan created works: Fanfiction and beyond. In David, M. and Halbert, D. (eds.), *The Sage Handbook of Intellectual Property.* Sage, London, pp. 391–403.

Light, D. and Warburton, R. (2005) Extraordinary claims require extraordinary evidence. *Journal of Health Economics,* 24: 1030–1033.

Lippmann, W. (2009/1920) *Liberty and the News.* Dover Publications Inc., New York.

Love, C. (2000) *The Love Manifesto.* http://www.reznor.com/commentary/loves_manifesto1.html.

Lyon, D. (2001) *Surveillance Society.* Open University Press, Buckingham.

McRobbie, A. and Thornton, S. (1995) Rethinking 'moral panic' for multi-mediated social worlds. *British Journal of Sociology,* 46(4): 559–574.

Malcomson, S. (2015) *Splinternet.* OR Books, New York.

Malinowski, B. (2002/1922) *Argonauts of the Western Pacific.* Routledge, Abingdon.

Marshall, L. (2004) *Bootlegging*. Sage, London.

Marx, K. (1995/1867) *Capital: An Abridged Version*. Oxford Paperbacks, Oxford.

Mason, P. (2015) *Post-Capitalism*. Allen Lane, London

Mauss, M. (1990) *The Gift*. Routledge, Abingdon.

May, C. (2007) *Digital Rights Management*. Chandos, Oxford.

May, C. and Halbert, D. (2005) AIDS, pharmaceutical patents and the African state: Reorienting the global governance of intellectual property. In Petterson, A. (ed.), *The African State and the AIDS Crisis*. Ashgate, Burlington, pp. 195–217.

May, C. and Sell, S. (2005) *Intellectual Property Rights*. Lynne Reinner, Boulder.

Merton, R. K. (1968) The Matthew Effect in science. *Science*, 159: 56–63.

Merton, R. K. (1972/1942) The institutional imperatives of science. In Barnes, B. (ed.), *Sociology of Science*. Penguin, London, pp. 65–79.

Millaleo, S. and Cadenas, H. (2015) Intellectual property in Chile. In David, M. and Halbert, D. (eds.), *The Sage Handbook of Intellectual Property*. Sage, London, pp. 130–147.

Mills, C. W. (1959) *The Sociological Imagination*. Oxford University Press, Oxford.

Millward, P. (2011) *The Global Football League*. Palgrave, London.

Millward, P. and Poulton, G. (2014) Football fandom, mobilization and Herbert Blumer: A social movement analysis of FC United of Manchester. *Sociology of Sport Journal*, 31(1): 1–22.

Moody, G. (2002) *Rebel Code: Linux and the Open Source Revolution*. Penguin, London.

Mooney, P. (2000) Why we call it biopiracy. In Svarstad, H. and Dhillion, S. (eds.), *Responding to Bioprospecting: From Biodiversity in the South to Medicines in the North*. Spartacus Forlag, Oslo, pp. 37–44.

O'Brien, D. (2015) Creativity and copyright. In David, M. and Halbert, D. (eds.), *The Sage Handbook of Intellectual Property*. Sage, London, pp. 315–330.

Oguamanam, C. (2015) Farmers' rights and the intellectual property dynamic in agriculture. In David, M. and Halbert, D. (eds.), *The Sage Handbook of Intellectual Property*. Sage, London, pp. 238–257.

Olson, M. (1965) *The Logic of Collective Action*. Harvard University Press, Cambridge, MA.

Op den Kamp, C. (2015) Copyright and film historiography: The case of the orphan film. In David, M. and Halbert, D. (eds.), *The Sage Handbook of Intellectual Property*. Sage, London, pp. 404–417.

Ostrom, E. (1990) *Governing the Commons*. Cambridge University Press, Cambridge.

Pearl, M. (2013) Dickens vs America. *Intelligent Life*. http://moreintelligentlife.co.uk/story/dickens-vs-america.

Phythian-Adams, S. L. (2015) 'The economic foundations of intellectual property': An arts and cultural economist's perspective. In David, M. and Halbert, D. (eds.), *The Sage Handbook of Intellectual Property*. Sage, London, pp. 28–51.

Polanyi, K. (2001/1944) *The Great Transformation*. Beacon Press, Boston.

Qi, L. (2015) Media and Employees' Interpretations to GlaxoSmith Kline's Bribery Scandal in China. MSc dissertation, University of Durham.

Rifkin, J. (2014) *The Zero Marginal Cost Society*. Palgrave Macmillan, New York.

Rimmer, M. (2015) Intellectual property and global warming: Fossil fuels and climate justice. In David, M. and Halbert, D. (eds.), *The Sage Handbook of Intellectual Property*. Sage, London, pp. 727–753.

Robbins, L. (1935) *An Essay on the Nature and Significance of Economic Science*. Macmillan, London.

Rojek, C. (2011) *Pop Music, Pop Culture*. Polity, Cambridge.

Rojek, C. (2015) Counterfeit commerce: The illegal accumulation and distribution of intellectual property. In David, M. and Halbert, D. (eds.), *The Sage Handbook of Intellectual Property*. Sage, London, pp. 189–206.

Rose, J. (1985) Peter Pan, language and the state: Captain Hook goes to Eton. In Beechey, V. and Donald, J. (eds.), *Subjectivity and Social Relations*. Open University Press, Milton Keynes, pp. 250–261.

Rose, H. and Rose, S. (2012) *Genes, Cells and Brains*. Verso, London.

Rossman, G. (2010) Review of *Peer to Peer and the Music Industry: The Criminalization of Sharing* by Matthew David. *Contemporary Sociology*, 39(6): 691–692.

Sahlins, M. (1974) *Stone Age Economics*. Routledge, Abingdon.

Sancho, G. R. (2014) Networks, insurgencies and prefigurative politics: A cycle of global indignation. *Convergence*, 20(4): 387–401.

Sandall, R. (2007) Off the record. *Prospect Magazine*, 137 (August). http://www.prospectmagazine.co.uk/features/offtherecord.

Scudamore, R. (2009) Call it by its name: this is theft. *Guardian*, 23 November. http://www.guardian.co.uk/media/organgrinder/2009/nov/23/creativ-coaltion-digital-bill.

Sen, A. (2012) India, Brazil & China defend generic drugs at WTO. *The Economic Times*, 25 June. http://articles.economictimes.indiatimes.com/2012-06-25/news/32409062_1_counterfeit-medicines-fake-drugs-generic-drugs.

Shiva, V. (1997) *Biopiracy*. Green Books, London.

Silbey, J. (2015) *The Eureka Myth*. Stanford University Press, Stanford.

Smith, P. 2009 Interview: NetResult CEO Christopher Stokes on tackling football TV pirates. https://gigaom.com/2009/09/22/419-interview-netresult-ceo-christopher-stokes-on-tackling-football-tv-pira/.

Söderberg, J. (2008) *Hacking Capitalism*. Routledge, Abingdon.

Srnicek, N. and Williams, A. (2015) *Inventing the Future: Postcapitalism and a World Without Work*. Verso, London.

Sulston, J. and Ferry, G. (2009) *The Common Thread*. Corgi Books, London.

Tapscott, D. and Williams, A. D. (2008) *Wikinomics*. Atlantic Books, London.

Thomas, P. (2015) Copyright and copyleft in India: Between global agendas and local interests. In David, M. and Halbert, D. (eds.), *The Sage Handbook of Intellectual Property*. Sage, London, pp. 355–369.

Thompson, J. B. (2005) *Books in the Digital Age*. Polity, Cambridge.

Thompson, J. B. (2012) *Merchants of Culture*. Polity, Cambridge.

UNESCO (1949) UNESCO Public Library Manifesto 1949. http://unesdoc. unesco.org/images/0011/001121/112122eo.pdf.

Vaidhyanathan, S. (2003) *Copyrights and Copywrongs*. New York University Press, New York.

Vaidhyanathan, S. (2004). *The Anarchist in the Library*. Basic Books, New York.

Vaidhyanathan, S. (2012) *The Googlization of Everything (and Why We Should Worry)*. University of California Press, Los Angeles.

Wall, D. (2007) *Cybercrime*. Polity, Cambridge.

Weber, M. (1930) *The Protestant Work Ethic and the Spirit of Capitalism*. George Allen and Unwin, London.

Weisbrod, B. (1977) *The Voluntary Non-Profit Sector: An Economic Analysis*. Lexington Books, Lexington.

Wolf, E. (1982) *Europe and the People without History*. University of California Press, Berkeley.

Woolgar, S. (1988) *Science: The Very Idea*. Tavistock, London.

Yar, M. (2013) *Cybercrime and Society*. Sage, London.

Young, M. (1958) *The Rise of the Meritocracy*. Penguin, London.

Yu, P. (2015) Déjà vu in the international intellectual property regime. In David, M. and Halbert, D. (eds.), *The Sage Handbook of Intellectual Property*. Sage, London, pp. 113–129.

Zeitlyn, D., Bex, J. and David, M. (1998) Access denied: The politics of new communications media. *Telematics and Informatics*, 15(3): 219–230.

Zeitlyn, D., David, M. and Bex, J. (1999) *Knowledge Lost in Information*. Office for Humanities Communication, London.

Index

Hanita Kosher · Asher Ben-Arieh
Yael Hendelsman

Children's Rights and Social Work

 Springer

Hanita Kosher
Paul Baerwald School of Social Work
  and Social Welfare
The Hebrew University of Jerusalem
Jerusalem
Israel

Yael Hendelsman
Paul Baerwald School of Social Work
  and Social Welfare
The Hebrew University of Jerusalem
Jerusalem
Israel

Asher Ben-Arieh
Paul Baerwald School of Social Work
  and Social Welfare
The Hebrew University of Jerusalem
Jerusalem
Israel

ISSN 2195-9749   ISSN 2195-9757   (electronic)
SpringerBriefs in Rights-Based Approaches to Social Work
ISBN 978-3-319-43918-1   ISBN 978-3-319-43920-4   (eBook)
DOI 10.1007/978-3-319-43920-4

Library of Congress Control Number: 2016948270

Printed on acid-free paper

This Springer imprint is published by Springer Nature
The registered company is Springer International Publishing AG
The registered company address is: Gewerbestrasse 11, 6330 Cham, Switzerland

Foreword

Even though you and I are in different boats, you in your boat and we in our canoe, we share the same River of Life.

—Chief Oren Lyons, Onandaga Nation, USA

The rights of every man are diminished when the rights of one man are threatened.

—John F. Kennedy, Civil Rights Announcement, June 11, 1963

For over a century, social workers have worked to improve the lives and situations of individuals, families, and communities. Social workers, often acting on behalf of the state's interests, typically intervened according to what they themselves perceived to be deficits in the lives and behaviors of persons in need. This approach to working with people patronizes, stigmatizes, and too often revictimizes those we seek to assist. It is long past time to revitalize and reframe our approach to working with those we seek to serve. The books in this series reframe deficit models used by social work practitioners and instead propose a human rights perspective. Rights-based social work shifts the focus from human needs to human rights and calls on social workers and the populations they work with to actively participate in decision-making processes of the state so that the state can better serve the interests of the population. The authors in the series share their strategies for empowering the populations and individuals we, as social workers, engage with as clinicians, community workers, researchers, and policy analysts.

The roots of social work in the United States can be traced to the pioneering efforts of upperclass men and women who established church-based and secular charitable organizations that sought to address the consequences of poverty, urbanization, and immigration. These were issues that were ignored by the public sphere at the time. Little in the way of training or methods was offered to those who volunteered their resources, efforts, and time in these charitable organizations until later in the nineteenth century when concepts derived from business and industry were applied to distribution of relief efforts in what became known as "scientific charity." This scientific approach led to the use of investigation, registration, and supervision of applicants for charity, and in 1877, the first American Charity Organization Society (COS) was founded in Buffalo, New York. The popularity of the approach grew quickly across the country. COS leaders wanted to reform charity by including an agent's investigation of the case's "worthiness" before distributing aid because they believed that unregulated and unsupervised relief led to more calls for relief.

Around the same time, an alternative response to the impact of industrialization and immigration was introduced and tested by the settlement house movement. The first US settlement, the Neighborhood Guild in New York City, was established in 1886, and less than three years later, Jane Addams and Ellen Gates Starr founded Hull House in Chicago, which came to symbolize the settlement house movement in the United States. Unlike the individually oriented COS, the settlement house movement focused on the environmental causes of poverty, seeking economic and social reforms for the poor and providing largely immigrant and migrant populations with the skills needed to stake their claims in American society.

The settlement house movement spread rapidly in the United States and by 1910, there were more than 400 settlements (Trolander 1987; Friedman and Friedman 2006). Advocacy for rights and social justice became an important component of the settlement activities and led to the creation of national organizations like the National Consumers' League, Urban League, Women's Trade Union League, and the National Association for the Advancement of Colored People (NAACP). The leaders of the movement led major social movements of the period, including women's suffrage, peace, labor, civil rights, and temperance, and were instrumental in establishing a federal-level children's bureau in 1912, headed by Julia Lathrop from Hull House.

During this same period, the charity organization societies set to standardize the casework skills for their work with individuals. Their methods became a distinct area of practice and were formalized as a social work training program in 1898 known as the New York School of Philanthropy and eventually, the Columbia University School of Social Work. In 1908, the Chicago Commons offered a full curriculum through the Chicago School of Civics and Philanthropy (now the University of Chicago's School of Social Service Administration) based on the practices and principles of the settlement movement. By 1919, there were 17 schools of social work.

Efforts already underway to secure and strengthen pragmatically derived casework knowledge into a standardized format were accelerated following Abraham Flexner's provocative lecture in 1915 questioning whether social work was a profession because he believed it lacked specificity, technical skills, or specialized knowledge (Morris 2008). By the 1920s, casework emerged as the dominant form of professional social work in the United States and remained primarily focused on aiding impoverished children and families but was rapidly expanding to work with veterans and middle-class individuals in child guidance clinics.

As social work branched out to other populations, it increasingly focused on refining clinical treatment modalities and over time clinical work too often stood apart from community work, advocacy, and social policy. Although social work education standards today require all students to be exposed to clinical and case-work, community practice, advocacy, research and policy, most schools do not prioritize the integrated practice of these areas in the advanced year of social work education (Austin and Ezell 2004; Knee and Folsom 2012).

Despite the development of sophisticated methods for helping others, social work practice overly relies on charity and needs-based approaches. These approaches are built on the deficit model of practice in which professionals or individuals with greater means diagnose what is "needed" in a situation and the "treatment" or services required to yield the desired outcome that has been set by the profession or other persons of advantage. Judgments of need are based on professional research, practice wisdom, and theory steeped in values (Ife 2012). These values, research, theories, and practices typically reflect the beliefs of the persons pronouncing judgment, not necessarily the values and theories of the person who is being judged. This has the effect of disempowering and diminishing control of one's own life while privileging professionals (Ife 2012). In turn, this risks reinforcing passiveness and perpetuating the violation of rights among the marginalized populations we seek to empower and at best maintains the status quo in society.

Needs-based approaches typically arise from charitable intentions. In social welfare, charity-based efforts have led to the labeling of persons worthy and unworthy of assistance, attributing personal behaviors as the cause of marginal-ization, poverty, disease, and disenfranchisement, and restricted the types of aid available accordingly. Judgments are cast by elites regarding who is deserving and who is not based on criteria that serve to perpetuate existing social, economic, and political relationships in charity-based approaches. Needs-based approaches attempt to introduce greater objectivity into the process of selecting who is helped and how by using evidence to demonstrate need and introducing effective and efficient interventions to improve the lot of the needy and society as a whole. Yet the solutions of needs-based efforts like charity-based ones are laden with the values of professionals and the politically elite and do not necessarily reflect the values and choices of the persons who are the object of assistance. Needs-based approaches prioritize the achievement of professionally established goals over the process of developing the goals, and, too often, the failure of outcomes is attributed to personal attributes or behaviors of individuals or groups who receive assistance. For example, the type of services a person diagnosed with a mental disorder receives in a needs-based approach will be often decided by authorities or experts according to their determination of what is best for the person and is likely to assume that a person with a mental disorder is incapable of making choices or at least not "good" choices. Programmatic success would then be evaluated according to adherence to the treatment plan prescribed by the persons with authority in the situation and may omit consumers' objections or own assessments of well-being.

Unlike needs-based and charity-based approaches, a rights-based approach places equal value on process and outcome. In rights-based work, goals are tem-porary markers that are adjusted as people perpetually re-evaluate and understand rights in new ways calling for new approaches to social issues. For example, having nearly achieved universal access to primary education, a re-evaluation of the right to education might lead to a new goal to raise the quality of education or promote universal enrollment in secondary education among girls. Rights-based approaches are anchored in a normative framework that are based in a set of internationally agreed upon legal covenants and conventions, which in and of themselves can provide a different and potentially more powerful approach. A key aspect of this approach posits the right of all persons to participate in societal decision-making, especially those persons or groups whom are affected by the decisions. For example, Article 12 of the United Nations Convention on the Rights of the Child (UNCRC) asserts that states "shall assure to the child who is capable of forming his or her own views the right to express those views freely in all matters affecting the child, the views of the child being given due weight in accordance with the age and maturity of the child" (UNCRC 1989). Likewise, the preamble to the United Nations Convention on the Rights of Persons with Disabilities (UNCRPD) holds states responsible for "redressing the profound social disadvantage of persons with disabilities and (to) promote their participation in the civil, political, economic, social, and cultural spheres with equal opportunities" (UNCRPD 2006).

A rights-based approach requires consideration of the universally recognized principles of human rights: the equality of each individual as a human being, the inherent dignity of each person and the rights to self-determination, peace, and security. Respect for all human rights sets the foundation for all civil, political, social, and economic goals that seek to establish certain standards of well-being for all persons. Rights-based efforts remove the charity dimension by recognizing people not only as beneficiaries, but as active rights holders.

One of the areas of value added by the human rights approach is the emphasis it places on the *accountability* of policy makers and other actors whose actions have an impact on the rights of people. Unlike needs, rights imply duties, and duties demand accountability (UN OHCHR 2002: paragraph 23). Whereas needs may be met or satisfied, rights are realized and as such must be respected, protected, facilitated, and fulfilled. Human rights are indivisible and interdependent and unlike needs that can be ranked, all human rights are of equal importance. A central dynamic of a rights-based approach is thus about identifying root causes of social issues and empowering rights holders to understand and if possible claim their rights while duty bearers are enabled to meet their obligations. Under international law, the state is the principal duty bearer with respect to the human rights of the people living within its jurisdiction. However, the international community at large also has a responsibility to help realize universal human rights. Thus, monitoring and accountability procedures extend beyond states to global actors—such as the donor community, intergovernmental organizations, international non-governmental organizations (NGOs) and transnational corporations—whose actions bear upon the enjoyment of human rights in any country (UN OHCHR 2002: paragraph 230).

Table 1 summarizes the differences between charity-, needs-, and rights-based approaches.

Table 1 Comparison of charity-, needs-, and rights-based approaches to social issues

	Charity-based	Needs-based	Rights-based
Goals	Assistance to deserving and disadvantaged individuals or populations to relieve immediate suffering	Fulfilling an identified deficit in individuals or community through additional resources for marginalized and disadvantaged groups	Realization of human rights that will lead to the equitable allocation of resources and power
Motivation	Religious or moral imperative of rich or endowed to help the less fortunate who are deserving of assistance	To help those deemed in need of help so as to promote well-being of societal members	Legal obligation to entitlements
Accountability	May be accountable to private organization	Generally accountable to those who identified the need and developed the intervention	Governments and global bodies such as the donor community, intergovernmental organizations, international NGOs, and transnational corporations
Process	Philanthropic with emphasis on donor	Expert identification of need, its dimensions, and strategy for meeting need within political negotiation. Affected population is the object of interventions	Political with a focus on participatory process in which individuals and groups are empowered to claim their rights
Power relationships	Preserves status quo	Largely maintain existing structure, change might be incremental	Must change
Target population of efforts	Individuals and populations worthy of assistance	Disadvantaged individuals or populations	All members of society with an emphasis on marginalized populations
Emphasis	On donor's benevolent actions	On meeting needs	On the realization of human rights
Interventions respond to	Immediate manifestation of problems	Symptomatic deficits and may address structural causes	Fundamental structural causes while providing alleviation from symptomatic manifestations

It can be argued that rights-based practice is not strikingly different from the way many social workers practice. For example, the strengths perspective that has become a popular approach in social work practice since the 1990s focuses on strengths, abilities, and potential rather than problems, deficits, and pathologies (Chapin 1995; Early and GlenMaye 2000; Saleebey 1992a) and "interventions are directed to the uniqueness, skills, interests, hopes, and desires of each consumer, rather than a categorical litany of deficits" (Kisthardt 1992: 60–61). In the strengths-based approach, clients are usually seen as the experts on their own situation and professionals are understood as not necessarily having the "best vantage point from which to appreciate client strengths" (Saleebey 1992b, p. 7). The focus is on "collaboration and partnership between social workers and clients" (Early and GlenMaye 2000: 120).

The strengths perspective has provided a way for many social workers to engage themselves and the populations they work with in advocacy and empowerment that builds upon capabilities and more active processes of social change. Indeed, strengths-based and rights-based approaches build upon the strengths of individuals and communities and both involve a shift from a deficit approach to one that reinforces the potential of individuals and communities. Both approaches acknowledge the unique sets of strengths and challenges of individuals and communities and engage them as partners in developing and implementing interventions to improve well-being giving consideration to the complexities of environments. However, the strengths-based perspective falls short of empowering individuals to claim their rights within a universal, normative framework that goes beyond social work to cut across every professional discipline and applies to all human beings. Rights-based approaches tie social work practice into a global strategy that asserts universal entitlements as well as the accountability of governments and other actors who bear responsibility for furthering the realization of human rights.

The link between social work and human rights normative standards is an important one as history has repeatedly demonstrated. In many ways, social work has been moving toward these standards (Healy 2008) but has yet to fully embrace it. Social work has been a contradictory and perplexing profession functioning both to help and also to control the disadvantaged. At times social workers have engaged in roles that have furthered oppression (Ife 2012) and served as a "handmaiden" to those who seek to preserve the status quo (Abramovitz 1998, p. 512). Social benefits can be used to integrate marginalized populations but also be used to privilege and exclude, particularly when a charity-based approach is utilized. When conditional, benefits can also be used as a way to modify behaviors and as a means of collecting information on private individual and family matters.

This contradictory and perplexing role of social work is shown albeit, in an extreme case, by social work involvement in the social eugenics movement specifically promulgated by National Socialists leaders in the 1930s and 1940s (Johnson and Moorehead 2011). Leading up to and during World War II, social workers were used as instruments to implement Nazi policies in Europe. Though the history of social work and social work education is different in each European country, in at least Germany, Austria, Switzerland, Czechoslovakia, and Hungary, authorities used social workers to exclude what the state considered at the time to be undesirable populations from assistance, to reward those who demonstrated loyalty and pledged to carry forth the ideology of the state, and to collect information on personal and family affairs for the state (Hauss and Schulte 2009). University-based and other forms of social work training were closed down in Germany in 1933 when the National Socialists assumed control because welfare was regarded as superfluous and a "waste for persons useless to the national community" (*Volksgemeinschaft* as quoted in Hauss and Schulte 2009, p. 9). "Inferiors" were denied support and social workers were re-educated in Nazi ideology to train mothers on how to raise children who were loyal and useful to the ambitions of the National Socialists (Kruse 2009). Similarly in Hungary, where social workers were referred to as "social sisters," social workers were re-educated to train mothers about the value of their contributions to the state (mainly their reproductive capacity and rearing of strong children for the state) and were instrumental in the implementation of Hungary's major welfare program that rewarded "worthy" clients with the redistribution of assets from Jewish estates (Szikra 2009). As Szrika notes, "In the 1930s social policy and social work constituted a central part of social and economic policy-making that was fueled by nationalist and anti-Semitic ideology, influenced by similar practices in Germany, Italy and Czechoslavakia" (p. 116). Following Nazi ideological inoculation based on eugenics and race hate, social workers in Austria were charged with the responsibility of collecting incriminating information regarding mental illness, venereal disease, prostitution, alcoholism, hereditary diseases, and disabilities that would then be used to deny social benefits, prohibit marriages, and even select children for Austria's euthanasia program (Melinz 2009).

Using social workers to realize state ideology was also employed to advance the Soviet agenda beginning in 1918 (Iarskaia-Smirnova and Romanov 2009). The provision of social services was distributed across multiple disciplines among the helping professions and the term social work was not used because of its association to Western social welfare (Iarskaia-Smirnova and Romanov 2009). These professionals, often referred to as social agents (workers in nurseries and youth centers, activists in women's organizations and trade unions, nurses, educators and domestic affairs officials), were charged with the double task of social care and control. Early on social agents contributed to the establishment of standards designating worthy and unworthy behavior and activities and practices such as censure and social exclusion designed to alienate those who did not comply with state goals (Iarskaia-Smirnova and Romanov 2009).

The use of social workers to carry out goals seemingly in contradiction of social work's ethics can be found in many examples in the United States as well (Abramovitz 1998). In his book, *The Child Savers: The Invention of Delinquency* (1965), Anthony Platt demonstrates that despite well-intentioned efforts to protect youth, the establishment of the juvenile justice system in the United States removed youth from the adult justice systems and in doing so created a class of delinquents who were judged without due process. Platt argues that "child savers should in no sense be considered libertarians or humanists" (Platt 1965, p. 176). The juvenile justice system that these reformers—many of who were social work pioneers—created in the United States purposefully blurred the distinction between delinquent and dependent young people. Labeling dependent children as delinquents, most of whom had committed no crime, robbed them of their opportunity to due process. The state and various religious organizations were given open reign to define delinquency as they saw fit and children who were perceived to be out of order or young women who were viewed as immoral were committed to institutions or other forms of state supervision with no means of redress.

More recently, Bumiller's analysis of domestic violence in the United States rouses our consciousness of the ways in which social workers engaged with persons involved in domestic violence and/or rape may inadvertently squash rather than empower individuals and families (Bumiller 2008). Bumiller (2008) uses sexual violence to demonstrate how lawyers, medical professionals, and social workers may be contributing to passivity of social service beneficiaries and in doing so, enlarge the state's ability to control the behaviors of its members. As Bumiller explains, our public branding of perpetrators of sexual violence as deserving of severe punishment and isolation allow us then to deem them incapable of reha-bilitation, and so we offer few opportunities for perpetrators to rejoin society as functioning members. In contrast, we expend resources toward "treating" victims to turn them into successful survivors and in the process of doing so instill their dependency on the state. We do this by requiring victims who seek support and protection from the state to comply with authorities, which in many cases are social workers, and acquiesce to the invasion of state control into their lives. In return for protection and assistance, needy women and children often relinquish control of their own lives and are forced to become individuals who need constant over-sight and regulation. "As women have become the subjects of a more expansive welfare state, social service agencies have viewed women and their needs in ways that have often discouraged them from resisting regulations and from being active participants in their own decisions" (Bumiller 2008). Some social workers use professional authority to support a deficit approach that allows social workers to scrutinize the parenting skills, education, housing, relationships, and psychological coping skills of those who have experienced sexual violence and then prescribe behaviors necessary to access to benefits. Those who voice complaints and resist scrutiny may be denied benefits such as disqualifying women from TANF benefits who fail to comply with work requirements or cutting off assistance to women who return to violent relationships. As key actors in this process, social workers have the opportunity to legitimize women's voice both within social welfare institutions and within the confines of relationships rather than reinforcing dependency and in some circumstances, revictimizing the individuals by making compliance a prerequisite for assistance.

The commonality of these examples lies in the omission of a normative frame that transcends national borders. The foundation of a rights-based approach is nested in universal legal guarantees to protect individuals and groups against the actions and omissions that interfere with fundamental freedoms, entitlements, and human dignity as first presented in the Universal Declaration of Human Rights (United Nations 1948). International human rights law is based on a series of international conventions, covenants, and treaties ratified by states as well as other non-binding instruments such as declarations, guidelines, and principles. Taken together these inalienable, interdependent, interrelated, and indivisible human rights are owned by people everywhere and responsibility to respect, protect, and fulfill these rights is primarily the obligation of the state.

Bonding social work practice to these international legal instruments obligates social workers to look beyond their own government's responses to social issues, to empower the populations they work with to have their voice heard, and to recast the neglected sovereignty of marginalized individuals and communities. It moves social workers away from being agents of the state to being change agents in keeping with the founding vision of social work. It reunites the different methods of social work practice by obligating all social workers to reflect on how public policies affect the rights of individuals and communities as well as how individual actions affect the rights of others (see Table 2). A rights-based approach compels social workers to look beyond existing methods of helping that too often exist to justify state intervention without addressing the root causes of the situation. It calls upon social workers who often act as agents of the state to acknowledge and act on their responsibility as moral duty bearers who have the obligation to respect, protect, and fulfill the rights of rights holders.

Rights-based approaches in social work have gained international acceptance in the past two decades more so outside of the United States than within. Social

Table 2 Rights-based approaches to social work practice at different levels of intervention

Individuals seeking assistance are not judged to be worthy or unworthy of assistance but rather are viewed as rights holders. Social workers assist others in claiming their rights and helping others understand how individual rights have been violated. Interventions offered are not patronizing or stigmatizing, rather methods provide assistance based on the dignity of and respect for all individuals
Example of individual-centered change: *Sexually trafficked persons are viewed as rights holders whose rights were violated rather than as criminals and are offered healing services and other benefits to restore their wholeness*

Community/group/organization efforts are redirected away from proving that they deserve or need a resource toward learning about how they can claim their entitlements to resources. Social workers facilitate human rights education among group members including knowledge of human rights instruments, principles, and methods for accessing rights
Example of group-centered change: *Groups are offered opportunities to learn about their housing rights, the change process in their community and learn skills so that they can claim their right to participation in community decisionmaking*

Society redirects its social policies and goals to facilitate the realization of human rights including addressing human needs. Macropracticing social workers affect the policy process and goals by expanding means for all members of a society to have their voices heard in the decision-making process
Example of society-centered change: *Persons with disabilities are able to participate in the policy-making process through the use of technology that allows them to participate in meetings from their homes*

workers in the United States are relatively new to human rights practice, in part because of longstanding resistance known as "American exceptionalism" which allows the United States to initiate and even demand compliance of human rights abroad while repeatedly rejecting the application of international standards for human rights in the United States (Hertel and Libal 2011). Most Americans are knowledgeable about civil and political rights, yet far fewer are as familiar with economic, social, and cultural rights. Relatively limited engagement in this area by social workers also stems from the perception that human rights activism is best led and achieved by lawyers or elite policy advocates. The books in this series are written to facilitate rights-based approaches to social work practice both in the United States and around the world and recognize that exposure to human rights multilateral treaties and applications may vary depending on where the reader was educated or trained.

A rights-based approach brings a holistic perspective with regards to civil, political, social, economic, and cultural roles we hold as human beings and a more holistic understanding of well-being that goes beyond the meeting of material needs. Our understanding of human rights is always evolving, and our methods, practices, research, interventions, and processes should evolve as our understanding deepens. The purpose of this series is to assist social work practitioners, educators, and students toward operationalizing a new approach to social work practice that is grounded in human rights. It is hoped that the books will stimulate discussion and the introduction of new methods of practice around maximizing the potential of individuals, communities, and societies. The books, like social work, reflect the wide range of practice methods, social issues, and populations while specifically addressing an essential area of social work practice. By using current issues as examples of rights-based approaches, the books facilitate the ability of social workers familiar with human rights to apply rights-based approaches in their practice. Each book in the series calls on social work practitioners in clinical, community, research, or policy-making settings to be knowledgeable about the laws in their jurisdiction but to also look beyond and hold states accountable to the international human rights laws and framework.

Fordham University, New York, NY   Shirley Gatenio Gabel

References

Abramovitz, M. (1998). Social work and social reform: An arena of struggle. *Social Work, 43*(6), 512–526.

Austin, M. J., & Ezell, M. (2004). Educating future social work administrators. *Administration in Social Work, 28*(1), 1–3.

Bumiller, K. (2008). *In an abusive state: How neoliberalism appropriated the feminist movement against sexual violence*. Durham: Duke University Press.

Chapin, R. (1995). Social policy development: The strengths perspective. *Social Work, 40*(4), 506–514.

Early, T., & GlenMaye, L. (2000). Valuing families: Social work practice with families from a strengths perspective. *Social Work, 45*(2), 118–130.

Friedman, M., & Friedman, B. (2006). *Settlement houses: Improving the welfare of America's immigrants.* New York: Rosen Publishing.

Hauss, G., & Schulte, D. (Eds.). (2009). *Amid social contradictions: Towards a history of social work in Europe.* Opladen, Farmington Hills, MI: Barbara Budrich Publishers.

Healy, L. M. (2008). Exploring the history of social work as a human rights profession. *International Social Work, 51*(6), 735–746.

Hertel, S., & Libal, K. (2011). *Human Rights in the United States: Beyond Exceptionalism.* Cambridge.

Iarskaia-Smirnova, E., & Romanov, P. (2009). Rhetoric and practice of modernisation: Soviet social policy (1917–1930). In G. Hauss & D. Schulte (Eds.), *Amid social contradictions: Towards a history of social work in Europe.* MI: Barbara Budrich Publishers.

Ife, J. (2012). *Human rights and social work: Towards rights-based practice.* Cambridge: Cambridge University Press.

Johnson, S., & Moorhead, B. (2011). Social eugenics practices with children in Hitler's Nazi Germany and the role of social work: Lessons for current practice. *Journal of Social Work Values and Ethics, 8*(1). http://www.jswve.org

Kisthardt, W. (1992). A strengths model of case management: The principles and functions of a helping partnership with persons with persistent mental illness. In D. Saleebey (Ed.), *The strengths perspective in social work practice.* New York: Longman.

Knee, R. T., & Folsom, J. (2012). Bridging the crevasse between direct practice social work and management by increasing the transferability of core skills. *Administration in Social Work, 36,* 390–408.

Kruse, E. (2009). Toward a history of social work training Germany—discourses and struggle for power at the turning points. In G. Hauss & D. Schulte (Eds.), *Amid social contradictions: Towards a history of social work in Europe.* MI: Barbara Budrich Publishers.

Melinz, G. (2009). In the interest of children: Modes of intervention in family privacy in Austria (1914–1945). In G. Hauss & D. Schulte (Eds.), *Amid social contradictions: Towards a history of social work in Europe.* MI: Barbara Budrich Publishers.

Morris, P. M. (2008). Reinterpreting Abraham Flexner's speech, 'Is social work a profession?' Its meaning and influence on the field's early professional development. *Social Service Review, 82* (1), 29–60.

Platt, A. M. (1965). *The child savers: The invention of delinquency.* Chicago, IL: University of Chicago Press.

Saleebey, D. (1992a). Introduction: Beginnings of a strengths approach to practice. In D. Saleebey (Ed.), *The strengths perspective in social work practice.* New York: Longman.

Saleebey, D. (Ed.). (1992b). *The strengths perspective in social work practice.* New York: Longman.

Szikra, D. (2009). Social policy and anti-semitic exclusion before and during WW II in Hungary: The case of productive social policy. In G. Hauss & D. Schulte (Eds.), *Amid social contradictions: Towards a history of social work in Europe.* MI: Barbara Budrich Publishers.

Trolander, J. A. (1987). *Professionalism and social change: from the settlement house movement to neighborhood centers, 1886 to the present.* New York: Columbia University Press.

United Nations. (1948, December 9). *Convention on the prevention and punishment of genocide.* Retrieved from http://www.ohchr.org/EN/ProfessionalInterest/Pages/CrimeOfGenocide.aspx

United Nations. (1989, November 20). *Convention on the rights of the child.* New York: United Nations. Retrieved from http://www2.ohchr.org/english/law/pdf/crc.pdf

United Nations Office of the High Commissioner for Human Rights (UN OHCHR). (2002). Draft
    Guidelines for a Human Rights Approach to Poverty Reduction Strategies 2002.
United Nations. (2006, December 13). *Convention on the rights of persons with disabilities*.
    NewYork: United   Nations.   Retrieved   from   http://www2.ohchr.org/english/law/pdf/
    disabilitiesconvention.pdf

Contents

Introduction

Recent years have witnessed a substantial increase in social and public commitment to the notion of children's rights. After centuries of ignoring children's rights and of children being treated as property and as objects, in the last century children gradually began to gain the status of human beings entitled to rights and dignity. The increased international awareness of children's rights is expressed in the United Nations Convention on the Rights of the Child (CRC). The principles and values of the CRC have had a remarkable impact on the status of children around the world, particularly on social policy, legislation, institutions and services for children.

The idea of children's rights has had considerable influence on professions involved with children, such as social work, and on organizations and institutions in the field of child welfare. Child welfare services have been required to adopt new approaches suitable to the new status of children in society as persons with human rights. Similarly, the social work profession now faces demands to consider children's rights in its practices, values and principles.

Social work's roots and principle combine well with the notion of human rights and, indeed, the pioneers of social work were leaders in promoting and protecting human rights (Healy 2008). Numerous national and international documents containing the definition, values and code of ethics of social work show that human rights have always been part of the social work mission. And, social workers are by definition "human rights workers", whose role is to help people realize their individual as well as collective rights.

Similarly, the connection between the social work profession and the idea of children's rights originated in the 19th century with the start of the profession. At that time social work strongly influenced the children's rights movement, with social workers at the forefront of efforts to recognize children as worthy of rights and to protect children from abuse in the workplace. The best evident for it is the involvement of social workers in the efforts leading up to the Convention on the Rights of the Child (Healy 2008). Because of this, the social work profession has an historic commitment to protect children through efforts to ensure their safety and healthy development. Thus, children are an important group of social work service users and social workers are key players in the lives of children and their families. Today, if the social work profession wishes to fulfill its duty and responsibilities of child care and protection, it is essential that the social work profession embrace a core principle of child welfare—the notion of children's rights.

The influence of social work on the children's rights movement is not uni-directional, as children's rights have also contributed greatly to the social work profession. A children's rights-based approach provides a conceptual framework, as well as specific strategies and opportunities for social workers. They must respect and protect children's rights at all levels of practice, from working with individual children to working with broader systems to influence public policy.

The purpose of this publication is to show how children's rights can contribute to and influence social work. Human rights, as well as children's rights, are most commonly seen as the concern of lawyers and those working in international bodies like the United Nations. Social work is left behind. This essay thus attempts to highlight the natural connection between social work and children's rights. It also aims to emphasize the special role of social workers in promoting children's rights, as well as in implementing children's rights in their everyday practice.

After introducing the connection between social work and human rights, (Chap. 1), Chap. 2 delves into the concept of children's rights, its history in human development and its typology and various aspects. Chapter 3 deals with the connection between social work and children's rights, the history of social work with children and children's rights in social work today. Chapter 4 deals directly with implications for practice, focusing on rights-based approaches for working with children and on implementing children's rights to participation in social work practice. The final chapter discusses how the children's rights concept can influence social work research.

At the end of each chapter is an exercise box, whose exercises aim to help students and other readers to practice and further discuss the ideas presented in each chapter.

Chapter 1
Social Work and Human Rights

The Concept of Human Rights

Children's rights theory and practice are based on a broader understanding and interpretation of general theories about human rights, therefore we first provide a general review of the concept of human rights. Human rights are considered to be a new and modern concept and one of the most powerful ideas in contemporary discourse (Ife 2012). At the most basic level, human rights are those rights that belong to all just because we are human (Healy 2008). This is based on the understanding that all people are inherently and naturally equal and deserve fundamental rights, such as social and civil rights (Ife 2012). Human rights are in essence justified claims. Having rights is meaningful only if there is someone who has the duty to fulfill them (Ladd 2002).

It is common to consider human rights as having developed in three waves or generations. According to Ife (2012), **first generation rights** are civil and political rights, like the right to vote, freedom of speech, freedom from discrimination, fair trial, etc. They are individually based and concern the fundamental freedoms seen as essential to the effective and fair organization of democracy and civil society. First generations rights are sometimes also referred to as negative rights, rights that need to be protected rather than realized, rights that people are seen as somehow possessing and the state is required to ensure that they are not threatened or violated. They are often also defined as natural rights, meaning rights human beings possess or inherit as part of the natural order (Ife 2012).

Second generation rights are economic, social, and cultural rights, like the right to health, housing, social security, education, etc. These are rights of the individual or group to receive various forms of social provision or services in order to realize their full potential as human beings. Rather than arising from 18th century liberalism, second generation rights have their intellectual origin more in the 19th and 20th century with the tradition that the collective, in the form of the state, should provide for the needs of the individual, at least at a minimal level. These rights are

© The Author(s) 2016
H. Kosher et al., *Children's Rights and Social Work*,
SpringerBriefs in Rights-Based Approaches to Social Work,
DOI 10.1007/978-3-319-43920-4_1

referred to as positive rights because they imply a much more active and positive role for the state. Rather than simply protecting rights, the state is required to take a stronger role in actually ensuring that these rights are realized through various from of social provision (Ife 2012).

Ife broadened the conceptualization of human rights even further and suggested **third generation rights**. These rights emerged only during the last three decades of the 20th century in response to the critique of human rights as being overly individual and based on Western liberalism and therefore of less relevance to cultures with more collective norms. The third generation rights are thus collective rights. These involve rights that are only meaningful if defined at a collective level; they are the rights of a community, population, society or nation, rather than being readily applicable to an individual. Such rights include the right to economic development, the right to benefit from world trade and economic growth, the right to live in a cohesive and harmonious society, and environmental rights, such as the right to breathe unpolluted air, the right to access to clean water, etc. Third generation rights represent an important arena for the human rights struggle and a significant arena for debate (Ife 2012).

Human rights have now become a significant notion integrated into many discourses, affecting laws, political institutions, science, research, universities, bureaucracy, military strategy, schools and more. As this idea integrated into the everyday life of the individual and in the human service professions, it began to merge into social work ideas. Yet, social work originally emerged from what today are known as human rights ideas (Ife 2012). To fully understand the beginning of the social work profession let us look at the processes that led to its formation.

Human Rights and Social Work: An Historical Point of View

Human rights are most commonly seen as the concern of lawyers and those working in international bodies like the United Nations, leaving the social work profession in the shadow. Nevertheless, the strong connection between social work and human rights should not be underestimated, noting the essential role of social workers as advocates of human rights for their clients at the level of the individual, family, and community (Calma and Priday 2011). Social work was extensively involved in human rights in its formative years and can claim important areas of leadership, especially before the UN Declaration of Human Rights in 1948 (Healy 2008).

To understand the historical role of social work in the promotion of human rights we must elaborate on the social problems which emerged in the 19th century in the Western world. From approximately 1780–1830 the West experienced the Industrial Revolution which caused massive changes in society. Urbanization and industrialization changed the basis of family structure from a dependence on the family household garden or farm to dependence on factories, paid work and the economic market. Increasing urbanization resulted in massive new problems of poor sanitary conditions and diseases that spread throughout the cities, causing families now living in large cities to struggle to survive and sustain themselves (De Vries 1984). These social changes led to "new" social problems, which increased and became more common, spreading among different groups within the society, such as extensive child labor, poor sanitation, urban epidemics, child assault and exploitation, criminality and prostitution (Hart 1991).

The social problems emerging from the Industrial Revolution in the 19th century formed the basis for social work itself. At that time in England and the US it was not called social work, rather it was considered and referred to as charity. Yet, it was a broad and diverse activity that included many areas today considered the core of social work, like advocacy, policy change and supporting individuals and groups who were excluded and weak within the general society. In the reality of the problems of the early 19th century—rapid urbanization, poorly built urban housing, poor sanitation and no regard for human rights or the people's wellbeing—the social work profession arose as a completely new approach (Skehill 2008), in which social workers became and remained active in international and social justice issues concerning issues of human rights (Reichert 2011).

In the early 20th century the founders of the social work profession were involved in the significant human rights movements of their day (Healy 2008). These first social workers were actually volunteers, upper class women with affluent backgrounds willing to devote a portion of their lives to the service of others. Some of these women realized the difficult everyday reality only through their first encounters with impoverished working-class life. Powerful voluntary organizations emerged—Prison Discipline Society, Anti-Slavery Society, the Vice Society, and many others (Hill and Aldgate 1996). In addition, in response to social ills of the time two social movements in social welfare—the Charity Organization Societies (COSs) and the Settlements House establishments arose in the 19th century and shaped the development of the profession of social work. The COS workers, with their emphasis on the needy individual and the combination of "scientific" record-keeping and friendly visiting, were the forerunners of social caseworkers (Healy 2001).

Some of the central leaders and founders of social work were human rights' advocates (Healy 2008). Women's issues, world peace and the labor conditions of the early 20th century were concerns at the international level, and members of the new profession of social work were active in each of the related social movements (Healy 2001).

Jane Addams, one of the founders of modern social work, expressed human rights ideas without using the concept itself. In her work at the Settlement Houses in the USA she socialized with the poor who struggled in their everyday life. She saw the inequality and lack of opportunities and she encouraged women who had the economic and social ability to act to help those in need. She wrote many times about the basic rights of each individual in society, she shared her thoughts on welfare services and their necessity in order to provide each individual the option to do better in his or her life. She referred to the democratic structure of the state and society and drew a direct line between that and the individual, basic rights (Freedberg 2009; Reichert 2011). The content of Addams' words is mostly identical to today's concept of human rights.

Jane Addams was at the forefront of the struggles for women's suffrage, immigrant education, health care, children's rights, housing, peace, and progressive education. She helped organize a number of national and international human rights organizations, including the American Civil Liberties Union (ACLU), the National Association for the Advancement of Colored People (NAACP) and the Women's International League for Peace and Freedom. Jane Addams is thus a symbol of the strong and initial connection between social work values and the concept of human rights.

Joining Jane Addams in these international human rights movements was **Sophonisba Breckinridge**, a US social work pioneer, who was treasurer of the Women's Peace party in 1915 and part of the women's peace delegation to The Hague in 1915. She was particularly active in international child welfare movements of the 1920s and 1930s. **Julia Lathrop and Grace Abbott** were also colleagues of Addams in the USA, who served on League of Nations human rights committees. Grace Abbott led the efforts of the League Committee on Trafficking Women and Children and served as the first US delegate to the International Labor Organization. **Alice Salomon**, championing women's rights, was founder of social work and social work education in Germany and first president of the International Association of Schools of Social Work. **Eglantyne Jebb** founded the Save the Children Fund in England. She moved from her early experiences with a charity organization to become a pioneer of children's rights. She wrote the first Declaration of the Rights of the Child in 1923, adopted by the League of Nations in 1924 as the Declaration of Geneva.

All these examples indicate that social workers were familiar with human rights concepts and used human rights language long before the UN Declaration of Human Rights in 1948 (Healy 2008; Reichert 2011). Social work also strongly influenced the children's rights movement, with social workers at the forefront of the earlier struggles to recognize children as worthy of rights and to protect them from abuse in the workplace. The efforts of social workers to protect children led to the establishment of government agencies and an array of laws and special services in most countries. Also, social work was strongly involved in the efforts leading to the Convention on the Rights of the Child (Healy 2008).

Although the social work profession began to examine human rights issues in the early 1900s, its involvement slowed or even stopped with the World War II (Reichert 2011). Active collaboration with the Nazi-controlled government in Germany is certainly the darkest episode in social work history. But, it should be noted that there were also many instance of positive, even heroic, efforts by European social workers (Healy 2008). After World War II social workers again started to play a role in the human rights movement of the time. This is clearly evident in the goals of the profession which were defined then, many of these goals stemming from human rights concepts (Reichert 2011). Over the years social work has continued to develop and become increasingly focused on the advancement of society's excluded groups and has taken on the role of promoting rights and advocacy for those who need it. Nevertheless, it seems that this aspect of modern social work has not gained the appropriate recognition, and external recognition of the contributions of social work remains limited (Healy 2008).

In summary, social work is based on human rights ideas, its pioneers were leaders in promoting and protecting human rights and there is an ideological and historical connection between social work and human rights. Yet, today the connection between social work and human rights has become obscure, as this area is now usually considered more a legal than a social one.

Ethics and Values in Social Work

The claim that human rights is a part of the social work mission (McPherson and Abell 2012) is evident in national and international documents on the definition, the values and the code of ethics of social work. The **International Federation of Social Work (IFSW)** declared that the principles of human rights are the core of the definition of social work (Hare 2004). From the late 1980s **IFSW** adopted a strong programmatic focus on human rights; through case advocacy, policy and member education, the federation is making an impact in this important arena (Healy 2001). The **International Association of Schools of Social Work (IASSW)** claims that: "Principles of human rights and social justice are fundamental to social work" (IASSW 2004, p.1). **The National Association of Social Workers (NASW)** writes that "human rights and social work are natural allies" (NASW 2009) and that the struggle for human rights remains a vital priority for the social work profession in the twenty-first century (Reichert 2011). Moreover, the **United Nations (UN)** has identified social work as a "crucial profession" in the promotion and protection of human rights (UN, Center for Human Rights 1994, p. iii; McPherson and Abell 2012). **The Global Agenda for Social Work and Social Development** (which is a combination of IASSW, IFSW and the International Council of Social Welfare) states that social work must "... seek universal implementation of the international conventions and other instruments on social, economic, cultural and political rights for all peoples, including, among others, the rights of children, older people, women, persons with disabilities and indigenous peoples..." (Global Agenda 2012, p. 3).

Human rights are also evident in the professional codes of ethics (Ife 2012). The **IFSW Statement of Ethical Principles** states in Article 3 that social workers should take into account International Conventions: "1.3 International human rights declarations and conventions form common standards of achievement, and recognize rights that are accepted by the global community." (http://ifsw.org/policies/statement-of-ethical-principles/). The code of ethics of **NASW** states that "... social workers will pursue social change, particularly with and on behalf of vulnerable and oppressed individuals and groups of people. ... social workers will strive to ensure equality of opportunity and meaningful participation in decision making for all people." We can clearly see that in these two statements alone social work ethics are directly linked to human right values (Ife 2012). According to the code of ethics, it lies within the responsibility of each social worker to trace and advance those whose basic rights (human rights) are unfulfilled.

Although this deep moral connection between social work and human rights is clear, the social work profession is not widely regarded as a leader within the global human rights movement (Healy 2008). Healy explains that the limited visibility of social work in the global human rights movement is due to: (1) the profession's emphasis on social and economic rights, rather than on civil and political rights that command more public attention; (2) the focus on vulnerable and socially excluded groups and not on the rights of all populations; (3) social work has a preference for the case approach rather than macro issues, which are more related to human rights; (4) the strict observance of confidentiality impeding use of cases to serve the wider cause; (5) social workers usually pay more attention to human needs than to human rights; and (6) the lack of sustained global leadership on human rights by the organizations representing the profession.

Social Work Practice and Human Rights

Nevertheless, human rights are very important for the human service profession, particularly for social workers. It has long been argued that human rights offer a normative base for social work. Ife (2001, 2012), at the forefront of connecting human rights and social work, argues that human rights provide social workers with a moral basis for their practices at all levels-individual, community-based and social policy and advocacy practices. Social workers often deal with vulnerable and marginalized populations and with those whose human rights are violated. Therefore, human rights are not only an academic or political concept for social workers; rather they are grounded in the practice of the profession (Ife 2012).

As noted in this chapter it is common to consider human rights as having developed in three waves or generations. Ife (2012) argues that this construction of human rights provides a useful framework for thinking about the place of social work practice with a human rights agenda. Social work practice can be seen as applying to all three generations. Realizing first generation rights—civil and political rights—in social work practice means advocacy either on behalf of individuals or disadvantaged groups. Some social workers play an important role in working for the protection of civil and political rights through work with advocacy groups, work with refugees, prison reform, attempting to secure adequate legal representation for people, etc.

Working to realize second generation rights—economic, social and cultural rights—involves helping clients realize their most basic rights, like the right to education, health care, housing, income, and so on. In fact, this is the main job of social workers; most, if not all, social workers are concerned with helping people realize second generation rights. Every time a social worker helps a client obtain income support or find accommodation, or refers them to a community health centre for physical, social, or emotional support, they are engaging in a form of human rights work.

Third generation rights, collective rights, intersect perfectly with the social work practice of community development. Community development is a way of working with, rather than for, communities to increase their capacity and ability to find their own solutions to problems. This community work is a minor aspect of social work in many Western countries or it is even defined as outside the concern of social work (Calma and Priday 2011; Ife 2012).

Reichert (2011) argues that the social work profession has developed interventions that are closely tied to human rights. First, there are interventions that aim to assist individuals and to bring about change with respect to social problems. Social workers have traditionally considered the oppressed and marginalized as their core focus. They are responsible for challenging individuals and social relations that create and maintain oppression. Second, another intervention used by social workers is that of empowerment, which is related to human rights. This intervention examines circumstances contributing to differential treatment with respect to ethnicity, age, class, national origin, religion, gender and sexual orientation. Third, the strength perspective is another social work intervention closely related to human rights, which require a focus on individual or group strength in order to help and assist. This intervention acknowledges that structural injustices have isolated many individuals and groups from necessary resources.

Academics also recognize the role of social work role in advancing human rights (McPherson and Abell 2012). This is evident in many publication in the field of social work and human rights (for example, Healy 2008; Healy and Link 2012; Ife 2001, 2012; Witkin 1998; Mapp 2008; Reichert 2003, 2007). A significant accomplishment was the publication of a manual on human rights and social work in the early 1990s by the UN, in collaboration with IFSW and IASSW. The document states:

> Human rights are inseparable from social work theory, values and ethics, and practice … Advocacy of such rights must therefore be an integral part of social work, even if in countries living under authoritarian regimes such advocacy can have serious consequences for social work professionals (United Nations Center for Human Rights 1992, p. 10).

Exercise Box 1

1. It is common to refer to three generations of human rights. Look for three case studies in your country or on the international level in which human rights have been violated. Each case study should express a different generation of human rights. Explain which right in the case is being violated. Relate your answer to the typology of the three generations of rights.

2. Find the code of ethics of social work in your own country. Analyze and discuss how the human rights discourse has influenced and is expressed in this code of ethics.
3. Social work and the human rights movement have a long and strong mutual relationship. Please outline at least three contributions of the social work profession to the human rights movement and three contributions of the human rights movement to the social work profession.

Chapter 2
The History of Children's Rights

Historical Perspective

The discourse on children's rights is relatively new, even within the modern human rights discussion. Not long ago it seemed absurd to talk about children's rights; the concept of children's rights gained widespread support only in the last few decades. Not only are children's rights relatively new ideas, but the very concepts of childhood and the child are relatively recent achievements (Hart 1991). Today, children's rights are a serious social issue (Chirsholm cited in Alaimo 2002).

Like the concept of childhood, the history of children's rights has been shaped by changing economic, social, cultural and political circumstances (Alaimo 2002). It is common to address three periods in the evolution of the concepts of children's rights—the pre-industrial period, the industrial period and from the mid-20th century to the present.

The Pre-industrial Period

Prior to the 16th century there appears to have been no conception of childhood as a unique or distinct period of life. Most children beyond six years of age were considered to be small adults and were not separated from adults as a class (Aries 1962; Hart 1991). Children were considered legally and socially as the property of their parents; they were not seen as human beings with their own status and rights (Hart 1991).

Even up to the first quarter of the 19th century children were mostly still viewed as the personal property or extensions of their parents with few or no legal rights whatsoever (Stier 1978). Parents, mainly fathers, were given unlimited power and control over them and were allowed to treat them as they wished; corporal punishment was almost universal and was accepted as appropriate.

© The Author(s) 2016
H. Kosher et al., *Children's Rights and Social Work*,
SpringerBriefs in Rights-Based Approaches to Social Work,
DOI 10.1007/978-3-319-43920-4_2

During the early period of modernization infant and child mortality was very common—one of four children died before their first birthday, making child mortality the most common cause of death (Hart 1991). Many historians argue that this high mortality was one of the causes for the emotional distance of parents from their children. They claim that parents suppressed the ability to feel empathy for their children to avoid emotional attachment to a baby with a low chance of survival (Aries 1960; deMause 1974). Adults were not expected to have close relationships to children and could be cruel and distrustful towards them. Many children were unwanted and negative parent-child relationships led to serious abuse and neglect (deMause 1974; Hart 1991; Stone 1977). Children had more duties towards their parents and society than they had rights (Alaimo 2002). They were characterized by a lack of identity and were considered expendable (Hart 1991). The poor status of children in society created a situation, in which they were neglected, abused and sold as slaves and were invisible in the eyes of society.

Child labor was a widespread phenomenon in the pre-industrial period and children were a significant part of the economic system all over the world (Hart 1991). Until and during the 19th century children over six years old were perceived as young adults and were therefore required to contribute to society according to their abilities. From about the age of 7 they began a slow initiation into the world of work, a world inhabited by both adults and children. Children as young as four and five could already be working in the factories, and at least some of the child laborers did not work with their families (Alaimo 2002). The concepts of education, schools, protection against hazards and special rights were rare or non-existent (Hart 1991).

The Industrial Period (the 19th Century up to the Mid-20th Century)

The technological and socioeconomic changes of the early 20th century resulted in a change in the conceptualization of childhood. Children were considered to be endangered by conditions of immigration, industrialization and urbanization in ways that would create undesirable behavior and threaten society (Hart 1991). This brought about a new agenda in regard to children's status and led to the emergence of the idea of protecting children and providing them rights.

The main development in children's rights arose in connection with industrial child labor (Alaimo 2002). Child labor began to be perceived as a social problem due to the fact that children were now recognized as a vulnerable group all over the Western world. They were working under hazardous conditions and were at risk, not only physical and life threatening risk, but also of moral damage (Hart 1991). Factory work was physically exhausting for children as young as seven years old, who worked sixteen hours a day in a damp, poorly ventilated workplace and corporal punishment was common. Foremen used harsh method to keep exhausted children awake. In addition, working in a factory, unlike at the family farm or craft shop, exposed the children to large numbers of strangers who might molest and corrupt them (Alaimo 2002).

The child labor reform movement, based on the view of child laborers as defenseless victims of industrialization, launched an eventually successful campaign to regulate and ultimately eliminate industrial child labor. The 19th century movement against child labor and in favor of child schooling was a significant shift in thinking, helping to bring about a key transformation in the conception of childhood and in the formulation of children's rights. The child labor reform movement opened a public discussion about the social meaning of childhood, specifically opening the door to the radical reform that perhaps children should not work at all and that they have the right to different childhood—one of physical, moral, intellectual and social development (Alaimo 2002).

Schooling became an alternative model of social existence for children, when the protection rights—laws against industrial child labor—were joined to provision rights—entitlement to education (Alaimo 2002). Life in cities brought crime, poor conditions of hygiene that led to the spreading of diseases, and the development of social alienation. Schools were considered a way of isolating children from all of these issues. It was further feared that working children would become adults lacking necessary education and who would be intellectually and morally hampered (Archard 1993).

Laws controlling child labor and the introduction of universal education in the 19th century recognized the need for children's protection and acknowledged that they had rights. As school gradually took the place of work, and regular schooling became compulsory (around 1900 in Europe), the attitudes toward the place and role of children also changed. Childhood could last longer and children could be seen as more dependent (Hill and Aldgate 1996).

The 19th century is considered the "child-saving" era. Particularly in the half-century from 1870 to 1920 the rights of children in relation to parents, employers and others expanded in the form of rights to protection and services that presupposed a vision of childhood as a distinctive phase under the patronage of the state (Alaimo 2002). Gradually, children began to be perceived as a separate class and not as property. The perception that children have no more than economic value began to change and be replaced by the concept that children are a unique group that society has the responsibility to maintain and protect from various dangers to which this group is exposed (Hart 1991).

Another change in this period is the protection of children from abuse and neglect by their parents. Parental neglect and abuse were subjected to intense scrutiny and challenged, not only by private philanthropies, but increasingly by government authorities. The state also increasingly challenged parental authority and autonomy in child rearing. In 1889 both France and Great Britain passed laws against child endangerment, including that caused by their parents (Alaimo 2002). The state with its professionals became the guarantor of children's rights. The child's right to protection led to the child's rights to provision of various sorts, with the state responsible for providing services. Health, care, acceptable housing, playgrounds, together with freedom from work and access to public schooling emerged as elements of children's rights (Alaimo 2002).

The 20th century became the period when legislation concerning children was introduced in many countries. This was frequently introduced in connection with child labor and education, but also to acknowledge a public responsibility toward orphans and other destitute children. By the end of the 19th century, life for most children was more than just a mere struggle for survival. Hence, the 20th century was characterized by concern and efforts to establish and formulate children's right to nurturance. After centuries of being dismissed, ignored, manipulated and looked upon as "objects", children were finally granted legal recognition as "persons" (Cohen 2002).

However, despite the worldwide recognition of children's rights, this approval of children's rights was based on the view of children either as passive, weak, and vulnerable creatures, and therefore in need of protection, or as unruly and threatening and therefore in need of control (Hallett and Prout 2003). Children were perceived as "becoming human" and were not yet recognized as full human beings with freedoms (Alaimo 2002).

Society was mostly concerned with children's protection and provision rights. Much attention was paid to children's physical survival and basic needs, focusing often on threats to children's survival. Such social perceptions spurred programs to save children's lives or supply their basic needs. Infant and child mortality, school enrollment and dropout rates, immunizations, and childhood disease are examples of areas in which these programs arose (Archard 1993; Brandon et al. 1998). Safeguarding and protecting children gave rise to a dependent childhood, highly regulated by adult guardians and characterized by children's loss of autonomous action. While these policies were important for saving children, they deprived children of the rights of self-determination.

Society adopted the concept of "saving children" and this idea continued to grow well into the 20th century. This concept became even more meaningful as children began to be perceived as the resources of the future. Society understood that, in their adulthood, today's children will determine the future of the world. Thus, not only are adults responsible for saving and protecting the child from a variety of hazards, but they are also required to take care of the positive aspects of the child's life for the sake of future generations. These ideas and changes created the new perception of a "person in the making" (Ben-Arieh et al. 2014).

It was only in the second half of the 20th century that the child's existing status, rather than the potential person, received concrete support. The emerging person status of children provided justification for rights to protection and for the first time also for self-determination.

Liberalism and Romanticism

Changes in the status of children cannot be attributed solely to the social and economic changes in the 19th century. Some streams of philosophical thinking emerging in the 17th and the 18th century also contributed to generating the notion of children's rights. From the 17th–19th century numerous Enlightenment thinkers focused on childhood education and how children learn. Indeed, the 18th century showed the emergence of a pronounced sensitivity to childhood, with a clear articulation of childhood as a distinct stage of life with its own ethos and in need of its own institutions. The Enlightenment's attention to the development of the individual child was an important milestone leading to the 20th century concept of the rights of the child (Ladd 2002).

John Locke (1632–1704), the founding philosopher of English liberalism, published his famous book "*Some Thoughts Concerning Education*" in 1663. This had a significant influence on how children were conceptualized in the 17th century. One of his core ideas was that the child is born a "blank slate" without innate ideas and that all knowledge comes from experience. Based on this idea, he argued that education is a powerful tool to shape the child. This was a groundbreaking way of thinking and it contributed to the idea and to the importance of children's right to education. Locke appeared to recognize the individuality of each child, arguing that parents and educators need to treat children as rational creatures. He rejected corporal punishment as inappropriate to the raising of a wise and good child.

Locke's thinking marks an important shift in the conceptualization of childhood in the West (Alaimo 2002). In spite of this great contribution, we should bear in mind that Locke's viewpoint was limited; he was primarily concerned with the adult in the future and not with the child in the present.

Another important philosopher on the path to children's rights was Jean-Jacques Rousseau (1712–1778), who, particularly in "Emile" (1762), associated children with nature and natural goodness. He implied that children have a right to a happy childhood, characterized by freedom and closeness to nature and saw childhood as an innocent, carefree and happy period of life. Reacting to Lock's assertion that the child is a rational creature, Rousseau stressed that children should be children before they are adults and that childhood has its own methods of seeing, thinking and feeling. He was genuinely concerned with the process of growing up.

Rousseau's ideas, which are considered pre-romantic, were later endorsed by the Romantic Movement, which took up this theme of children's original innocence. The Romantics proclaimed childhood as the best part of life and attributed qualities of purity and innocence to the child. The British Romantic poets, such as Wordsworth and Coleridge, saw children as innocents gradually corrupted by society (Cunningham 1995). Ironically, this idealization of childhood coincided with the emergence of the first industrial societies which encouraged the exploitation of children. Nevertheless, the Romantic conception of childhood, derived from Rousseau, greatly contributed to the nation of children's rights (Alaimo 2002).

The Middle of the 20th Century to the Present

Throughout the first half of the 20th century the concept of children's rights still embodied the idea of a child's right to protection against harm and access to certain basic entitlements, such as schooling and health care. A noticeable change in the thinking on children's rights occurred in the second half of the 20th century, with a shift from issues dealing solely with children's protection or nurturance rights to those dealing with children's right to self-determination or self-expression. Increasing awareness of children's rights to participation (Ruck and Horn 2008) have led to a global move toward giving children and adolescents a greater degree of autonomy in the decisions affecting their own lives and development (Cherny and Shing 2008). This new approach is based on the assertion that children are not property of their parents or the state, but are legal persons entitled to many of the same rights as adults (Peterson-Badali et al. 2004; Peterson-Badali and Ruck 2008). Worldwide focus shifted to struggles over how to develop a framework that would allow active child participation in civil society (Cohen 2002).

In a landmark decision for children (in re Gault 1967) the U.S. Supreme Court noted that, "...neither the Fourteenth Amendment nor the Bill of Rights is for adults alone" (p. 13). Two years later the court noted that "children are 'persons' under the Constitution (Tinker v. des Moines Independent Community School District 1969), and almost a decade later, the Supreme Court stated, "Constitutional rights do not mature and come into being magically only when one attains the state defined age of majority" (Planned Parenthood v. Danforth 1976, p. 5204). Thus, after centuries of being dismissed, ignored, manipulated, and looked upon as "objects", children were finally granted legal recognition as "persons".

Today the status of children (globally and in the Western world) is better than ever, their rights are detailed and implemented by governments in various countries, allowing children a childhood that is protected and separated from the adult world. Note that most of the rights are still related to child protection; children are still not fully accepted as active participants in their own lives.

The various rights and limited freedoms given to children clearly do not exactly correspond to the myriad of rights given to adults (Hart 1991). Even if children are considered 'equal', they may still not receive the attention or the respect for their dignity and integrity which are accorded to adults. Hitting a child is legal in most countries, while hitting an adult may lead the offender to prison. Working conditions for adults are secured by law—not so for children. Even in schools, where the children vastly outnumber the adults, there are rarely rules applying to the "working conditions" of the pupils. As a general rule, when children do have legalized rights, these are indirect, in the sense that others (most often the parents/guardians) have rights on behalf of the child, and even explicit rights are conditional or controlled by others.

International Treaties and Conventions on the Rights of the Child

In the aftermath of the First World War the protection-provision view of children's rights expanded into the international arena. In 1924, Eglantyne Jebb, founder of Save the Children International, persuaded the League of Nations to adopt **the Declaration of Geneva on Children's Rights**. This declaration is short, containing only 5 statements but these provide a concise list of what society "owed the child" and established the notion that children should have certain types of "rights". They were not rights to "do" or to "act" independently as individuals. Instead they were rights to "receive" in the form of things that should be done for the child.

The Second World War brought a new wave of interest in children's well-being. In 1959 the United Nations General Assembly accepted the **Declaration of the Rights of the Child**, asserting that each child has a right to a "happy childhood". This declaration is also still characterized by the provision-protection view of children's rights based on the assumption of childhood dependency and vulnerability. Its language reflects the then prevailing concept of children as "objects" in need of "services"; in other words, it did not mention or support the child's individual rights to participation (Cohen 2002).

In 1979 the UN designated the International Year of the Child to celebrate the twentieth anniversary of the 1959 declaration. As part of the celebration writing a new treaty for children's rights was proposed. Although drafting was begun that year, the convention was not completed until ten years later in 1989. The UN General Assembly adopted the **Convention on the Rights of the Child** (CRC) on November 1989. The text is reprinted in Appendix.

The CRC was adopted unanimously. In spite of possible negative reactions, a large majority of the nations of the world have now ratified the CRC, signifying that they subscribe to and will defend the rights of the child (Hart 1991). Outlining children's political, civil, social, and economic rights (Ruck and Horn 2008), the CRC is the most comprehensive international convention, and addresses a full range of rights for children (Ben-Arieh 2005). It particularly emphasizes children's rights in relation to decision-making processes that concern their lives (Kirk 2007; Melton 2005; Munro et al. 2005).

The CRC has been a record breaker in every sense of the word. Cohen (2002) noted its unique aspects: first, on the day of its signing ceremony in 1990, the Convention was signed by the greatest number of signatories to ever sign a human rights convention. Second, the convention went into force faster than any previous human rights treaty. Third, it achieved universal ratification by 1997, making it the most ratified of all human rights treaties. Finally, it is the only human rights treaty to combine civil/political, economic, social, cultural and humanitarian rights in a single instrument.

The CRC affirms not only the child's right to protection from harm and abuse, but also the right to childhood, to develop into an autonomous adult, and to have a voice in matters affecting and concerning the individual child (Alaimo 2002).

The CRC highlights that the child is a human being with the right to be respected as a unique individual with his/her own perspective and personal intentions by fellow human beings and also by the state, its institutions and other organizations (Krappmann 2010).

Typologies of Children's Rights

Because there are so many substantive articles covering so many types of rights, there have been numerous efforts over the years to cluster the articles and categorize them (Cohen 2002). Contemporary literature on children's rights identifies several categories and typologies of children's rights. One of the most popular children's right typologies discusses four categories or principles derived from the 54 articles of the CRC: non-discrimination; the best interests of the child; the right to life, survival and development; and participation rights.

The right to life, survival and development—children have the inherent right to live, and the state has an obligation to ensure the child's survival and development. This group of rights deals with rights to health, education, social security, as well as the right to a standard of living. It also includes the right to be protected from abuse, neglect and any form of exploitation;

Non-discrimination rights—This principle asserts the state's obligation to protect children from any form of discrimination and to take positive action to promote their rights, meaning that all rights apply to all children without exception;

The best interests of the child—according to this principle all actions concerning the child should take full account of his/her best interests;

Participation rights—Nearly a quarter of the substantive articles deal with participation and self-determination rights, assuring access to information, freedom of movement, association, belief and expression, privacy, liberty and development toward independence.

Another popular typology found in the contemporary literature of children's rights is known as the **"three Ps"**: Protection, Provision and Participation rights (Lansdown 1994; Troope 1996).

Provision rights—The CRC includes articles outlining young people's right to the adequate provision of services and resources to enable children to develop their abilities (Ruck and Horn 2008). The CRC calls for fullest provision, which refers to rights to necessary goods, services and resources, including standard care, health, care review when looked after, the right to an adequate standard of living, to education and childcare, to cultural life and to the arts, and to know about the CRC;

Protection rights—This category includes the right to be protected from neglect, abuse, exploitation, violence, cruel and degrading treatment, discrimination, invasion of privacy, exploitation and hazardous work, armed conflict, invasive research and ecological changes.

Participation rights—This principle, as noted above, refers to the right of children to be respected as active members of and contributors to the family, community, and society from their first years (Alderson 2008).

Another accepted typology is **nurturance rights versus self-determination rights**. The nurturance orientation entails the provision and protection by society of rights that are beneficial to children (e.g., right to education). In contrast, the self-determination orientation focuses on children's right to have some measure of control over their own lives (e.g., the right to choose their own religion) (Horn and Ruck 2008).

The nurturance orientation is based on the paternalistic assumption that society or the state ascertains what is in the best interest of the child. In contrast, the self-determination orientation is based on the child's decision of what is or is not in the child's own best interest or within its own personal prerogative (Rogers and Wrightsman 1978; Walker et al. 1999). This distinction underscores some of the tensions inherent in children's rights. For example, if adults take responsibility for protecting children, does this not potentially limit the children's freedom? (Alaimo 2002). Provision and protection rights enjoy wide support, but participation rights are more controversial.

More marginal approaches to children's rights relating to the two orientations are the **protective approach** and the **liberal approach**. The protective approach is based on the assumption that children require care and need to be protected from abuse and exploitation. That is, this approach is based on views of children as innocent and immature and is often regarded as a paternalistic model. By alleging that children are not rational, not capable of making their own decisions, liable to make mistakes and vulnerable, it justifies adult control and interference in children's lives (Archard 1993; Barnes 2009; Clifton and Hodgson 1997). The protectionist model denies children any voice in their lives and deprives them of their self-determination and participation rights (Barnes 2009).

The liberal approach to children's rights challenges the protectionist perspective, advocating an extreme position on children's rights. In line with other marginalized or minority groups championed in the 1970s, such as women and black people, children are regarded as an oppressed group. Farson (1974) and Holt (1975) advocated that children should have the same rights, privileges and responsibilities as adults if they so wish. This includes the right to vote, to live away from home and to manage their own education at whatever age. They argued that the segregated world of children and adults is discriminatory.

Exercise Box 2

1. Choose a book or a movie recounting children's lives during a historical period (e.g., a classic, like Charles Dickens' books, or a more modern work). Analyze the concept and status of the child that emerges from the work you have chosen, and discuss the rights that are given or withdrawn from children.

2. Look for an article in current newspapers dealing with the case of a child or children. Analyze the concept and status of the child that emerges from it, and discuss the rights that are given or withdrawn from children in the article.

3. Read the Convention of the Rights of the Child (Appendix). Choose three rights from the Convention: (1) The right that, in your opinion, is the most important for children's lives and well-being. Explain your choice. (2) A right that is most frequently withdrawn from children in your county. Support your answer with data and other sources. (3) A right that, in your opinion, is missing from the CRC. Explain your answer.

4. The Convention has four core principles. Please note an example for a violation of a right in regard to each principle that is relevant to your country. Please explain your answer and demonstrate your claims.

Chapter 3
Social Work and Children's Rights: A Theoretical and Ethical View

The History of Social Work with Children

From its beginnings as a profession in the early 20th century, social work has been strongly involved with children and families (Petr 2004). Children have remained an important group of social work service users and social workers are key players in their lives and those of their families.

The social work profession has an historic commitment to protecting children through its comprehensive efforts to ensure their safety and protect them from abuse in various practice settings, as well working to ensure their healthy development (Reichert 2011; Tilbury 2013). For many years the social work profession has focused on children's welfare, offering them protection and provision, while almost ignoring them as independent human beings and ignoring their participation rights. Today the social work profession is undergoing a rapid change, as social workers are required to take the status of children into account as subjects and as active agents. This means that social workers should view children as human beings in the present and not as becoming human in the future. The intervention of social workers with children, therefore, not only aims to ensure that children have a better future as adults but that children have a better life in the present. This brings complex challenges to a profession which has mainly focused on an agenda of protection and provision. The evolution of practice and policy for working with children in social work is discussed below.

Protection and Provision

Throughout its history, social work has clearly viewed children's rights as related to protection and provision. The dominant concern of social work organizations was originally to 'save' children so that they could enjoy a childhood. All the voluntary

© The Author(s) 2016
H. Kosher et al., *Children's Rights and Social Work*,
SpringerBriefs in Rights-Based Approaches to Social Work,
DOI 10.1007/978-3-319-43920-4_3

societies in the profession's early days operated to keep children out of bad environments, away from potentially harmful parents and other adult influences and to provide them with a good or new start where they could become children (Brandon et al. 1998).

During the 19th century, societal efforts on behalf of children and families focused on dependent and neglected children (Petr and Spano 1990). The period from the last third of the 19th century to the outbreak of the First World War was characterized by the forming of a large number of voluntary organizations and child rescue organizations working in parallel to cope with the abandoned, orphaned or deserted children of the urban working class or those with 'unfit' parents. There was also a large but uncoordinated sector of voluntary charities dedicated to child welfare (Brandon et al. 1998). All these organizations shared elements of the child rescue mission, most were founded by social activists (Skehill 2008). Thus, in its early days social work took upon itself to protect and defend children as a vulnerable group and represent them in the social structure (Ife 2001).

Until the 19th century Western world the family was regarded as the responsibility of the parents, thus there was minimal intervention in the family. It was only toward the end of the 19th century that laws across the Western world began to place the child's welfare before the conduct and wishes of its parents (Brandon et al. 1998). Between approximately 1870 and 1940 important markers were laid down in statute and in practice indicating a greater involvement of the state in the lives of disadvantaged or neglected children. The capacity of the state to remove a child from unfit parents was established, as was the state's power to regulate adoption activities (Skehill 2008).

Public attitudes towards child abuse changed, with concern growing, not just about infanticide, but also about the practices of neglectful families and the need to ensure that working-class children were raised as responsible citizens. A major example of this change were the laws empowering courts to issue warrants for any person to enter premises to search for a child, if that child was likely to be suffering unnecessarily, and to take the child to a 'place of safety'. These Acts also empowered courts to give custody of a child to a relation or other 'fit person' (Hill and Aldgate 1996). As it was thought that parents should build their children's characters, it followed that the parents of children with character flaws were unworthy parents who had no moral right to rear their children. By the 1920s, social work with children and families rested on this strong moral foundation that criticized and blamed parents for the maladies of their children (Petr 2004). It was assumed that the best interests of the child could be assured only by professional experts whose scientific training in emerging personality theories and child development qualified them to choose and monitor the type and quality of care for the child. Even today many professionals see themselves as the experts who best know what is in the best interests of the child and many professionals refuse to consider the strengths and competencies of the child itself (Petr 2004).

The response to dependent and needy children was thus to target the children themselves. Social work offered children and youth rehabilitation based on discipline and structure that were provided in institutions. These separated the child from the negative influences of its family and larger environment (Ehrenreich 2014). This approach led to the proliferation of large institutions whose purposes were to discipline, control, and reform troubled youth (Petr 2004).

In summary, since its beginnings, the social work profession took upon itself to ensure children's welfare by adopting a 'child rescue' model (Ehrenreich 2014). Although such interventions clearly promoted the children's rights, these efforts were mostly directed towards rescuing and protecting children and not at ensuring their rights. Throughout the history of the social work profession children were regarded as powerless victims of abuse and neglect or as objects that must be removed from their potentially harmful parents, and professionals were seen as the experts in the child's best interest. This mission of safeguarding children was intensively developed and became a dominant aspect of social work practice with children.

Social work was further characterized by supervision with a strongly authoritarian aspect. The child was seen as a passive, weak creature lacking any life-capabilities and therefore in need of maximum protection. There was a tendency to compare children at risk to animals in danger, revealing a one-dimensional and limited conception of the child. Social workers, who took upon themselves to protect weak and needy children, treat children in a very protective and paternalistic fashion, ironically excluding them from their own life decisions (Brandon et al. 1998; Hart 1991).

The profession clearly did not consider the children as subjects, as individuals with self-determination rights. Only towards the end of the 20th century did the idea of children's participation rights begin to be expressed in social work practice and policy.

Every Child Matters

Social work as a profession has never experienced so many changes or seen so many new and rapid developments in policy and practice as in the last decades. These changes have been particularly important in the field of child and family welfare. The renaissance in child care policy and practice has been dictated by political factors, societal pressures and general dissatisfaction with how cases of presumed child abuse were dealt with. A fundamental review was required to strike a balance between protection and prevention, to address a lack of involvement by parents in decision making about their children, and to ascertain why a growing number of children were entering the care system (Iwaniec and Hill 2000).

During the second half of the 20th century new theories appeared, especially theories of child development, such as Bowlby's attachment theory and Anna Freud's stages theory. This research hugely influenced social work practice with children, particularly affecting assessments of child–parent relationships and decisions on whether children should be placed in long-term fostering or adoption.

The understanding that the child has special and different needs from those of adults now became the basic concept of the social work profession and the number of social workers focusing on children's care greatly increased. Social work was no longer concerned only with removing children from their environment or viewing reception into care as an irrevocable step after which a permanent substitute home had to be found, as in the past. Now it became clear that children needed to maintain some link with their natural parents. Helping parents visit children placed some distance from their home became one of the social worker's chief tasks (Ben Arieh 2010).

Children and childhood have now become the target of massive interventions, with whole armies of health and social workers working to modify childhood. The concept of children's needs—derived from professionals' concepts, assumptions, priorities and goals—justifies interventions, including the education of mothers, health promotion and social work practice (Woodhead 1997). Yet, even these new directions and theories of childhood have predominantly conceptualized children as passive recipients of care, placed in the private sphere. Models of childhood still tended to take parental attitudes and adult ideals as their starting point (Hinton 2008).

The Late 20th Century to the Present—Children as Autonomous Persons

During the last two decades the focus of social work with children has shifted from children's need for protection to children's right to participation and their wishes for independence and legal autonomy. Basically, children are now eligible to more rights, rights that used to belong only to adults. The protective approach to child-based practice has been supplemented with the promotion of the rights of children to participate in decisions affecting their lives. There has been a move towards treating children as people and not as objects of concern (Brandon et al. 1998).

Recent years have further brought into focus the rights of children to self-determination, self-expression and participation (Peterson-Badali and Ruck 2008). The CRC emphasizes the importance of enabling children to express their opinions on important matters, particularly to express their opinions and to be actively involved in decision-making processes that affect their lives and in all matters concerning them, including in the social services arena (Sofer and Ben-Arieh 2014; Alderson 2008; Ruck and Horn 2008).

In the social services in the Western world, children are now recognized as independent beings with their own interests that need representation and also consultation. Realizing children's participation rights requires different principles and tools from the social worker than does realization of children's protection and provision rights. Practice methods have been developed to encourage social workers to take a much more active role in helping children express their inner feelings (Brandon et al. 1998; Iwaniec and Hill 2000).

Theoretical approaches have also influenced this shift in focus, mainly through the development of theories on childhood based on the children's perspective and on perceiving young people as independent 'social actors', beings who, like adults, should be regarded as autonomous (Dalrymple 2005).

One of the most deeply influential theoretical developments on how children are viewed is the "new sociology of childhood" or the "new social studies of childhood". Changing the definition of childhood, which for many years was dominated by socialization theory and developmental psychology (Hogan 2005), the sociology of childhood sees childhood as a social construction, as a specific structural and cultural component of society. The new sociology of childhood focuses on children as active social agents in their present lives and disagrees with the view of childhood as a phase towards reaching adulthood. Challenging the focus on children exclusively as "future adults" or members of the "next generation", it calls for a shift towards the idea of a child "being a child" (Qvortrup 1994). The new sociologists of childhood argue for the perspective emphasizing the current value for children of their lives and relationships (James and Prout 1990, 1997). That is, childhood is seen as a part of society not prior to it (Christensen and Prout 2005). Proponents of these theories, such as Prout and James (1997) argue that the binary divisions of child and adult, maturity and immaturity, are used arbitrarily to prevent children and young people from accessing their rights and from gaining equal treatment with adults (Barnes 2012; James et al. 1998; Prout and James 1997).

A second key feature of the new sociology of childhood is that children are, and must be seen as, active in the construction and determination of their own social lives. Children are not just passive subjects of social structures and processes. Children are seen as possessing different experiences and knowledge from adults and as being competent social actors, actively involved in responding to and shaping their social worlds (Waksler 1991; James and Prout 1997; Christensen and James 2000; Hutchby 2005). According to this perspective, children are active participants in the construction and determination of their experiences (James et al. 1998).

Taking children seriously as people leads to shifts in thinking. Children have moved from being seen as objects of adult work to being seen as competent, contributing social actors. The idea that adult views are sufficient for defining children's needs has had to give way to the understanding that children's own wishes and expressed needs are relevant to the construction and implementation of social policies and practices (Mayall 2000). The new paradigm of sociology and new trends in the children's rights discourse have brought the principle of children as persons to the forefront of the discourse on children's well-being. This especially highlights children's need to be involved in decision making that affects their lives, which must be now taken into account by the social work, health, and education professions.

Why Should the Social Work Profession Be Involved in Children's Rights Practice?

As shown above, social work has long been based on child welfare and children's need of protection and provision, but these concepts are being challenged with new approaches and ideas of children's rights. Even though social work shares some common principles and values with the idea of children's participation rights, the strong linkage between social work and the idea of children's rights, particularly children's participation rights, has not received sufficient attention. While social work already adheres to the concept of children's provision and protection rights, it cannot afford to be leave children's participation and self-determination rights behind. We believe that a children's rights agenda is fundamental to the theory, values and the practice of social work profession. We now give three main reasons why social work should be involved with the children's rights agenda.

Participation as a Value in Social Work

The social work profession is guided by a set of values defining the core principles of the profession. One of the most prominent core principles is the idea of participation, which is a basic aspect of social work. This is best expressed in the various codes of ethics of the profession throughout the world, which, in spite of some differences, all share the basic value of client participation.

The new NASW Code of Ethics, adopted in 1996, embodies current social work practice standards and can be seen as an important window onto the state of the social work profession (Brill 2001). It summarizes broad ethical principles that reflect the profession's core values and establishes a set of specific ethical standards that should be used to guide social work practice (NASW 2009). Article 1.02 states: "Self-Determination: **Social workers respect and promote the right of clients to self-determination and assist clients in their efforts to identify and clarify their goals**". Article 6.02 points out that: "Social workers should facilitate informed participation by the public in shaping social policies and institutions".

The International Federation of Social Work's (IFSW) Statement of Ethical Principles also notes in Article 4.1.1 that "Respecting the right to self-determination —**Social workers should respect and promote people's right to make their own choices and decisions, irrespective of their values and life choices,** provided this does not threaten the rights and legitimate interests of others". And Article 4.1.2 states: "Promoting the right to participation—**Social workers should promote the full involvement and participation of people using their services** in ways that enable them to be empowered in all aspects of decisions and actions affecting their lives".

The social work profession is now clearly directed towards empowerment, independence and personal choice of its clients, being obliged to advance clients' participation is shaping their lives. The concept of self-determination in social work typically entails the right of clients to chart a life path and act according to their own goals, desires and wishes. Social work thus recognizes clients' right to freedom in making their own choices and decisions in the casework process, and caseworkers are obliged to respect these rights, recognize the need for and help activate the potential for self-direction of the client (Reamer 1998).

Although the codes of ethics do not specifically refer to children, it can be argued that it is even more important to implement the principles of self-determination in the case of children. One cannot ignore the fact that children are powerless members of society, they are a marginal and deprived group in our society, mainly controlled by adults and the state. As social workers have a special obligation towards advancing deprived groups in society, it is only natural that their duty lies toward prompting children's participation and self-determination. Article 4.2.1 of the IFSW Statement of Ethical Principles states: "Social workers have a responsibility to challenge negative discrimination on the basis of characteristics such as ability, age, culture, gender or sex, marital status, socio-economic status...". This highlights the importance of not excluding any group and of treating all clients with equal respect. Children, just as adults, should be treated with respect for their rights to self-determination and participation.

Participation as Basic Practice in Social Work

Since the 1970s civic participation as a social concept has become a dominant idea in the political, social and public discourse. The emergence of participation as an issue among academics and policy makers is related to the move from centralized top-down policy-making to a decentralized, less hierarchical policy-making process with a wider array of partnerships and partners (Stoker 2006; Tisdall 2008). Participation has also deeply influenced social work practice, with social work for a long time playing a dominant role in promoting citizen participation, especially among deprived groups in the society. Scholars have long regarded participation as a basic skill unique to social work practice. In the 1960s and early 1970s, social workers directed considerable attention toward matters of social justice, social reform, and civil rights (Reamer 1998). This led to development of a new set of intervention tools, including participatory practice. This practice should not be confined only to parts of the population but should be also implemented with children, as individuals and as a group.

Social Work as a Profession of Authority and Supervision

Social work professionals are legally and socially empowered to supervise their clients, especially children. Thus, it can be said that social work comprises an element of paternalism (see Reamer 1998). The supervision and control that social workers impose upon children are not a goal in themselves but rather a means to protect and advance the well-being of children at risk and of helping families. This power and control must be used carefully. Adopting the principle of children's rights can help social workers use their power over children with dignity and direct them to respect children's self-determination rights. We argue that, because children are a target of supervision and protection by social workers, it is especially important to respect their self-determination rights and give them the opportunity to express their views and wishes in a process they do not always control.

In this regard it is interesting to note that the NASW ethical code Article 1.02 **stresses that** "Social workers may limit clients' right to self-determination when, in the social workers' professional judgment, clients' actions or potential actions pose a serious, foreseeable, and imminent risk to themselves or others". Given the fact that social workers seldom judge children as able or capable of making their own choices, it can be understood why children seldom receive the opportunity to participate in the process of intervention.

Participation is a core value of practice in social work and is crucial for keeping a balance of power between the social-worker and the child. Yet, the concept of children's right is a great challenge to social work practice based on an ethic of care and welfare. In the ethics of care approach social workers should work in the best interests of young people, whereas working from the rights approach they are expected to 'voice' young people's wishes and feelings, but not attempt to judge or act on what they believe to be in a young person's best interests.

Few theorists have considered how an ethic of care may be applied to children and their rights (Barne 2009). Arneil (2002) and Smart et al. (2001) point out the limitation of a rights model for children that portrays them as a set of individuals with separate interests and, therefore, separate rights. Drawing on the above arguments, a model for children's rights that incorporates an ethic of care would continue to place children and young people at the center of their worlds but would not assume they are autonomous individuals. This model would attach weight to relationality: children's relationships, especially with family and other care givers are vitally important to them, although it must be taken into account that some of these relationships are not positive and could be abusive. This means highlighting these activities as an important public duty, not restricting them to the private and personal sphere. This entails seeing children as individuals who are also part of a whole.

Exercise Box 3

1. Social work with children has passed through three key phases: provision and protection, "every child matters" and participation. In each of these phases social work was concerned with a different sort of children's rights. Present at least one right which is relevant for each of the phases. Explain your answer.

2. There are several reasons why social work should be involved with children's rights-based practice. Nevertheless, social workers today are reluctant to use rights-based practice, and most children's rights advocacy is by professionals from the legal discipline. Please discuses at least three possible reasons why social workers refrain from using a children's rights perspective to frame their practice.

Chapter 4
Social Work and Children's Rights: Implications for Practice

Rights-Based Approach for Working with Children

According to the BASW (2015), a human rights-based approach is directed to empower people to know and claim their rights, as well as to increase the ability and accountability of individuals and institutions responsible for respecting, protecting and fulfilling rights. This includes giving people the power and opportunity to participate in decisions that affect their lives and human rights. According to UNICEF (2009) a rights-based approach is a conceptual framework for the process of human development that is normatively based on international human rights standards and operationally directed to promoting and protecting human rights.

Embracing a rights-based approach means that human rights become the targets of intervention. The rights provide a framework, a set of priorities, and new objectives to guide programs and activities. Rights-based approaches have shifted the focus of practice from fulfilling needs to empowering and building the capacity of individuals and communities (BASW 2015).

A rights-based approach has emerged and been used over the years in international development work. Early international development assistance was often based on the assumption that improving economies and personal wealth alone would improve the lives of individuals. This work mainly used a needs-based approach, which looks at the needs of the poor and relies on generosity and benevolence. In the late 20th century criticism of this approach arose, claiming that it maintained the relationship of the generous giver and the needy recipient and that it placed little or no responsibility on the primary duty-bearers (Save the Children 2005).

More recently a trend to more 'people-centred', empowering, and participatory approaches has emerged—the rights-based approach. Today, development work around the world is guided by the imperative to achieve people's rights, and rights-based approaches have now become an important means by which agencies and organizations "do" development. There are many rights-based programs around

© The Author(s) 2016
H. Kosher et al., *Children's Rights and Social Work*,
SpringerBriefs in Rights-Based Approaches to Social Work,
DOI 10.1007/978-3-319-43920-4_4

the world which support rights holders—especially the poor, powerless and dis-criminated against—to claim their rights. These programs aim to increase impact and strengthen sustainability by addressing the underlying causes of violations of rights, bringing about policy and practice changes to make a sustained difference to the lives of individuals (Save the Children 2005). The underlying principles which are of fundamental importance in applying a human rights-based approach in practice are participation, accountability, non-discrimination and equality, empowerment and legality (UNICEF 2009).

A children's rights-based approach applies specifically to working to realize the rights of children in order to consider their special needs and vulnerabilities. Using a children's rights-based approach means using human rights principles and stan-dards in work with children, their families, carers and communities. This approach aims to improve the position of children so that can fully enjoy their rights and can live in societies that acknowledge and respect children's rights (Save the Children 2005).

There are two main reasons for using a children rights-based approach when working with children: (a) a moral or legal reason—the intrinsic rationale, acknowledging that a human rights-based approach is the right thing to do, morally or legally; and (b) an instrumental reason—recognizing that a human rights-based approach leads to better and more sustainable human development outcomes. In practice, the reason for pursuing a human rights-based approach is usually a blend of both (UNICEF 2009).

According to Save the Children (2005) some key principles of a children's rights-based approach are:

1. A clear focus on children, their rights and their role as social actors.
2. A holistic view of children: considering all aspects of a child while making strategic choices and setting priorities.
3. A strong emphasis on accountability for promoting, protecting and fulfilling children's rights across a range of duty-bearers from the primary duty bearer—the state (e.g., local and central government) to the private sector, the media, child-care professionals, and other individuals with direct contact with children.
4. Supporting duty bearers: consideration of how duty bearers could be helped to meet their obligations through technical assistance, budget support and other forms of partnership.
5. Advocacy: the importance of advocacy, public education and awareness raising as programming tools to ensure that duty bearers are held accountable.
6. Participation: the promotion of children's effective participation in program-ming (and beyond), according to children's developing capacities.
7. Non-discrimination: a commitment to the inclusion of the most marginalized children and to challenging discrimination on grounds such as gender, class, ethnicity, (dis)ability, etc.
8. The best interests of children: consideration (with children) of the impact on children of all program choices.

9. Survival and development: a focus on the immediate survival of children as well as a commitment to ensuring the development of their full potential.
10. Children as part of a community: an understanding of children's place in their families, communities and societies and the role that their parents and other carers have in defending their rights and guiding children's development.
11. Root causes and broad issues: a focus on the underlying causes as well as immediate violations.
12. Partnerships: building partnerships and alliances for the promotion, protection and fulfilment of children's rights.
13. Information and knowledge: Facilitating access to and understanding of children's rights for children themselves, their communities and key duty bearers, including government.

The Relevance of a Rights-Based Approach to Social Work

Although a rights-based approach is manly used in international development, its principle and values can guide us in how to implement children's rights in social work practice. Using a children's rights-based approach in social work practice means viewing children's rights, norms and standards as the primary frame of reference for every intervention at the macro or the micro level (BASW 2015). The AASW (2013) deals specifically with how to adopt a rights-based approach consistent with the CRC in social work. It suggests that social workers be committed to ensuring that: (1) the best interests of children be the primary concern; (2) all children be heard, consulted with, and take part in making decisions affecting their life in consideration of the child's age or ability to understand; (3) all children have the right to be given information about decisions and plans concerning their future with regard to the child's age or ability to understand; and (4) these rights be afforded to all children, regardless of their race, religion, abilities, gender, beliefs or any other factor.

Save the Children (2005) suggests using the four general principles of the CRC as guidelines for intervention with children. Although they are not directed specifically to social work, these guidelines can be used to better understand how social work practice should adopt the values of children's rights.

Non-discrimination. Non-discrimination is a core principle of the CRC best expressed in Article 2, which determines that all member parties to the CRC are obliged to provide equal rights and opportunities to all children. This means eliminating discrimination of individual children, specific groups of children (e.g., children with disabilities), and of the child population as a whole (e.g., stopping children from being treated worse than adults (e.g., in terms of the level of violence that society allows to be used against them) (Save the Children 2005).

Based on this principle, all welfare agencies working with children should ensure that their interventions and programs do not discriminate children. They should, for example, identify which groups of children are being excluded from or included within a particular program and why. Children's rights practice requires a particular focus on the most marginalized children in society (Save the Children 2005).

Although social workers intervene every day with marginalized groups of children, like poor children or children with disabilities, most social work practice is direct towards helping such children develop well and improve their well-being. A rights-based practice in social work would emphasize that social workers should also be involved with non-discrimination practices with these groups and individual children to better realize their rights. This can be a challenging task, as many social workers represent the state, while this kind of work can demand of them to act on behalf of the child's right against state authorities. Furthermore, this principle implies that social workers should be devoted not just to marginalized groups of children, but to all children in society, as children are a vulnerable group compared to adults.

The best interests of the child. The principle of the best interest of the child is connected to every aspect of a child's life. This principle implies that whenever decisions are taken that affect children's lives, the impact of that decision must be assessed. This means that the interests of others—such as parents, the community or the state—should not be an overriding concern, although they may influence the final outcome of a decision.

Acting in the child's best interest should be directed towards the realization of its rights and take serious account of the child's own views. This involves, for example, ensuring that children's opinions are sought and listened to in decisions affecting them, or making sure that a wide range of opinions are sought and listened to, including those of carers, community members, and professionals (Save the Children 2005).

The implementation of this principle in social work practice can be complex, as much of the work of the welfare services focuses on the idea that the best interest of the child is best evaluated and determined by adult professionals. Integrating children's rights practice into social work means viewing the child's best interest from a perspective which takes the child's views into account.

Survival and development. Children's right to survive and develop is fundamental. CRC states that children have an inherent right to life, thus members should maximally ensure the survival and development of the child, so that children can contribute to a peaceful, tolerant society. The right to survival and development includes a wide range of aspects—physical, mental, cultural, spiritual, moral and social development. It assumes that children carry within them the potential for their own development, yet they must live in the appropriate protective, caring and stimulating environment to realize their potential (Save the Children 2005). The duty of the welfare services here is to ensure that children's rights to development are met.

To do this, social work practice must, for example, recognize the holistic nature of children and that their development, more than physical growth and health, includes moral and spiritual growth. Social work practice should also recognize that children develop and undergo change as they move towards greater autonomy and maturity (i.e., they have "evolving capacities"). It should also recognize that the world is changing and that child development needs to keep pace with the changing environments that children will have to contend with as adults (Save the Children 2005).

Participation. The CRC is the first human rights treaty to explicitly assert children's civil rights. Every child has the right to information, has the right to the opportunity to express his or her views, to have these views heard in decision making affecting him or her, and to form or join associations. This principle will be discussed in more detail below.

Children's Rights Practice in Social Work

Having presented the ideas and principles of using a rights-based approach while working with children, we now present more practical tools for using the idea of children's rights in social work practice. Firstly, the idea of children's rights calls for advocacy work in social work. One may wrongly assume that this is the work or the responsibility of the legal sphere. We argue that social work should and must be involved in child advocacy work. Secondly, children's rights practices in social work can also be expressed in participatory practice with children expressed as participation with the individual child and participation with children as a group. We now discuss these three paths for implementing children's rights in social work practice.

Social Work and Children's Right at the Macro Level: Child Advocacy

Since the beginning of social work as a profession, social workers throughout the Western world have influenced social policy in a variety of ways. On the one hand, social work practice consists of therapeutic-individual care with families and individuals to assist them in their private lives. On the other hand, 'policy practice' is practice on the macro level focusing on changing policy and influencing the system to the benefit of social welfare (Weiss-Gal and Gal 2011). These are the two poles of social work practice and many kinds of practice lie between them.

One model of policy practice with children is child advocacy, which is relatively a recent phenomenon (Dalrymple 2003). After the Second World War, social work was grounded in a psychoanalytical model in which relationships were seen as central (Biestek 1961; Hollis 1964), and this model has continued to play a large role in both training and practice. Nevertheless, recent decades have brought greater emphasis on the practice of child advocacy in social work. Advocacy services have developed over the past few decades, focusing primarily on adults or older people. More recently it has been acknowledged that advocacy can play a role for children and young people, particularly those in care in the public care system (Boylan and Boylan 1998; Boylan and Ing 2005; Utting 1997).

Advocacy is often described in terms of 'voice'—'to advocate' meaning 'to give voice to' (Bateman 1995). Advocacy work is based on the assumption that children and young people, a marginal and socially silenced group in society, need opportunities to give voice to their experiences, needs and perceptions (Dalrymple 2003).

There are two main modes of advocacy, individual case-based and cause-based, the former more engaged with concerns raised by individuals, the latter seeking to generate systemic change but often informed by case-based issues. Advocacy for children can also combine these two modes.

How can we practice advocacy for children in social work? We illustrate the practice by introducing the most popular model of advocacy for children—the institution of a **children's ombudsman**.

An ombudsman for children is an official representative or organization charged with improving the life conditions of children as a group. Today, in Europe and in the United States ombudsmen act under the Children's Rights Convention as independent public authorities devoted to the realization of children's rights (Solomon 2006). The creation of the institution of ombudsman has three main goals; supervision and monitoring of the implementation of the children's and youth rights, promoting children's rights and the protection of those rights. To achieve these three goals the institution of the ombudsman holds four main function rights (Solomon 2006).

The first is to influence decision-makers and policy-makers to consider the rights of children. The ombudsman is thus responsible for exposing policy failures and violations of children's rights and must act to initiate bills related to the advancement of children's rights.

The ombudsman's second role is to promote an attitude which respects the views and participation of children in society. The ombudsman must ensure that the views of children are heard by the policy makers and will be reflected in the legislative processes of laws relating to children. The ombudsman should also see that children have the best tools and procedures for expressing their views to the various parties.

The third mission of the ombudsman is to raise awareness regarding children's rights among both children and adults. To fulfill this commitment, the institution of the ombudsman must produce and make information about rights accessible to children. It must process and analyze existing data on children and collect new data about them. In addition, it must train professionals who may contact children regarding their rights and it must hold events of various kinds to increase awareness.

Finally, the ombudsman should act to establish effective mechanisms through which children can complain about violation of their rights and ensure that children have easy access to these mechanisms. These may be concrete mechanisms for handling complaints from individual children or cases regarding children, or mechanisms acting on behalf of the children's group.

Some of the ombudsmen for children are general, meaning they direct their assistance to all children, while others focus on a specific group of children, for example children with disabilities. One of the important models of ombudsman for a specific group of children is the ombudsman for children in care, children in out-of-home placement. These children are under the supervision of the welfare system, they live far from their homes, their parents mostly cannot take care of them and therefore cannot represent their interests. Moreover, these children are exposed to many adults and professionals responsible for their safety. This vulnerability places them at risk of violation of their rights. For these reasons, children in residential care need a special instance to which they can complain about matters of concern to them.

Filing a complaint is an aspect of children's right to participation. The right to file a complaint allows children to better realize their rights and to improve the services and care provided to them. It assumes that their point of view is required to maintain or modify the out-of-home placement system. The right to file a complaint provides a means for children to express their opinions, their hardships and their problems in matters relating to their lives. This allows them to experience themselves and initiate a process to improve their situation. The resulting investigative procedures affect not only the life of the child who filed the complaint, but also the lives of a group or groups of children complaining about the same problem, either directly or indirectly (Benbenishty and Peled-Amir 2007).

Child Participation as a Practice in Social Work

Children's right to participation is the core of the 20th century children's right movement. There is growing recognition that children should participate in forming their lives in various aspect and contexts, including in recent years children's participation in the decision processes regarding their care and welfare. There is now a wide range of literature on this issue (e.g., Kirby and Bryson 2002; McNeish and Newman 2002; O'Quigley 2000; Shier 2001), including practical guides. Before discussing how social workers can implement children's rights to participate in practice, we first define children's participation and discuss the contribution of this idea to children's well-being.

What Is Child Participation?

The principle of the child's rights to participate in decision making is stated in Article 12 of the CRC:

State parties shall assure to the child who is capable of forming his or her own views the right to express those views freely in all matters affecting the child, the views of the child being given a due weight in accordance with the age and maturity of the child.

Article 12 has been identified as one of the most radical and far reaching aspects of the convention. It is also one of the provisions most widely violated and disregarded in almost every sphere of children's lives (Sheir 2001).

The right to participation is not only a technical procedure that must be followed in decision-making processes, it is a privilege that requires a change in thinking. It is a principle that should shape the child's environment in everyday life—in the family, at school and in the community. The premise is that if a child's voice is heard it could change outcomes, not only for the child, but also for adults. However, Article 12 does not give the child the right to decide or the right that his or her opinion will determine all matters. The final resolution is not imposed on the children and they are not responsible for the decision, but it requires their participation in the process of acceptance—they should be heard and taken seriously (Cherney and Shing 2008; Pecora et al. 2012).

Another idea important for the implementation of children's participation is the principle of the "evolving capacity of the child". Article 12 states that children's view should be given due weight according to the child's age and maturity. This means that participation depends on the capacities and capabilities of the individual child. It also means that the level of children's participation will vary depending on the decisions involved and the capability and choice of the child.

Why Should We Let the Child Participate?

The purposes of children's participation have been variously identified. Sinclair and Franklin (2000, cited in Sinclair 2004) offer the following contributions of children's participation:

- to uphold children's rights;
- to fulfil legal responsibilities;
- to improve services;
- to improve decision making;
- to enhance democracy;
- to promote child protection;
- to enhance children's skills;
- to empower and enhance self-esteem.

Matthews (2003) distinguishes three arguments for child participation; education for citizenship, fitting young people into society, and strengthening young people's status in relation to adults. In each case, he suggests, it is accepted that 'participation is an essential and moral ingredient of any democratic society, enhancing quality of life, enabling empowerment, encouraging psycho-social well-being, and providing a sense of inclusiveness' (p. 270).

It has long being recognized that participation contributes to child well-being. Children who experience participation will understand that their message was important and can develop a sense of self-value and efficacy. Participation enables them to acquire proper tools for learning actively, rather than passively. They also acquire the knowledge and tools to understand how decisions are made and how to act in a democratic society, knowledge which will help children to function as adults in the community (Flekkoy and Kaufman 1997). As children gain more experience by making decisions in ambiguous situations, they will develop a sense of control, their judgment will be strengthened and they will make more mature and better quality life choices (Flekkoy and Kaufman 1997). Significant participation also develops the ability to resolve conflicts, as well as developing negotiation skills and critical thinking. A child who learned from experience that she can influence the course of her life will feel more responsibility and control. Such a person will develop greater motivation to endure, persist, and believe in her abilities.

Participation also contributes to the community and society as a whole. Participating children grow up to be participating adults, believing in their ability to change their reality. Once children are allowed to express their views and participate in making daily decisions at home, in the community and at school, they will naturally want to become involved in legal proceedings or in education, medicine and policy decision making. This creates a democratic society based on proactive and caring citizens. Adults who have experienced childhood participation and active citizenship may be the adults who will spread the knowledge, skills and values necessary for strengthening and preserving democracy (Flekkoy and Kaufman 1997).

Finally, participation contributes to children's dignity and status. Participation carries with it a message to adults and through them to the whole community, that children have value and that society cares for them and their rights (Flekkoy and Kaufman 1997).

Models for Children's Participation

Article 12 is quite vague, thus over the years scholars have expended considerable effort to translate it into practical tools for children's participation and have developed a number of typologies of children's participation (Franklin 1997; Hart 1992; Matthews 2003; Shier 2001; Thoburn et al. 1995; Treseder 1997; West 2004). One of the most popular models is Hart's "ladder of participation". This is based on Arnstein's (1969) "eight rungs in the ladder of citizen participation". Like Arnstein, Hart's ladder contains a number of degrees of participation and non-participation, arranged linearly in eight levels. The lowest level is non-participating ('manipulation', 'decoration' and 'tokenism'), where adults have the initiative and control and children obey them. Intermediate stages are 'adult-initiated, shared decisions with children' and 'child-initiated and directed', while the top level is 'child-initiated, shared decisions with adults', where children are attached to decision-maker forums and are asked for their opinions. The highest stage is achieved when children are the initiators of the projects. This model has come to dominate discussion and thinking about children's participation, particularly among practitioners, to an extent that the author could never have intended.

Treseder's (1997) model with five aspects of participation skips over the three 'non-participation' rungs of Hart's ladder and removes the hierarchical element. His model is based on five types or degrees of participation in a circular layout: 'child-initiated, shared decisions with adults'; 'consulted and informed'; 'assigned but informed'; 'adult-initiated, shared decisions with children'; 'child-initiated and directed'. The rationale behind this model is that different kinds of participatory activities and relationships are appropriate to different settings and circumstances. In his opinion the lower degrees of power or engagement are not necessarily worth less than the highest levels of participation. There is no "better" way of participating and all means are legitimate. Treseder suggests that the child and the adults should choose the most suitable degree for the specific situation. Each situation has its own characteristics and the participation of the child should be adjusted to each child and each case individually. However, Treseder feels that children should not be participating at the highest level and sometimes not even at the intermediate levels.

Sheir's (2001) model is based on four levels of participation:

1. Children are listened to
2. Children are supported in expressing their views
3. Children's view are taken into account
4. Children share power and responsibility for decision-making.

At each level of participation individuals and organizations may have different degrees of commitment to the process of empowerment. This model seeks to clarify this by identifying three degrees of commitment at each level: opening, opportunities and obligations.

In spite of differences among the various models, they all cover a continuum of involvement in decision making. Participation is a range of possibilities, from non-participation to active initiation that can be implemented differently in diverse situations and times.

Note that participation is not the right to make the decisions or determine the outcomes, rather it is the right to be heard and having one's views taken seriously and treated with respect (Cashmore 2002).

Children's Participation as Individuals in the Child Welfare System

Children's and young people's participation in child welfare and protection services has been the focus of research, policy development and legislation and scholars have presented models for children's participation in the welfare system (van Bijleveld et al. 2013). Cashmore (2002) introduced a model for participation that includes: the opportunity and choice of means to participate; access to relevant information; a trusted advocate or mentor; policy and legislation that require children and young people to be consulted and informed; means to complain; means for services to evaluate their performance and how they encourage the involvement of children and young people.

Implementing children's participation in the child welfare or protection system is a complex and challenging mission, especially in regard to the child protection system. Child protection workers must operate within a context of tensions involving the rights of parents and of children and of the state to intervene in family life, when serious concerns are raised about a child's welfare (Fox Harding 1991).

It is highly important to enable children in care to participate in decision making that affects their life in the welfare system. Particularly for children and young people in care, participation has the potential to accord children recognition as well as protection. Participation is important for children in care for several further reasons (Cashmore 2002):

First, within the triad of social worker, parents and child, the child arguably occupies the least powerful position. The social worker can easily become absorbed in the parents' issues and lose sight of the child (Cossar et al. 2013).

Second, whereas decisions for children living at home are generally made by one or two adults with whom the child is in daily contact, decisions for children in care are often made by a number of adults—parents, carers, and workers from one or more agencies, judges, magistrates and lawyers. Some of these may not have even met the child or understand what is important to him/her (Cashmore 2002; Thomas and O'Kane 1999).

Third, not involving maltreated children may compound or reactivate feelings of powerlessness (Bell 2002). They can easily feel alienated from the process and merely an object of concern. Schofield and Thoburn (1996) argue that the effective participation of children and young people in child protection work can be an important part of the healing process. Participation may give abused or neglected children and young people some sense of being active agents in relation to their own care, rather than being powerless victims of the whims of adults. Children wish for more involvement in decisions related to their own welfare and, when they are excluded, they experience more harmful feelings (Boylan and Wyllie 1999; Butler and Williamson 1994; Cashmore 2002; Marshall 1997; Shemmings 2000). Participation is associated with an increased feeling of mastery and control (Bell 2002; Leeson 2007; McLeod 2007; Munro 2001). Children and young people reported that, when social workers valued their views, took their concerns seriously and provided realistic options, they felt good about themselves and felt valued (Bessell 2011; Leeson 2007). In contrast, the absence of participation created a sense of being ignored or overlooked, leading to a decrease in self-esteem and self-worth (Leeson 2007).

Fourth, participation correlates with high satisfaction with the decision made and shows good outcomes. Participating in decision making about their lives helps children feel connected and committed to the decisions taken (Woolfsen et al. 2010). For example, there is some evidence that when children and young people in care have some choice about their placement, the placement tends to be more stable (Lindsay 1995). Planning and decision-making which consider the children's views are likely to be both more appropriate and more acceptable to the child (Cashmore 2002). Many children, like adults, feel resentful about having decisions imposed upon them, and children placed in out-of-home placements against their will may be so resistant as to cause the placement to break down (Aldgate and Statham 2001; Cashmore 2002). Taking children's views, wishes and expectations into account may make interventions more responsive and therefore more effective (McLeod 2007; Barnes 2012).

Finally, children in care are required to make the transition to independent living at a much younger age than their counterparts living with their families of origin. Participation is important for these children because it prepares them for future independence and for the autonomous decision making they will be required to deal with when they leave care (Cashmore 2002).

In spite of the importance of children's participation in the welfare system for their well-being and for social work practice, it is barely implemented. Most children and young people think they have had limited opportunities to be involved in how important decisions were made, such as where they lived, and when and how often they saw their parents. Some were not even well informed about why they had entered care (Cashmore 2002; Gilligan 2000). All studies show that although there is an intention to involve children, social workers express ambiguities and reservations about doing so (Archard and Skivenes 2009; van Bijleveld et al. 2013).

Even when children have been involved in their care process, their experience has not always been positive. Although consulted, children and young people found that they had insufficient or inconsistent opportunities to express their views on matters affecting them while in care. Some did not feel that their views were necessarily valued or acted upon. (Bell 2002; Bessell 2011). Children further reported that they were allowed to influence trivial decisions, but that the professionals did not let them participate in the decisions they considered important, such as where they lived, contact with their parents and siblings, and choice of school (Bessell 2011; Cashmore 2002; Leeson 2007; Munro 2001). Formal decisions about the lives of children and young people are commonly made at case conferences, review meetings and family group conferences (Cashmore 2002; van Bijleveld et al. 2013). Although a number of children and young people did attend such meetings, they were often only observing rather than actually participating (Leeson 2007).

Van Bijleveld and colleagues (2013) explain that there are a number of challenges to children's participation in child protection services, which are inherent in how the social work and case management systems are organized within statutory practice. Social workers and case managers need to determine what is in the child's best interests in a context where different stakeholders have their conflicting interests, rights and needs (Archard and Skivenes 2009; Barnes 2012; Bell 2002;

Pinkney 2011; Sanders and Mace 2006). Also, the tensions between children's rights to protection and their rights to participation limit implementation of children's participation. The view of children as social actors, as autonomous and as active agents constructing their lives, challenges the view of the child as inherently vulnerable and in need of protection, stemming from developmental psychology as well as social work practice (Cossar et al. 2013; Such and Walker 2005). Sanders and Mace (2006) explain that conflicts arise between the government's guidance to implement the child's right to have a voice in decision-making with its duty to protect the child from significant harm. It is a conflict between the CRC principle of participation and the welfare culture typical of child protection services (Vis et al. 2012). The professionals must maintain a balance (van Bijleveld et al. 2013). However, these views are challenged today by the fact that participation can actually be protective for vulnerable children, leading to increased confidence, self-efficacy and self-worth (Cossar et al. 2013; Limber and Kaufman 2002; Schofield 2005).

Concerns have also been expressed that involving children in social work processes may be potentially harmful, for instance, by exposing them to hostility during meetings (Cossar et al. 2014; Healy and Darlington 2009). Professionals also worry about exposing children to inappropriate information and responsibilities. Professionals are concerned that children may be present at child protection conferences where the behavior of their parents is being scrutinized. In a child protection context, this may be a burden, depriving the child of what is perceived as a proper childhood. The presence of parents in conferences in the welfare system may also challenge children's participation (Sanders and Mace 2006).

Examples from Around the World

In the last two decades there have been increasing efforts to establish children's participation in care and protection processes, mainly in legislation and policy guidelines, as a means of promoting acceptance of the principle of children's participation. The legislation in some countries includes the requirement that children and young people be able to express their views on matters affecting them, especially their care, and that these views be taken seriously when decisions are made. This does not necessarily guarantee that the child's views will be heard (Cashmore 2002), but it is important to note these models.

Examples of such legislation can be found in **England and Wales**: the Children Act 1989 incorporated principles requiring participation by children and young people. The law requires local authorities and courts to take into account the wishes and feelings of children and young people when making decisions concerning their welfare, to provide them with information and legal representation, and to establish complaints procedures for "looked after" children (Cashmore 2002).

In **Finland** the newest Child Welfare Act (2007) strongly emphasizes the principle of participation along with protection, devoting a whole chapter to this. The Act contains new sections concerning how a child should be heard in child-protection procedures and how the child needs to be allowed to influence matters concerning her or his own life (Polkki et al. 2012; Sinko 2008). Other examples can be found in **Norway**, **France**, **New Zealand**, and various states and provinces in **Australia** and **Canada**.

Children's Participation in the Public Context—How Is This Relevant for Social Workers?

The wording of Article 12 of the CRC seems to indicate that the right to be heard is a right of the individual child. However, Krappman (2010) argues that the use of the expression "the child" does not necessarily mean that an individual child only can exercise the right. This right does not only belong to the individual child, but also to groups of children, the children of a classroom, the children of a neighborhood, the children of a city, all children can be heard, when matters affect them collectively. In its General Comment the CRC Committee explains that children, who as individuals are indubitably regarded as capable of forming a view, cannot be denied the right to be heard, when they decide to express a concern as a group (Krappman 2010).

Nonetheless, children's participation has been implemented mainly in individual contexts concerning the private life of the child, mainly in health issues, divorce of the parents and child protection process. Children's participation in the broader social context has been neglected. Historically, national and local social policies have developed with children and young people being 'objects of concern' rather than persons with views to be taken seriously. Children and young people have tended to be regarded either as vulnerable and in need of protection or as unruly and threatening and in need of control (Partidge 2005). Children are still enmeshed in policy as passive recipients and arguably oppressed by certain policies. Their voices remain generally excluded from social policy design at the national and local levels and from the institutions they attend, for example, schools, voluntary organization, residential institutions, and so on. When heard in local government settings and national government processes, children's views are frequently disregarded (Hill et al. 2004).

Why Is It Important to Promote Children's Participation as a Group in the Public Context?

Children are one of the groups most governed by both the state and civic society, and they are some of the highest users of state services—health, education, and social security—and thus a primary focus of state intervention (Hill et al. 2004).

Many social policies are directed at young children, yet their voice is rarely heard in shaping these policies. It is important to give them the opportunity and power to influence the policies concerning them and the institutions they will be part of. This can be achieved through the practice of children's participation.

Children have their own perspectives and views about what they need, which mostly differ from adults' perceptions (Ben-Arieh 2005). Yet, most of the social policy for children is designed, delivered and evaluated by adults, who are not familiar with what is important to children. Social policy for children in the welfare sphere is concerned with promoting children's welfare and reducing their exposure to the many risks associated with material disadvantage. They are intended to be protective towards children, but often leave adult-child power relations untouched (Hill et al. 2004). For example, Ridge (2002) found that children living in poverty define their poverty in terms of the 'normal' things that they cannot afford but which their peers and their families can pay for, e.g., not being able to share activities with friends, not being able to reciprocate, not being able to go on school trips, not having the right clothes. Performance indicators of importance to adults often do not incorporate indicators important to children, which range from clean and private toilets to adequate play space.

Child participation in social policy design includes discussing with children what is important to them and what they think about social issues concerning them. Their participation helps policy makers better understand the lives of children and young people (Cockburn 2005; Hill et al. 2004). Children's participation can reform and direct social policy to be responsive to children's needs, rather than adults wishes. Child participation in forming social policy thus improves policy by making it more sensitive to social needs and more likely to succeed.

Children's participation in the public sphere improves their well-being. Participating in policy-making brings children and young people benefits, such as increased confidence and self-esteem, new knowledge and skills, improved achievement at school and lower rates of exclusion (Hannam 2000; Partridge 2005).

Nonetheless, from the limited evidence available it appears that where children are involved in public decision-making, they have a relatively minimal impact on that decision making (Partridge 2005). Frequently children's views, even if sought, are still disregarded within everyday institutions (e.g., schools), local government settings (e.g., social service departments) and national government processes (Hill et al. 2004). Surveying 146 organizations engaged in participation activity with children and young people, Kirby and colleagues (2003) found that most participation was on the local level in small organizations or agencies, the most common age group being 12–16 year olds, and most participation focused on service development or delivery. They concluded that young people were having little impact on public decision-making.

The role or significance of the social worker in the process of involving children in designing social policy has not yet been clarified. We argue that social workers, as advocators for children's rights, should take part in the participatory practice of children in the public context. As noted above, social workers have been advocators for children as a group since the beginning of the profession and promoting excluded groups is embedded in the ethical code of social work. Thus, social work as a discipline must lead in bringing children to participate in the public arena. This includes involving children in welfare policy design at the national and the local level, in the design of social and welfare services and especially in the forming of institutions for children in care. Social worker as promoters of children's rights, particularly children's right to participation, should lead the initiative for children's participation in these arenas. Social workers should help bring children's voices, views, desire and interests into the public sphere and advocate for the importance of involving children in design of policy and services.

Exercise Box 4

1. Discuss the benefits and advantages of using a rights-based approach in social work practice with children. Explain the benefits of rights-based interventions for society as a whole, as well as for children.
2. Advocacy is a means of implementing children's rights to participation. Present an example of advocacy work on behalf of children in your country. Describe the role of social workers in it. Also, discuss how this advocacy work improves children's well-being.
3. Present an example of children's participation in social work practice in your country. Describe the level of children's participation, the benefits for children and the benefits for practice. Also discuss whether the principles of children's rights can conflict with one another, for example, the best interest of the child and child participation.
4. Children's participation can also take place in the public sphere. Give two examples in which social workers can facilitate children's participation in the public sphere. For each example, explain why social workers should be involved in it.

Chapter 5
Social Work and Children's Rights: Implications for Research

Introduction

The empirical study of issues related to children's rights has grown considerably since its beginnings in the late 1980s (Peterson-Badial and Ruck 2008). The adoption of the CRC was followed by an increase in publications in the early 1990s, and their number has increased ever since. Fifty-nine articles were published over the five year period 1990–1994, while 463 articles were published in the period 2005–2009. Now children's rights research is an established and legitimate field of study. However, despite this growth, research in children's rights is still very limited in volume and scope (Quennerstedt 2013).

The research conducted over the past 20 years has enlarged our knowledge of what rights for children are, has identified important questions and opened up new areas for study. Children's rights research has been a driving force in upgrading the status of children in society, and strengthening the claim that children are 'people in their own right' (Quennerstedt 2013).

Studies on children's rights have focused on four main domains. The first is an evolving body of empirical research on the perception and attitudes of children and adults towards the concept of children's rights. In the early 1980s researchers began to examine children's own thinking about children's rights issues (Melton 1908, 1983; Melton and Limber 1992; Helwig 1995a, b; Ruck et al. 1998), as well as how adults perceive this concept (Bohrnstedt Freedman and Smith 1981; Morton et al. 1982; Peterson-Badali et al. 2004; Rogers and Wrightsman 1978).

A second domain is a focus on children's participation rights (Reynaert et al. 2009). Studies have examined children's participation in the community, in civic society, and in the political arena (e.g., Browning et al. 2004; Chavis and Wandersman 1990; Delhey and Newton 2002; Finn and Checkoway 1998; Fogel 2004; Glaeser et al. 2000; Kelly 2009; Kwak et al. 2004; Lichter et al. 1999; Newton 2001; Newton and Pippa 2000; O'Toole et al. 2003; Torney-Purta et al. 2008; Rasinski et al. 1993).

© The Author(s) 2016
H. Kosher et al., *Children's Rights and Social Work*,
SpringerBriefs in Rights-Based Approaches to Social Work,
DOI 10.1007/978-3-319-43920-4_5

Another body of studies, discussed above, is that examining children's participation in child protection processes in the welfare system. These studies have
examined social workers' attitudes towards the idea of children's rights (Polkki
et al. 2012; Shemmings 2000; van Bijleveld et al. 2013; Vis et al. 2012; Vis and
Thomas 2009), the scope and nature of children's participation in the welfare
system (Bell 2002; Sinclair and Boushel 1998; Thomas 2005; Thomas and O'Kane
1999; Vis and Thomas 2009), and the obstacles to children's participation
(Alderson 2008; Sanders and Mace 2006; Vis et al. 2012).

A fourth domain of implementation research is investigating how the rights
recognized in the Convention have been realized in practice in the various areas of
society (Reynaert et al. 2009). The Convention is viewed as a standard-setting
instrument and has formed the basis of a vast amount of implementation research
(Quennerstedt 2013).

Children's Right to Participation—Implications for Social Work Research

Children's right to have due weight given their views extends "to all matters
affecting the child" and thus necessarily applies in the context of research projects
relating to children. The Committee of the CRC asserted that the right to express
views should be "anchored in the child's daily life… including through research
and consultation" (Lundy and 2011). Thus, the most important implication of the
idea of children's rights for social work research is the concept of children's participation. Social work research itself should adhere to the recognition of children's
rights of participation and should involve children directly. Cousins and Milner
(2007) argue that incorporating the value of children's participation into social work
research is an invaluable means of enabling children and young people to express
their views and to have these views taken seriously without discrimination.

Although there is a rich tradition of children's studies in social work, studies on
children' worlds have been largely about children rather than with them, treating
them as object of study and not as subjects (Hill 1997). Also, over the years
children's lives have been explored through the views and understandings of their
adult caretakers or their views have been included within research on the family
(Christensen and James 2000). Until recently much research on children's lives was
focused on efforts at objective description, treating children as passive objects that
are acted upon by the adult world (Ben-Arieh 2005). This approach is based on the
belief that children lack the verbal skills, conceptual abilities and competence to
convey their experiences and to express their opinion and thoughts. Therefore,
parents, caregivers, and other adults have typically been the informants in research
focused on children (Faux et al. 1988).

In contrast, over the last two decades there has been a change in how research
treats children. Now it increasingly involves children and young people directly in

research and this has become the dominant trend in studying children. This new trend in children's studies is deeply influenced by the concept that children's right to participation and the new sociology of childhood must be integrated into social work research.

Today studying children as subjects of concern and asking them directly about their lives, experiences, feelings and thoughts is both more acceptable and common (Kirk 2007), and children's perspectives have become an important focus for research (Christensen and James 2000; Lewis and Lindsay 2000). We can see that more and more researchers value children's perspectives, wish to understand their lived experience, and are motivated to find out more about how children understand and interpret, negotiate and feel about their daily lives (Greene and Hill 2005).

Recent years have brought a growing body of research developing new ways of undertaking research with children. Drawing upon the increasingly important children's rights movement, researchers have been developing inclusive and participatory children-centered methodologies, which place the voices of children, as social actors, at the center of the research process (Ben-Arieh 2005).

Children's Participation in Social Work Research

Children's participation in social work research can be expressed in several ways: first, by hearing *children's perspective on any subject of study concerning their lives.* It seems obvious that the best source of information for studying children's lives and well-being is the children themselves. Ben-Arieh (2005) argues that, while the legal and public systems may very well accept children as persons, the scientific community is still reluctant. He explains that many of the major studies examining children's well-being or quality of life have too easily given up on children's subjective perceptions. Until recently much research on children's lives has been focused on efforts at objective description, treating children as passive objects that are acted upon by the adult world. To gain accurate measures and achieve meaningful monitoring of children's well-being, we need to develop means of gathering children's subjective perceptions of their world and insights into their experiences

Second, *children can be the data collectors.* Children's active role in data collection can be achieved through participatory research and specifically through their direct involvement in data collection (Ben-Arieh 2005). Third, *children can be part of the data analysis*: designing a study, identifying the sources of information and collecting the data are all worthless without the phase of data analysis and its interpretation. In any study, all perspectives require interpretation. Information is part of a context and is directed towards a cultural and social framework. Understanding the context requires the help of children in interpreting it (Ben-Arieh 2005). Thomas and O'Kane (1998) present several ways in which they tried to create opportunities for children to participate in the interpretation and analysis of their research data.

Exercise Box

Please find an article presenting a study in the field of social work focusing on the subject of children. Based on the article, discuss the following points:

1. What is the subject of the research?
2. Which research method has been used (sample, data collection, research design etc.)?
3. What is the status of children in the study design?
4. Discuss the paradigm of the study as you understand it: is it a conservative study in which children are the object of study or is it a new paradigm-based study in which children are the subject in the research process?
5. If the study has involved children, please discuss the advantages and disadvantage of this for the study. If the study did not involve children, please discuss the advantages and disadvantage of this for the study.

Appendix
Convention on the Rights of the Child

Preamble

The States Parties to the present Convention,

Considering that, in accordance with the principles proclaimed in the Charter of the United Nations, recognition of the inherent dignity and of the equal and inalienable rights of all members of the human family is the foundation of freedom, justice and peace in the world,

Bearing in mind that the peoples of the United Nations have, in the Charter, reaffirmed their faith in fundamental human rights and in the dignity and worth of the human person, and have determined to promote social progress and better standards of life in larger freedom,

Recognizing that the United Nations has, in the Universal Declaration of Human Rights and in the International Covenants on Human Rights, proclaimed and agreed that everyone is entitled to all the rights and freedoms set forth therein, without distinction of any kind, such as race, colour, sex, language, religion, political or other opinion, national or social origin, property, birth or other status,

Recalling that, in the Universal Declaration of Human Rights, the United Nations has proclaimed that childhood is entitled to special care and assistance,

Convinced that the family, as the fundamental group of society and the natural environment for the growth and well-being of all its members and particularly children, should be afforded the necessary protection and assistance so that it can fully assume its responsibilities within the community,

Recognizing that the child, for the full and harmonious development of his or her personality, should grow up in a family environment, in an atmosphere of happiness, love and understanding,

Considering that the child should be fully prepared to live an individual life in society, and brought up in the spirit of the ideals proclaimed in the Charter of the United Nations, and in particular in the spirit of peace, dignity, tolerance, freedom, equality and solidarity,

Bearing in mind that the need to extend particular care to the child has been stated in the Geneva Declaration of the Rights of the Child of 1924 and in the

© The Author(s) 2016
H. Kosher et al., *Children's Rights and Social Work*,
SpringerBriefs in Rights-Based Approaches to Social Work,
DOI 10.1007/978-3-319-43920-4

Declaration of the Rights of the Child adopted by the General Assembly on 20 November 1959 and recognized in the Universal Declaration of Human Rights, in the International Covenant on Civil and Political Rights (in particular in articles 23 and 24), in the International Covenant on Economic, Social and Cultural Rights (in particular in article 10) and in the statutes and relevant instruments of specialized agencies and international organizations concerned with the welfare of children,

Bearing in mind that, as indicated in the Declaration of the Rights of the Child, "the child, by reason of his physical and mental immaturity, needs special safe-guards and care, including appropriate legal protection, before as well as after birth",

Recalling the provisions of the Declaration on Social and Legal Principles relating to the Protection and Welfare of Children, with Special Reference to Foster Placement and Adoption Nationally and Internationally; the United Nations Standard Minimum Rules for the Administration of Juvenile Justice (The Beijing Rules); and the Declaration on the Protection of Women and Children in Emergency and Armed Conflict, Recognizing that, in all countries in the world, there are children living in exceptionally difficult conditions, and that such children need special consideration,

Taking due account of the importance of the traditions and cultural values of each people for the protection and harmonious development of the child, Recognizing the importance of international co-operation for improving the living conditions of children in every country, in particular in the developing countries,

Have agreed as follows:

Part I

Article 1

For the purposes of the present Convention, a child means every human being below the age of eighteen years unless under the law applicable to the child, majority is attained earlier.

Article 2

1. States Parties shall respect and ensure the rights set forth in the present Convention to each child within their jurisdiction without discrimination of any kind, irrespective of the child's or his or her parent's or legal guardian's race, colour, sex, language, religion, political or other opinion, national, ethnic or social origin, property, disability, birth or other status.
2. States Parties shall take all appropriate measures to ensure that the child is protected against all forms of discrimination or punishment on the basis of the

status, activities, expressed opinions, or beliefs of the child's parents, legal guardians, or family members.

Article 3

1. In all actions concerning children, whether undertaken by public or private social welfare institutions, courts of law, administrative authorities or legislative bodies, the best interests of the child shall be a primary consideration.
2. States Parties undertake to ensure the child such protection and care as is necessary for his or her well-being, taking into account the rights and duties of his or her parents, legal guardians, or other individuals legally responsible for him or her, and, to this end, shall take all appropriate legislative and administrative measures.
3. States Parties shall ensure that the institutions, services and facilities responsible for the care or protection of children shall conform with the standards established by competent authorities, particularly in the areas of safety, health, in the number and suitability of their staff, as well as competent supervision.

Article 4

States Parties shall undertake all appropriate legislative, administrative, and other measures for the implementation of the rights recognized in the present Convention. With regard to economic, social and cultural rights, States Parties shall undertake such measures to the maximum extent of their available resources and, where needed, within the framework of international co-operation.

Article 5

States Parties shall respect the responsibilities, rights and duties of parents or, where applicable, the members of the extended family or community as provided for by local custom, legal guardians or other persons legally responsible for the child, to provide, in a manner consistent with the evolving capacities of the child, appropriate direction and guidance in the exercise by the child of the rights recognized in the present Convention.

Article 6

1. States Parties recognize that every child has the inherent right to life.
2. States Parties shall ensure to the maximum extent possible the survival and development of the child.

Article 7

1. The child shall be registered immediately after birth and shall have the right from birth to a name, the right to acquire a nationality and. as far as possible, the right to know and be cared for by his or her parents.
2. States Parties shall ensure the implementation of these rights in accordance with their national law and their obligations under the relevant international instruments in this field, in particular where the child would otherwise be stateless.

Article 8

1. States Parties undertake to respect the right of the child to preserve his or her identity, including nationality, name and family relations as recognized by law without unlawful interference.
2. Where a child is illegally deprived of some or all of the elements of his or her identity, States Parties shall provide appropriate assistance and protection, with a view to re-establishing speedily his or her identity.

Article 9

1. States Parties shall ensure that a child shall not be separated from his or her parents against their will, except when competent authorities subject to judicial review determine, in accordance with applicable law and procedures, that such separation is necessary for the best interests of the child. Such determination may be necessary in a particular case such as one involving abuse or neglect of the child by the parents, or one where the parents are living separately and a decision must be made as to the child's place of residence.
2. In any proceedings pursuant to paragraph 1 of the present article, all interested parties shall be given an opportunity to participate in the proceedings and make their views known.
3. States Parties shall respect the right of the child who is separated from one or both parents to maintain personal relations and direct contact with both parents on a regular basis, except if it is contrary to the child's best interests.
4. Where such separation results from any action initiated by a State Party, such as the detention, imprisonment, exile, deportation or death (including death arising from any cause while the person is in the custody of the State) of one or both parents or of the child, that State Party shall, upon request, provide the parents, the child or, if appropriate, another member of the family with the essential information concerning the whereabouts of the absent member(s) of the family unless the provision of the information would be detrimental to the well-being of the child. States Parties shall further ensure that the submission of such a request shall of itself entail no adverse consequences for the person(s) concerned.

Article 10

1. In accordance with the obligation of States Parties under article 9, paragraph 1, applications by a child or his or her parents to enter or leave a State Party for the purpose of family reunification shall be dealt with by States Parties in a positive, humane and expeditious manner. States Parties shall further ensure that the submission of such a request shall entail no adverse consequences for the applicants and for the members of their family.
2. A child whose parents reside in different States shall have the right to maintain on a regular basis, save in exceptional circumstances personal relations and direct contacts with both parents. Towards that end and in accordance with the obligation of States Parties under article 9, paragraph 1, States Parties shall respect the right of the child and his or her parents to leave any country, including their own, and to enter their own country. The right to leave any country shall be subject only to such restrictions as are prescribed by law and which are necessary to protect the national security, public order (ordre public), public health or morals or the rights and freedoms of others and are consistent with the other rights recognized in the present Convention.

Article 11

1. States Parties shall take measures to combat the illicit transfer and non-return of children abroad.
2. To this end, States Parties shall promote the conclusion of bilateral or multi-lateral agreements or accession to existing agreements.

Article 12

1. States Parties shall assure to the child who is capable of forming his or her own views the right to express those views freely in all matters affecting the child, the views of the child being given due weight in accordance with the age and maturity of the child.
2. For this purpose, the child shall in particular be provided the opportunity to be heard in any judicial and administrative proceedings affecting the child, either directly, or through a representative or an appropriate body, in a manner consistent with the procedural rules of national law.

Article 13

1. The child shall have the right to freedom of expression; this right shall include freedom to seek, receive and impart information and ideas of all kinds, regardless of frontiers, either orally, in writing or in print, in the form of art, or through any other media of the child's choice.
2. The exercise of this right may be subject to certain restrictions, but these shall only be such as are provided by law and are necessary:

(a) For respect of the rights or reputations of others; or
(b) For the protection of national security or of public order (ordre public), or of public health or morals.

Article 14

1. States Parties shall respect the right of the child to freedom of thought, conscience and religion.
2. States Parties shall respect the rights and duties of the parents and, when applicable, legal guardians, to provide direction to the child in the exercise of his or her right in a manner consistent with the evolving capacities of the child.
3. Freedom to manifest one's religion or beliefs may be subject only to such limitations as are prescribed by law and are necessary to protect public safety, order, health or morals, or the fundamental rights and freedoms of others.

Article 15

1. States Parties recognize the rights of the child to freedom of association and to freedom of peaceful assembly.
2. No restrictions may be placed on the exercise of these rights other than those imposed in conformity with the law and which are necessary in a democratic society in the interests of national security or public safety, public order (ordre public), the protection of public health or morals or the protection of the rights and freedoms of others.

Article 16

1. No child shall be subjected to arbitrary or unlawful interference with his or her privacy, family, or correspondence, nor to unlawful attacks on his or her honour and reputation.
2. The child has the right to the protection of the law against such interference or attacks.

Article 17

States Parties recognize the important function performed by the mass media and shall ensure that the child has access to information and material from a diversity of national and international sources, especially those aimed at the promotion of his or her social, spiritual and moral well-being and physical and mental health.

To this end, States Parties shall:

(a) Encourage the mass media to disseminate information and material of social and cultural benefit to the child and in accordance with the spirit of article 29;

(b) Encourage international co-operation in the production, exchange and dissemination of such information and material from a diversity of cultural, national and international sources;
(c) Encourage the production and dissemination of children's books;
(d) Encourage the mass media to have particular regard to the linguistic needs of the child who belongs to a minority group or who is indigenous;
(e) Encourage the development of appropriate guidelines for the protection of the child from information and material injurious to his or her well-being, bearing in mind the provisions of articles 13 and 18.

Article 18

1. States Parties shall use their best efforts to ensure recognition of the principle that both parents have common responsibilities for the upbringing and development of the child. Parents or, as the case may be, legal guardians, have the primary responsibility for the upbringing and development of the child. The best interests of the child will be their basic concern.
2. For the purpose of guaranteeing and promoting the rights set forth in the present Convention, States Parties shall render appropriate assistance to parents and legal guardians in the performance of their child-rearing responsibilities and shall ensure the development of institutions, facilities and services for the care of children.
3. States Parties shall take all appropriate measures to ensure that children of working parents have the right to benefit from child-care services and facilities for which they are eligible.

Article 19

1. States Parties shall take all appropriate legislative, administrative, social and educational measures to protect the child from all forms of physical or mental violence, injury or abuse, neglect or negligent treatment, maltreatment or exploitation, including sexual abuse, while in the care of parent(s), legal guardian(s) or any other person who has the care of the child.
2. Such protective measures should, as appropriate, include effective procedures for the establishment of social programmes to provide necessary support for the child and for those who have the care of the child, as well as for other forms of prevention and for identification, reporting, referral, investigation, treatment and follow-up of instances of child maltreatment described heretofore, and, as appropriate, for judicial involvement.

Article 20

1. A child temporarily or permanently deprived of his or her family environment, or in whose own best interests cannot be allowed to remain in that environment, shall be entitled to special protection and assistance provided by the State.
2. States Parties shall in accordance with their national laws ensure alternative care for such a child.
3. Such care could include, inter alia, foster placement, kafalah of Islamic law, adoption or if necessary placement in suitable institutions for the care of children. When considering solutions, due regard shall be paid to the desirability of continuity in a child's upbringing and to the child's ethnic, religious, cultural and linguistic background.

Article 21

States Parties that recognize and/or permit the system of adoption shall ensure that the best interests of the child shall be the paramount consideration and they shall:

(a) Ensure that the adoption of a child is authorized only by competent authorities who determine, in accordance with applicable law and procedures and on the basis of all pertinent and reliable information, that the adoption is permissible in view of the child's status concerning parents, relatives and legal guardians and that, if required, the persons concerned have given their informed consent to the adoption on the basis of such counselling as may be necessary;
(b) Recognize that inter-country adoption may be considered as an alternative means of child's care, if the child cannot be placed in a foster or an adoptive family or cannot in any suitable manner be cared for in the child's country of origin;
(c) Ensure that the child concerned by inter-country adoption enjoys safeguards and standards equivalent to those existing in the case of national adoption;
(d) Take all appropriate measures to ensure that, in inter-country adoption, the placement does not result in improper financial gain for those involved in it;
(e) Promote, where appropriate, the objectives of the present article by concluding bilateral or multilateral arrangements or agreements, and endeavour, within this framework, to ensure that the placement of the child in another country is carried out by competent authorities or organs.

Article 22

1. States Parties shall take appropriate measures to ensure that a child who is seeking refugee status or who is considered a refugee in accordance with applicable international or domestic law and procedures shall, whether unaccompanied or accompanied by his or her parents or by any other person, receive appropriate protection and humanitarian assistance in the enjoyment of applicable rights set forth in the present Convention and in other international human rights or humanitarian instruments to which the said States are Parties.

2. For this purpose, States Parties shall provide, as they consider appropriate, co-operation in any efforts by the United Nations and other competent inter-governmental organizations or non-governmental organizations co-operating with the United Nations to protect and assist such a child and to trace the parents or other members of the family of any refugee child in order to obtain information necessary for reunification with his or her family. In cases where no parents or other members of the family can be found, the child shall be accorded the same protection as any other child permanently or temporarily deprived of his or her family environment for any reason, as set forth in the present Convention.

Article 23

1. States Parties recognize that a mentally or physically disabled child should enjoy a full and decent life, in conditions which ensure dignity, promote self-reliance and facilitate the child's active participation in the community.
2. States Parties recognize the right of the disabled child to special care and shall encourage and ensure the extension, subject to available resources, to the eligible child and those responsible for his or her care, of assistance for which application is made and which is appropriate to the child's condition and to the circumstances of the parents or others caring for the child.
3. Recognizing the special needs of a disabled child, assistance extended in accordance with paragraph 2 of the present article shall be provided free of charge, whenever possible, taking into account the financial resources of the parents or others caring for the child, and shall be designed to ensure that the disabled child has effective access to and receives education, training, health care services, rehabilitation services, preparation for employment and recreation opportunities in a manner conducive to the child's achieving the fullest possible social integration and individual development, including his or her cultural and spiritual development.
4. States Parties shall promote, in the spirit of international cooperation, the exchange of appropriate information in the field of preventive health care and of medical, psychological and functional treatment of disabled children, including dissemination of and access to information concerning methods of rehabilitation, education and vocational services, with the aim of enabling States Parties to improve their capabilities and skills and to widen their experience in these areas. In this regard, particular account shall be taken of the needs of developing countries.

Article 24

1. States Parties recognize the right of the child to the enjoyment of the highest attainable standard of health and to facilities for the treatment of illness and rehabilitation of health. States Parties shall strive to ensure that no child is deprived of his or her right of access to such health care services.

2. States Parties shall pursue full implementation of this right and, in particular, shall take appropriate measures:

   (a) To diminish infant and child mortality;
   (b) To ensure the provision of necessary medical assistance and health care to all children with emphasis on the development of primary health care;
   (c) To combat disease and malnutrition, including within the framework of primary health care, through, inter alia, the application of readily available technology and through the provision of adequate nutritious foods and clean drinking-water, taking into consideration the dangers and risks of environmental pollution;
   (d) To ensure appropriate pre-natal and post-natal health care for mothers;
   (e) To ensure that all segments of society, in particular parents and children, are informed, have access to education and are supported in the use of basic knowledge of child health and nutrition, the advantages of breastfeeding, hygiene and environmental sanitation and the prevention of accidents;
   (f) To develop preventive health care, guidance for parents and family planning education and services.

3. States Parties shall take all effective and appropriate measures with a view to abolishing traditional practices prejudicial to the health of children.
4. States Parties undertake to promote and encourage international co-operation with a view to achieving progressively the full realization of the right recognized in the present article. In this regard, particular account shall be taken of the needs of developing countries.

Article 25

States Parties recognize the right of a child who has been placed by the competent authorities for the purposes of care, protection or treatment of his or her physical or mental health, to a periodic review of the treatment provided to the child and all other circumstances relevant to his or her placement.

Article 26

1. States Parties shall recognize for every child the right to benefit from social security, including social insurance, and shall take the necessary measures to achieve the full realization of this right in accordance with their national law.
2. The benefits should, where appropriate, be granted, taking into account the resources and the circumstances of the child and persons having responsibility for the maintenance of the child, as well as any other consideration relevant to an application for benefits made by or on behalf of the child.

Article 27

1. States Parties recognize the right of every child to a standard of living adequate for the child's physical, mental, spiritual, moral and social development.
2. The parent(s) or others responsible for the child have the primary responsibility to secure, within their abilities and financial capacities, the conditions of living necessary for the child's development.
3. States Parties, in accordance with national conditions and within their means, shall take appropriate measures to assist parents and others responsible for the child to implement this right and shall in case of need provide material assistance and support programmes, particularly with regard to nutrition, clothing and housing.
4. States Parties shall take all appropriate measures to secure the recovery of maintenance for the child from the parents or other persons having financial responsibility for the child, both within the State Party and from abroad. In particular, where the person having financial responsibility for the child lives in a State different from that of the child, States Parties shall promote the accession to international agreements or the conclusion of such agreements, as well as the making of other appropriate arrangements.

Article 28

1. States Parties recognize the right of the child to education, and with a view to achieving this right progressively and on the basis of equal opportunity, they shall, in particular:
   (a) Make primary education compulsory and available free to all;
   (b) Encourage the development of different forms of secondary education, including general and vocational education, make them available and accessible to every child, and take appropriate measures such as the introduction of free education and offering financial assistance in case of need;
   (c) Make higher education accessible to all on the basis of capacity by every appropriate means;
   (d) Make educational and vocational information and guidance available and accessible to all children;
   (e) Take measures to encourage regular attendance at schools and the reduction of drop-out rates.
2. States Parties shall take all appropriate measures to ensure that school discipline is administered in a manner consistent with the child's human dignity and in conformity with the present Convention.
3. States Parties shall promote and encourage international cooperation in matters relating to education, in particular with a view to contributing to the elimination of ignorance and illiteracy throughout the world and facilitating access to scientific and technical knowledge and modern teaching methods. In this regard, particular account shall be taken of the needs of developing countries.

Article 29

1. States Parties agree that the education of the child shall be directed to:

    (a) The development of the child's personality, talents and mental and physical abilities to their fullest potential;
    (b) The development of respect for human rights and fundamental freedoms, and for the principles enshrined in the Charter of the United Nations;
    (c) The development of respect for the child's parents, his or her own cultural identity, language and values, for the national values of the country in which the child is living, the country from which he or she may originate, and for civilizations different from his or her own;
    (d) The preparation of the child for responsible life in a free society, in the spirit of understanding, peace, tolerance, equality of sexes, and friendship among all peoples, ethnic, national and religious groups and persons of indigenous origin;
    (e) The development of respect for the natural environment.

2. No part of the present article or article 28 shall be construed so as to interfere with the liberty of individuals and bodies to establish and direct educational institutions, subject always to the observance of the principle set forth in paragraph 1 of the present article and to the requirements that the education given in such institutions shall conform to such minimum standards as may be laid down by the State.

Article 30

In those States in which ethnic, religious or linguistic minorities or persons of indigenous origin exist, a child belonging to such a minority or who is indigenous shall not be denied the right, in community with other members of his or her group, to enjoy his or her own culture, to profess and practise his or her own religion, or to use his or her own language.

Article 31

1. States Parties recognize the right of the child to rest and leisure, to engage in play and recreational activities appropriate to the age of the child and to participate freely in cultural life and the arts.
2. States Parties shall respect and promote the right of the child to participate fully in cultural and artistic life and shall encourage the provision of appropriate and equal opportunities for cultural, artistic, recreational and leisure activity.

Article 32

1. States Parties recognize the right of the child to be protected from economic exploitation and from performing any work that is likely to be hazardous or to interfere with the child's education, or to be harmful to the child's health or physical, mental, spiritual, moral or social development.
2. States Parties shall take legislative, administrative, social and educational measures to ensure the implementation of the present article. To this end, and having regard to the relevant provisions of other international instruments, States Parties shall in particular:

   (a) Provide for a minimum age or minimum ages for admission to employment;
   (b) Provide for appropriate regulation of the hours and conditions of employment;
   (c) Provide for appropriate penalties or other sanctions to ensure the effective enforcement of the present article.

Article 33

States Parties shall take all appropriate measures, including legislative, administrative, social and educational measures, to protect children from the illicit use of narcotic drugs and psychotropic substances as defined in the relevant international treaties, and to prevent the use of children in the illicit production and trafficking of such substances.

Article 34

States Parties undertake to protect the child from all forms of sexual exploitation and sexual abuse. For these purposes, States Parties shall in particular take all appropriate national, bilateral and multilateral measures to prevent:

(a) The inducement or coercion of a child to engage in any unlawful sexual activity;
(b) The exploitative use of children in prostitution or other unlawful sexual practices;
(c) The exploitative use of children in pornographic performances and materials.

Article 35

States Parties shall take all appropriate national, bilateral and multilateral measures to prevent the abduction of, the sale of or traffic in children for any purpose or in any form.

Article 36

States Parties shall protect the child against all other forms of exploitation prejudicial to any aspects of the child's welfare.

Article 37

States Parties shall ensure that:

(a) No child shall be subjected to torture or other cruel, inhuman or degrading treatment or punishment. Neither capital punishment nor life imprisonment without possibility of release shall be imposed for offences committed by persons below eighteen years of age;
(b) No child shall be deprived of his or her liberty unlawfully or arbitrarily. The arrest, detention or imprisonment of a child shall be in conformity with the law and shall be used only as a measure of last resort and for the shortest appropriate period of time;
(c) Every child deprived of liberty shall be treated with humanity and respect for the inherent dignity of the human person, and in a manner which takes into account the needs of persons of his or her age. In particular, every child deprived of liberty shall be separated from adults unless it is considered in the child's best interest not to do so and shall have the right to maintain contact with his or her family through correspondence and visits, save in exceptional circumstances;
(d) Every child deprived of his or her liberty shall have the right to prompt access to legal and other appropriate assistance, as well as the right to challenge the legality of the deprivation of his or her liberty before a court or other competent, independent and impartial authority, and to a prompt decision on any such action.

Article 38

1. States Parties undertake to respect and to ensure respect for rules of international humanitarian law applicable to them in armed conflicts which are relevant to the child.
2. States Parties shall take all feasible measures to ensure that persons who have not attained the age of fifteen years do not take a direct part in hostilities.
3. States Parties shall refrain from recruiting any person who has not attained the age of fifteen years into their armed forces. In recruiting among those persons who have attained the age of fifteen years but who have not attained the age of eighteen years, States Parties shall endeavour to give priority to those who are oldest.
4. In accordance with their obligations under international humanitarian law to protect the civilian population in armed conflicts, States Parties shall take all feasible measures to ensure protection and care of children who are affected by an armed conflict.

Article 39

States Parties shall take all appropriate measures to promote physical and psychological recovery and social reintegration of a child victim of: any form of neglect, exploitation, or abuse; torture or any other form of cruel, inhuman or degrading treatment or punishment; or armed conflicts. Such recovery and reintegration shall take place in an environment which fosters the health, self-respect and dignity of the child.

Article 40

1. States Parties recognize the right of every child alleged as, accused of, or recognized as having infringed the penal law to be treated in a manner consistent with the promotion of the child's sense of dignity and worth, which reinforces the child's respect for the human rights and fundamental freedoms of others and which takes into account the child's age and the desirability of promoting the child's reintegration and the child's assuming a constructive role in society.
2. To this end, and having regard to the relevant provisions of international instruments, States Parties shall, in particular, ensure that:

   (a) No child shall be alleged as, be accused of, or recognized as having infringed the penal law by reason of acts or omissions that were not prohibited by national or international law at the time they were committed;
   (b) Every child alleged as or accused of having infringed the penal law has at least the following guarantees:

      (i)   To be presumed innocent until proven guilty according to law;
      (ii) To be informed promptly and directly of the charges against him or her, and, if appropriate, through his or her parents or legal guardians, and to have legal or other appropriate assistance in the preparation and presentation of his or her defence;
      (iii) To have the matter determined without delay by a competent, independent and impartial authority or judicial body in a fair hearing according to law, in the presence of legal or other appropriate assistance and, unless it is considered not to be in the best interest of the child, in particular, taking into account his or her age or situation, his or her parents or legal guardians;
      (iv) Not to be compelled to give testimony or to confess guilt; to examine or have examined adverse witnesses and to obtain the participation and examination of witnesses on his or her behalf under conditions of equality;
      (v)   If considered to have infringed the penal law, to have this decision and any measures imposed in consequence thereof reviewed by a higher competent, independent and impartial authority or judicial body according to law;

    (vi) To have the free assistance of an interpreter if the child cannot understand or speak the language used;

    (vii) To have his or her privacy fully respected at all stages of the proceedings.

3. States Parties shall seek to promote the establishment of laws, procedures, authorities and institutions specifically applicable to children alleged as, accused of, or recognized as having infringed the penal law, and, in particular:

    (a) The establishment of a minimum age below which children shall be presumed not to have the capacity to infringe the penal law;

    (b) Whenever appropriate and desirable, measures for dealing with such children without resorting to judicial proceedings, providing that human rights and legal safeguards are fully respected. 4. A variety of dispositions, such as care, guidance and supervision orders; counselling; probation; foster care; education and vocational training programmes and other alternatives to institutional care shall be available to ensure that children are dealt with in a manner appropriate to their well-being and proportionate both to their circumstances and the offence.

Article 41

Nothing in the present Convention shall affect any provisions which are more conducive to the realization of the rights of the child and which may be contained in:

(a) The law of a State party; or

(b) International law in force for that State.

Part II

Article 42

States Parties undertake to make the principles and provisions of the Convention widely known, by appropriate and active means, to adults and children alike.

Article 43

1. For the purpose of examining the progress made by States Parties in achieving the realization of the obligations undertaken in the present Convention, there shall be established a Committee on the Rights of the Child, which shall carry out the functions hereinafter provided.

2. The Committee shall consist of eighteen experts of high moral standing and recognized competence in the field covered by this Convention.1/The members of the Committee shall be elected by States Parties from among their nationals and shall serve in their personal capacity, consideration being given to equitable geographical distribution, as well as to the principal legal systems.

3. The members of the Committee shall be elected by secret ballot from a list of persons nominated by States Parties. Each State Party may nominate one person from among its own nationals.

4. The initial election to the Committee shall be held no later than six months after the date of the entry into force of the present Convention and thereafter every second year. At least four months before the date of each election, the Secretary-General of the United Nations shall address a letter to States Parties inviting them to submit their nominations within two months. The Secretary-General shall subsequently prepare a list in alphabetical order of all persons thus nominated, indicating States Parties which have nominated them, and shall submit it to the States Parties to the present Convention.

5. The elections shall be held at meetings of States Parties convened by the Secretary-General at United Nations Headquarters. At those meetings, for which two thirds of States Parties shall constitute a quorum, the persons elected to the Committee shall be those who obtain the largest number of votes and an absolute majority of the votes of the representatives of States Parties present and voting.

6. The members of the Committee shall be elected for a term of four years. They shall be eligible for re-election if renominated. The term of five of the members elected at the first election shall expire at the end of two years; immediately after the first election, the names of these five members shall be chosen by lot by the Chairman of the meeting.

7. If a member of the Committee dies or resigns or declares that for any other cause he or she can no longer perform the duties of the Committee, the State Party which nominated the member shall appoint another expert from among its nationals to serve for the remainder of the term, subject to the approval of the Committee.

8. The Committee shall establish its own rules of procedure.

9. The Committee shall elect its officers for a period of two years.

10. The meetings of the Committee shall normally be held at United Nations Headquarters or at any other convenient place as determined by the Committee. The Committee shall normally meet annually. The duration of the meetings of the Committee shall be determined, and reviewed, if necessary, by a meeting of the States Parties to the present Convention, subject to the approval of the General Assembly.

11. The Secretary-General of the United Nations shall provide the necessary staff and facilities for the effective performance of the functions of the Committee under the present Convention.

12. With the approval of the General Assembly, the members of the Committee established under the present Convention shall receive emoluments from United Nations resources on such terms and conditions as the Assembly may decide.

Article 44

1. States Parties undertake to submit to the Committee, through the Secretary-General of the United Nations, reports on the measures they have adopted which give effect to the rights recognized herein and on the progress made on the enjoyment of those rights

   (a) Within two years of the entry into force of the Convention for the State Party concerned;
   (b) Thereafter every five years.

2. Reports made under the present article shall indicate factors and difficulties, if any, affecting the degree of fulfilment of the obligations under the present Convention. Reports shall also contain sufficient information to provide the Committee with a comprehensive understanding of the implementation of the Convention in the country concerned.

3. A State Party which has submitted a comprehensive initial report to the Committee need not, in its subsequent reports submitted in accordance with paragraph 1 (b) of the present article, repeat basic information previously provided.

4. The Committee may request from States Parties further information relevant to the implementation of the Convention.

5. The Committee shall submit to the General Assembly, through the Economic and Social Council, every two years, reports on its activities.

6. States Parties shall make their reports widely available to the public in their own countries.

Article 45

In order to foster the effective implementation of the Convention and to encourage international co-operation in the field covered by the Convention:

(a) The specialized agencies, the United Nations Children's Fund, and other United Nations organs shall be entitled to be represented at the consideration of the implementation of such provisions of the present Convention as fall within the scope of their mandate. The Committee may invite the specialized agencies, the United Nations Children's Fund and other competent bodies as it may consider appropriate to provide expert advice on the implementation of the Convention in areas falling within the scope of their respective mandates. The Committee may invite the specialized agencies, the United Nations Children's Fund, and other United Nations organs to submit reports on the implementation of the Convention in areas falling within the scope of their activities;

(b) The Committee shall transmit, as it may consider appropriate, to the specialized agencies, the United Nations Children's Fund and other competent bodies, any reports from States Parties that contain a request, or indicate a need, for technical advice or assistance, along with the Committee's observations and suggestions, if any, on these requests or indications;

(c) The Committee may recommend to the General Assembly to request the Secretary-General to undertake on its behalf studies on specific issues relating to the rights of the child;

(d) The Committee may make suggestions and general recommendations based on information received pursuant to articles 44 and 45 of the present Convention. Such suggestions and general recommendations shall be transmitted to any State Party concerned and reported to the General Assembly, together with comments, if any, from States Parties.

Part III

Article 46

The present Convention shall be open for signature by all States.

Article 47

The present Convention is subject to ratification. Instruments of ratification shall be deposited with the Secretary-General of the United Nations.

Article 48

The present Convention shall remain open for accession by any State. The instruments of accession shall be deposited with the Secretary-General of the United Nations.

Article 49

1. The present Convention shall enter into force on the thirtieth day following the date of deposit with the Secretary-General of the United Nations of the twentieth instrument of ratification or accession.

2. For each State ratifying or acceding to the Convention after the deposit of the twentieth instrument of ratification or accession, the Convention shall enter into force on the thirtieth day after the deposit by such State of its instrument of ratification or accession.

Article 50

1. Any State Party may propose an amendment and file it with the Secretary-General of the United Nations. The Secretary-General shall thereupon communicate the proposed amendment to States Parties, with a request that they indicate whether they favour a conference of States Parties for the purpose of

considering and voting upon the proposals. In the event that, within four months from the date of such communication, at least one third of the States Parties favour such a conference, the Secretary-General shall convene the conference under the auspices of the United Nations. Any amendment adopted by a majority of States Parties present and voting at the conference shall be submitted to the General Assembly for approval.

2. An amendment adopted in accordance with paragraph 1 of the present article shall enter into force when it has been approved by the General Assembly of the United Nations and accepted by a two-thirds majority of States Parties.
3. When an amendment enters into force, it shall be binding on those States Parties which have accepted it, other States Parties still being bound by the provisions of the present Convention and any earlier amendments which they have accepted.

Article 51

1. The Secretary-General of the United Nations shall receive and circulate to all States the text of reservations made by States at the time of ratification or accession.
2. A reservation incompatible with the object and purpose of the present Convention shall not be permitted.
3. Reservations may be withdrawn at any time by notification to that effect addressed to the Secretary-General of the United Nations, who shall then inform all States. Such notification shall take effect on the date on which it is received by the Secretary-General.

Article 52

A State Party may denounce the present Convention by written notification to the Secretary-General of the United Nations. Denunciation becomes effective one year after the date of receipt of the notification by the Secretary-General.

Article 53

The Secretary-General of the United Nations is designated as the depositary of the present Convention.

Article 54

The original of the present Convention, of which the Arabic, Chinese, English, French, Russian and Spanish texts are equally authentic, shall be deposited with the Secretary-General of the United Nations. In witness thereof the undersigned plenipotentiaries, being duly authorized thereto by their respective Governments, have signed the present Convention.

Bibliography

Alaimo, K. (2002). Historical roots of children's rights in Europe and the United States. In K. Alaimo & B. Klug (Eds.), *Children as equals: Exploring the rights of the child* (pp. 1–24). Lanham, MD: University Press of America.

Alderson, P. (2008). *Young children's rights: Exploring beliefs, principles and practice*. London: Jessica Kingsley Publishers.

Aldgate, J., & Statham, J. (2001). *The Children Act now: Messages from research*. London: The Stationery Office.

Archard, D. (1993). *Children: Rights and childhood*. UK: Routledge.

Aries, P. (1962). *Centuries of childhood: A social history of family life*. New York: Vintage Books.

Arneil, B. (2002). Becoming versus being: A critical analysis of the child in liberal theory. In D. Archard & C. M. Macleod (Eds.), *The moral and political status of children* (pp. 71–94). Oxford, UK: Oxford University Press.

Arnstein, S. (1969). Eight rungs on the ladder of citizen participation. *Journal of the American Institute of Planners, 35*, 216–224.

Australian Association of Social Workers (AASW) (2013). *Child well-being and protection. A position paper.* Retrieved from http://www.aasw.asn.au/document/item/2215.

Barnes, K. V. (2009). *Caring for rights: Social work and advocacy with looked after children and young people.* A thesis submitted in partial fulfillment of the requirements for the degree of Doctor of Philosophy in Health and Social Studies University of Warwick, Department of Health and Social Studies.

Barnes, K. V. (2012). Social work and advocacy with young people: Rights and care in practice. *British Journal of Social Work, 42*, 1275–1292.

Bateman, N. (1995). *Advocacy skills: A Handbook for human service professionals*. Arena: Aldershot.

Bell, M. (2002). Promoting children's rights through the use of relationship. *Child and Family Social Work, 7*, 1–11.

Ben-Arieh, A. (2005). Where are the children? Children's role in measuring and monitoring their well-being. *Social Indicators, 74*, 573–596.

Ben-Arieh, A. (2010). Developing indicators for child well-being in a changing context. In C. McAuley, & W. Rose (Eds.), *Child well-being understanding children's lives* (pp. 129–142). London: Jessica Kingsley Publishers.

Ben-Arieh, A., Casas, F., Frønes, I., & Korbin, J. E. (Eds.). (2014). *Handbook of child well-being: Theories, methods and policies in global perspective*. Springer.

Benbenishty, R., & Peled- Amir, T. (2007). *Complaint mechanisms for children in out of home placements: A policy proposal*. Jerusalem: Paul Baerwald School of Social Work & Social Welfare. [In Hebrew].

Bessell, S. (2011). Participation in decision-making in out-of home care in Australia: What do young people say? *Children and Youth Services Review, 33*, 496–501.

Biestek, F. P. (1961). *The casework relationship*. London: Unwin University Books.

© The Author(s) 2016
H. Kosher et al., *Children's Rights and Social Work*,
SpringerBriefs in Rights-Based Approaches to Social Work,
DOI 10.1007/978-3-319-43920-4

Bohrnstedt, G. W., Freedman, H. E., & Smith, T. (1981). Adult perspectives on children's autonomy. *Public Opinion Quarterly, 45,* 443–462.

Boylan, J., & Boylan, P. (1998). Empowering young people: Advocacy in North Wales. *Representing Children, 11*(1), 42–49.

Boylan, J., & Ing, P. (2005). Seen but not heard: Young people's experience of advocacy. *International Journal Social Welfare, 14,* 2–12.

Boylan, J., & Wyllie, J. (1999). Advocacy and child protection. In N. Parton & C. Wattam (Eds.), *Child sexual abuse: Responding to the experiences of children.* Chichester: Wiley/NSPCC.

Brandon, M., Schofield, G., & Trinder, L. (1998). *Social work with children.* London: Macmillan Press.

Brill, C. K. (2001). Looking at the social work profession through the eye of the NASW code of ethics. *Research on Social Work Practice, 11*(2), 223–234.

Browning, C. R., Feinberg, S. L., & Dietz, R. D. (2004). The paradox of social organization: Networks, collective efficacy and violent crime in urban neighborhoods. *Social Forces, 83,* 503–534.

Butler, I., & Williamson, H. (1994). *Children speak: Trauma and social work.* Harlow: Longman.

Calma, T., & Priday, E. (2011). Putting Indigenous human rights into social work practice. *Australian Social Work, 64,* 147–155.

Cashmore, J. (2002). Promoting the participation of children and young people in care. *Child Abuse & Neglect, 26,* 837–847.

Chavis, D. M., & Wandersman, A. (1990). Sense of community in urban environment: A catalyst for participation and community development. *American Journal of Community Psychology, 18,* 55–81.

Cherney, I. D., & Shing, Y. L. (2008). Children's nurturance and self-determination rights: A cross-cultural perspective. *Journal of Social Issues, 64,* 835–856.

Clifton, J., & Hodgson, D. (1997). Rethinking practice through a children's rights perspective. In C. Cannan & C. Warren (Eds.), *Social action with children and families* (pp. 43–65). London: Routledge.

Cockburn, T. (2005). Children's participation in social policy: Inclusion, chimera or authenticity? *Social Policy and Society, 4*(2), 109–119.

Cohen, C. P. (2002). United Nations Convention on the Rights of the Child: Developing international norms to create a new world for children. In K. Alaimo & B. Klug (Eds.), *Children as equals: Exploring the rights of the child* (pp. 49–72). Lanham, MD: University Press of America.

Cossar, J., Brandon, M., and Jordan, P. (2014). You've got to trust her and she's got to trust you': children's views on participation in the child protection system. *Child and Family Social Work.* Advance online publication. doi:10.1111/cfs.12115.

Cousins, W., & Milner, S. (2007). Children's rights: A cross-border study of residential care. *Irish Journal of Psychology, 27,* 88–96.

Dalrymple, J. (2003). Professional advocacy as a force for resistance in child welfare. *British Journal of Social Work, 33,* 1043–1062.

Dalrymple, J. (2005). Constructions of child and youth advocacy: Emerging issues in advocacy practice. *Children & Society, 19,* 3–15.

Dalrymple, J., & Hough, P. (1995). *Having a voice: An exploration of children's rights and advocacy.* Birmingham: Venture Press.

De Vries, J. (1984). *European urbanization, 1500–1800.* Cambridge: Harvard University Press.

Delhey, J., & Newton, K. (2002). *Who trusts? The origins of social trust in seven nations.* Berlin, Germany: Social Structure and Social Reporting, Social Science Research Center.

deMause, L. (1974). *The history of childhood.* New York: Psychohistory Press.

Ehrenreich, J. H. (2014). *The altruistic imagination: A history of social work and social policy in the United States.* New York: Cornell University Press.

Farson, R. (1974). *Birthrights.* New York: Penguin Books.

Finn, J., & Checkoway, B. (1998). Young people as competent community builders: A challenge to social work. *Social Work, 43,* 335–345.

Flekkoy, M. G., & Kaufman, N. H. (1997). *The participation rights of the child: rights and responsibilities in family and society.* London: Jessica Kingsley Publishers.

Fogel, S. J. (2004). Risks and opportunities for success: Perceptions of urban youths in a distressed community and lessons for adults. *Families in Society, 85,* 335–344.

Fox Harding, L. (1991). *Perspectives in child care policy.* London: Longman.

Franklin, B. (1997). The Ladder of Participation in Matters Concerning Children. In J. Boyden & J. Ennew (Eds.), *Children in focus: A manual for participatory research with children.* Stockholm: Grafisk Press.

Freedberg, S. (2009). *Relational theory for Social Work practice: A feminist perspective.* New York: Routledge.

Gallagher, M., Smith, M., Hardy, M., & Wilkinsion, H. (2012). Children and families' involvement in social work decision making. *Children & Society, 26,* 74–85.

Gilligan, C. (1982). *In a different voice: Psychological theory and women's development.* Cambridge: Harvard University Press.

Gilligan, R. (2000). The developmental implications for children of life in public care: Irish and international perspectives. *Irish Journal of Psychology, 21,* 138–153.

Glaeser, E. L., Laibson, D., Scheinkman, J. A., & Soutter, C. L. (2000). Measuring trust. *Quarterly Journal of Economics, 115*(3), 811–846.

Hallett, C., & Prout, A. (Eds.). (2003). *Hearing the voices of children: Social policy for a new century.* London: Routledge.

Hare, I. (2004). Defining social work for the 21st century: The international federation of social workers' revised definition of social work. *International Social Work, 47,* 407–424.

Hart, R. A. (1992). *Children's Participation: From Tokenism to Citizenship, Innocenti Essays, 4.* Florence: UNICEF.

Hart, S. N. (1991). From property to person status: Historical perspective on children's rights. *American Psychologist, 46*(1), 53.

Healy, K., & Darlington, Y. (2009). Service user participation in diverse child protection contexts: Principles for practice. *Child & Family Social Work, 14,* 420–430.

Healy, L. M. (2001). *International social work: Professional action in an interdependent world.* New York: Oxford University Press.

Healy, L. M. (2008). Exploring the history of social work as a human rights profession. *International Social Work, 51,* 735–748.

Healy, L. M., & Link, R. J. (Eds.). (2012). *Handbook of international social work: Human rights, development, and the global profession.* Oxford, England: Oxford University Press.

Helwig, C. C. (1995a). Adolescents' and young adults' conceptions of civil liberties: Freedom of speech and religion. *Child Development, 66,* 152–166.

Helwig, C. C. (1995b). Social contexts in social cognition: Psychological harm and civil liberties. In M. Killen & D. Hart (Eds.), *Morality in everyday life: Developmental perspectives* (pp. 166–200). Cambridge: Cambridge University Press.

Hill, M., & Aldgate, J. (1996). *Child welfare services: Developments in law, policy, practice, and research.* Jessica Kingsley Publishers.

Hill, M., Davis, J., Prout, A., & Tisdall, K. (2004). Moving the participation agenda forward. *Children & Society, 18*(2), 77–96.

Hollis, F. (1964). *A Psycho-Social therapy.* New York: Random House.

Holt, J. (1974). *Escape from childhood—The needs and rights of children.* Middlesex: Penguin books.

Ife, J. (2001). *Human rights and social work.* Cambridge: Cambridge University Press.

Ife, J. (2012). *Human rights and social work* (3rd ed.). New York: Cambridge University Press.

International Federation of Social Workers & International Association of Schools of Social Work. (2004). *Ethics in social work, statement of principles.* Bern, Switzerland: Author.

Iwaniec, D., & Hill, M. (2000). Issues emerging from child care research: Post-implementation of the Children Act 1989. In D. Iwaniec & M. Hill (Eds.), *Child welfare policy and practice* (pp. 9–22). London: Jessica Kingsley.

James, A., Jenks, C., & Prout, A. (1998). *Theorizing childhood.* Cambridge, UK: Polity Press.

John, M. (2003). *Children's rights and power: Gearing up for a new century.* Gateshead: Jessica Kingsley.

Kelly, D. C. (2009). In reparation for adulthood: Exploring civic participation and social trust among young minorities. *Youth & Society, 40,* 526–540.

Kirby, P., & Bryson, S. (2002). *Measuring the magic? Evaluating and researching young people's participation in public decision making.* London: Carnegie Young People Initiative.

Kirby, P., Lanyon, C., Cronin, K., & Sinclair., R. (2003). *Building a Culture of Participation: Involving children and young people in policy, service planning, delivery and evaluation.* Department for Education & Science.

Kirk, S. (2007). Methodological and ethical issues in conducting qualitative research with children and young people: A literature review. *International Journal of Nursing Studies, 4,* 1250–1260.

Krapmann, L. (2010). The weight of the child's view (Article 12 of the Convention on the Rights of the Child). *International Journal of Children's Rights, 18,* 501–513.

Kwak, N., Shah, D. V., & Holbert, R. L. (2004). Connecting, trusting and participating: The direct and interactive effects of social associations. *Political Research Quarterly, 57,* 643–652.

Ladd, R. E. (2002). Rights of the child: A philosophical approach. In K. Alaimo & B. Klug (Eds.), *Children as equals: Exploring the rights of the child* (pp. 89–101). Lanham, MD: University Press of America.

Lansdown, G. (1994). Children's rights. In B. Mayall (Ed.), *Children's childhoods: Observed and experienced* (pp. 33–44). London: The Falmer Press.

Leeson, C. (2007). My life in care: Experiences of non-participation in decision-making processes. *Child & Family Social Work, 12,* 268–277.

Lichter, D. T., Shanahan, M. J., & Gardner, E. L. (1999). *Becoming a good citizen? The longterm consequences of poverty and family instability during childhood (Research Paper).* New York: Russell Sage.

Limber, S., & Kaufman, N. H. (2002). Civic participation by children and youth. In N. Kaufman & I. Rizzini (Eds.), *Globalization and Children's.* New York: Kluwer Academic.

Lindsay, M. J. (1995). Involving young people in decision-making. *Children Australia, 20,* 39–42.

Lundy, L., McEvoy, L., & Byrn, B. (2011). Working with young children as co-researchers: An approach informed by the United Nations Convention on the Rights of the Child. *Early Education and Development, 22*(5), 714–736.

Mapp, S. C. (2008). *Human rights and social justice in a global perspective: An introduction to international social work.* New York, NY: Oxford University Press.

Marshall, K. (1997). *Children's rights in the balance: The participation-protection debate.* Edinburgh: The Stationery Office.

Matthews, H. (2003). Children and regeneration: Setting an agenda for community participation and integration. *Children & Society, 17,* 264–276.

Mayall, B. (2000). The sociology of childhood in relation to children's rights. *The International Journal of Children's Rights, 8,* 243–259.

McLeod, A. (2007). Whose agenda? Issues of power and relationship when listening to looked-after young people. *Child and Family Social Work, 12,* 278–286.

McNeish, D., & Newman, T. (2002). Involving children and young people in decision making. In D. Mcneish, T. Newman, & H. Roberts (Eds.), *What works for children? effective services for children and families* (pp. 186–204). Buckingham: Oxford University Press.

McPherson, J., & Abell, N. (2012). Human rights engagement and exposure: New scales to challenge social work education. *Research on Social Work Practice, 22*(6), 704–713.

Melton, G. B. (1980). Children's concepts of their rights. *Journal of Clinical Child Psychology, 9,* 186–190.

Melton, G. B. (1983). *Child advocacy.* New York: Plenum.

Melton, G. B. (2005). Treating children like people: A framework for research and advocacy. *Journal of Clinical Child and Adolescent Psychology, 34,* 646–657.

Melton, G. B., & Limber, S. (1992). What children's rights mean to children: Children's own view. In M. Freeman & P. Veerman (Eds.), *The ideologies of children's rights* (pp. 167–187). Dordercht: Martinus Nijhoff Publishers.

Morton, T. L., Dubanoski, R. A., & Blaine, D. D. (1982). Cross-cultural perceptions of children's rights. In J. S. Henning (Ed.), *The rights of children: Legal and psychological perspectives* (pp. 141–160). Springfield, IL: Charles & Thomas.

Munro, E. (2001). Empowering looked-after children. *Child and Family Social Work, 6,* 129–137.

Munro, W. R., Holmes, L., & Harriet, W. (2005). Researching vulnerable groups: Ethical issues and the effective conduct of research in local authorities. *British Journal of Social Work, 35,* 1023–1038.

National Association of Social Workers. (2009). *Social work speaks: National Association of Social Workers policy statements, 2009–2012.* Washington, DC: NASW Press.

Newman, J., Barnes, M., Sullivan, H., & Knops, A. (2004). Public participation and collorative governance. *Journal of social Policy, 33*(2), 203–233.

Newton, K. (2001). Trust, social capital, civic society and democracy. *International Political Science Review, 22,* 201–214.

Newton, K., & Pippa, N. (2000). Confidence in public institutions: Faith, culture or performance? In S. Pharr & R. Putnam (Eds.), *Disaffected democracies* (pp. 52–73). Princeton, NJ: Princeton University Press.

O'Quigley, A. (2000). *Listening to Children's Views: The findings and recommendations of recent research.* York: Joseph Rowntree Foundation.

O'Toole, T., Lister, M., Marsh, D., Jones, S., & McDonagh, A. (2003). Turning out or left out? Participation and non-participation among young people. *Contemporary Politics, 9,* 45–61.

Parker, R., Ward, H., Jackson, S., Aldgate, J., & Wedge, P. (1991). *Looking after children: Assessing outcomes in child care.* London: HMSO.

Partridge, A. (2005). Children and young people's inclusion in public decision-making. *Support for Learning, 20,* 181–189.

Pecora, P. J., Whittaker, J. K., Maluccio, A. N., & Barth, R. P. (2012). *The child welfare challenge: Policy, practice, and research.* AldineTransaction.

Peterson-Badali, M., & Ruck, M. D. (2008). Studying children's perspectives on self-determination and nurturance rights: Issues and challenges. *Journal of Social Issues, 64,* 749–769.

Peterson-Badali, M., Morine, S. L., Ruck, M. D., & Slonim, N. (2004). Predictors of maternal and early adolescent attitudes toward children's nurturance and self-determination rights. *Journal of Early Adolescence, 24,* 159–179.

Peterson-Badali, M., Ruck, M. D., & Ridley, E. (2003). College students' attitudes towards children's nurturance and self-determination rights. *Journal of Applied Social Psychology, 30,* 730–755.

Petr, C. G., & Spano, R. N. (1990). Evolution of social services for children with emotional disorders. *Social Work, 35*(3), 228–234.

Petr, C. G. (2004). *Social work with children and their families: Pragmatic foundations* (2nd ed.). Oxford: University Press.

Pinkney, S. (2011). Participation and emotions: Troubling encounters between children and social welfare professionals. *Children and Society, 25,* 37–46.

Pölkki, P., Vornanen, R., Pursiainen, M., & Riikonen, M. (2012). Children's participation in child protection processes as experienced by foster children and social workers. *Child Care in Practice, 18,* 107–125.

Prout, A., & James, A. (1997). A new paradigm for the sociology of childhood? Provenance, promise and problems. In A. James & A. Prout (Eds.), *Constructing and reconstructing childhood* (2nd ed., pp. 1–33). London: Falmer.

Quennerstedt, A. (2013). Children's Rights Research Moving into the Future—Challenges on the Way Forward. *International Journal of Children's Rights, 21,* 233–247.

Rasinski, K. A., Ingels, S. J., Rock, D. A., Pollack, J. M., & Wu, S. (1993). *America's high school sophomores: A ten year comparison.* Washington, DC: U.S. Government Printing Office.

Reamer, F. G. (1998). The Evolution of Social Work Ethics. *Social Work, 43,* 488–500.

Reichert, E. (2003). *Social work and human rights: A foundation for policy and practice.* New York, NY: Columbia University Press.

Reichert, E. (2007). *Challenges in human rights: A social work perspective.* New York: Columbia University Press.

Reichert, E. (2011). *Social work and human rights: A foundation for policy and practice* (2nd ed.). New York: Colombia University Press.

Reynaert, D. M., Bouverne-de-Bie, & Vandevelde, S. (2009). A Review of Children's Rights Literature since the Adoption of the United Nations Convention on the Rights of the Child. *Childhood, 16,* 518–534.

Ridge, T., & Millar, J. (2000). Excluding children: Autonomy, friendship and the experience of the care system. *Social Policy and Administration, 34*(2), 160–175.

Ridge, T. (2002). *Childhood poverty and social exclusion: From a child's perspective.* Bristol: The Policy Press.

Rogers, C. M., & Wrightsman, L. S. (1978). Attitudes toward children's rights. *Journal of Social Issues, 34*(2), 59–68.

Ruck, M. D., & Horn, S. S. (2008). Charting the landscape of children's rights. *Journal of Social Issues, 64*(4), 685–699.

Ruck, M. D., Keating, D. P., Abramovitch, R., & Koegl, C. J. (1998). Adolescents' and children's knowledge about rights: Some evidence for how young people view rights in their lives. *Journal of Adolescence, 21,* 275–289.

Sanders, R., & Mace, S. (2006). Agency Policy and the Participation of Children and Young People in the Child Protection Process. *Child Abuse Review, 15,* 89–109.

Save the Children (2005). *Child rights programming: how to apply rights-based approaches to programming.* Save the children. Retrieved from http://resourcecentre.savethechildren.se/library/child-rights-programming-handbook-how-apply-rights-based-approaches-programming.

Schofield, G. (2005). The voice of the child in family placement decision-making a developmental model. *Adoption and Fostering, 29,* 29–43.

Shemmings, D. (2000). Professional attitudes to children's participation in decision-making: Dichotomous accounts and doctrinal contests. *Child and Family Social Work, 5,* 235–243.

Shier, H. (2001). Pathways to participation: Openings, opportunities and obligations. *Children and Society, 15,* 107–117.

Sinclair, R. (2004). Participation in Practice: Making it Meaningful, Effective and Sustainable. *Children and Society, 18,* 106–118.

Sinclair, R., & Boushel, M. (1998). Involving children in planning their care. *Child and Family Social Work, 3,* 137–142.

Sinko, P. (2008). The New Child Welfare Act in Finland. Retrieved from http://www.childrenwebmag.com/articles/child-care-articles/the-new-child-welfare-act-in-finland.

Skehill, C. (2008). The history of social work. *British journal of social work, 38,* 619–837.

Smart, C., Neale, B., & Wade, A. (2001). *The changing experience of childhood: Families and divorce.* Cambridge: Polity Press.

Solomon, L. (2006). *The institution of Ombudsman: As a means of protecting the human rights of children and adolescents.* Jerusalem: Paul Baerwald School of Social Work & Social Welfare. [In Hebrew].

Stier, S. (1978). Children's rights and society's duties. *Journal of Social Issues, 34,* 46.

Stoker, G. (2006). *Why politics matters: Making democracy work.* Basingstoke: Palgrave.

Such, E., & Walker, R. (2005). Young citizens or policy objects? Children in the rights and responsibilities debate. *Journal of Social Policy, 34*(1), 39–57.

The British Association of Social Workers (BASW) (2015). *BASW human rights policy.* Retrieved from http://cdn.basw.co.uk/upload/basw_30635-1.pdf.

Thoburn, J., Lewis, A., & Shemmings, D. (1995). *Paternalism or Partnership? Family Involvement in the Child Protection Process.* London: HMSO.

Thomas, N., & O'Kane, C. (1998). *A first report on the children and decision-making research.* International Centre for Childhood Studies: University of Wales, Swansea.

Thomas, N. (2005). Has anything really changed? Managers' views of looked after children's participation in 1997 and 2004. *Adoption and Fostering, 29,* 67–77.

Tilbury, C. (2013). Social work with children and young people. *Australian Social Work, 66*(3), 311–313.

Tisdall, E. K. M. (2008). Is the honeymoon over? Children and young people's participation in public decision making. *International Journal of Children's rights, 16,* 419–429.

Torney-Purta, J., Wilkenfeld, B., & Barber, C. (2008). How adolescents in 27 countries understand, support, and practice human rights. *Journal of Social Issues, 64,* 857–880.

Treseder, P. (1997). *Empowering children and young people: Promoting involvement in decision making—Training manual.* London: Save the Children Fund and Children's Rights Office.

Troope, S. (1996). The Convention of the Right of the Child: Implications for Canada. In M. Freeman (Ed.), *Children's rights.* Aldershot, UK: Dartmouth Publishing Company.

UNICEF Toolkit on Diversion and Alternatives to Detention 2009 (2009). Part A: UNICEF position on a human rights-based approach to programming in relation to children. Retrieved February 15, 2016 from http://www.unicef.org/tdad/index_56511.html.

Utting, W. (1997). *People like us: The report of the review of the safeguards for children living away from home.* London: HMSO.

van Bijleveld, G. G., Dedding, C. W. M., & Bunders-Aelen, J. F. (2013). Children's and young people's participation within child welfare and child protection services: A state-of-the-art review. *Child and Family Social Work, 20,* 129–138.

Vis, S. A., & Thomas, N. (2009). Beyond talking—children's participation in Norwegian care and protection cases. *European Journal of Social Work, 12,* 155–168.

Vis, S. A., Holtan, A., & Thomas, N. (2012). Obstacles for Child Participation in Care and Protection Cases: Why Norwegian social workers find it Difficult. *Child Abuse Review, 21,* 7–23.

Vis, S. A., Strandbu, A., Holtan, A., & Thomas, N. (2010). Participation and health—A research review of child participation in planning and decision-making. *Child and Family Social Work, 16,* 325–335.

Walker, N. E., Brooks, C. M., & Wrightsman, L. S. (1999). *Children's rights in the United States: In search of a national policy.* Thousand Oaks, CA: Sage.

West, A. (2004). Children and participation: Meaning, motives and purpose. In D. Crimmens & A. West (Eds.), *Having their say: Young people and participation: European experiences.* Russell House: Lyme Regis.

Williams, F. (2001). In and beyond New Labour: Towards a new political ethics of care. *Critical Social Policy, 21*(4), 467–493.

Willow, C. (2002). *Participation in practice: Children and young people as partners in change.* London: The Children Society.

Wises-Gal, I., & Gal, J. (2011). *The practice of social work policy.* Jerusalem: The Hebrew University Magnes Press. [In Hebrew].

Witkin, S. (1998). Editorial: Human rights and social work. *Social Work, 43,* 197–201.

Woodhead, M. (1997). Psychology and the cultural construction of children's needs. In A. James & A. Prout (Eds.), *Constructing and reconstructing childhood: Contemporary issues in the sociological study of childhood.* London: Falmer Press.

Woolfson, R. C., Heffernan, E., Paul, M., & Brown, M. (2010). Young people's views of the child protection system in Scotland. *British Journal of Social Work, 40,* 2069–2085.

The Global Agenda for Social Work and Social Development (2012). Retrieved March 2016 from http://cdn.ifsw.org/assets/globalagenda2012.pdf.

Printed by Printforce, the Netherlands